Valleys to Mountaintops

Inspirational Health Journeys

TERESA MEINERT

iUniverse, Inc.
Bloomington

Valleys to Mountaintops
Inspirational Health Journeys

iUniverse books may be ordered through booksellers or by contacting:

iUniverse
1663 Liberty Drive
Bloomington, IN 47403
www.iuniverse.com
1-800-Authors (1-800-288-4677)

Because of the dynamic nature of the Internet, any web addresses or links contained in this book may have changed since publication and may no longer be valid. The views expressed in this work are solely those of the author and do not necessarily reflect the views of the publisher, and the publisher hereby disclaims any responsibility for them.

Any people depicted in stock imagery provided by Thinkstock are models, and such images are being used for illustrative purposes only.

Certain stock imagery © Thinkstock.

ISBN: 978-1-4620-1072-1 (sc)
ISBN: 978-1-4620-1070-7 (hc)
ISBN: 978-1-4620-1071-4 (ebk)

Library of Congress Control Number: 2011911883

Printed in the United States of America

iUniverse rev. date: 08/16/2011

Table of Contents

SECTION C: RELATED ISSUE

SECTION D: STORIES PLUS

INTRODUCTION

The stories you'll read as you continue may seem like "business as usual" situations for the people telling about their lives, but perhaps they and others who read this book will come to understand their heroism.

Teaching at an agency in Iowa, I helped new employees know how to aid those with disabilities. As I taught I became truly enlightened. The usual classroom lack of knowledge was disturbing; however, unless one must deal with a health-care situation, missing information is understandable. Thus, an interest was sparked for me to explain to people that unexpected health circumstances *can* occur in people's lives. They're unimaginable and unfortunate. However, when such circumstances actually happen, most people are able to accept, adapt, and move forward. Researching different situations and writing, through first hand testimony, has been very rewarding!

Multiple sclerosis, diagnosed in 1980, osteoporosis, diagnosed in 2004, and severe scoliosis are my health issues. When I was forty years old and working became impossible, I wondered what to do. After all, I was still a fairly young person! Seeking possible opportunities, school was an attractive option because I had attended a year of college already, albeit twenty-some years before. I loved it and eventually graduated with a bachelor's degree in psychology, then went on to earn a master's degree in rehabilitation counseling. Rehab counselors help people with disabilities find employment. After teaching about disabilities for three years, it became necessary to retire permanently.

Much personal experience with people with health challenges has stayed with me, so writing a book became intriguing. It has definitely been rewarding! I have learned so much in connecting with others, about many different situations, and have met many wonderful people. I have also found that people all over the world are friendly, courageous, and amazing! Worldwide acceptance, understanding, and story contributions have been extremely important to me. Heartfelt thanks to everyone.

As a person who has known what it is to go from being totally functional to almost totally dependent, I can safely say life has been undeniably interesting. This book has been written with speech recognition software and mostly with my left hand. I am naturally right-handed; however the right side of my body works minimally. I wear assistive devices to keep me upright as I use the power wheelchair. My personal assistant and I live in Iowa.

Working or otherwise, living with and without health challenges can provide one with innumerable experiences. For me, writing about the experiences of others has been so enjoyable! I have connected and reconnected with many wonderful people who are unquestionably friends. They deserve only praise.

This quote by Samuel Beckett, "Ever tried. Ever failed. No matter. Try again. Fail again. Fail better," appeals to me. My world has an upbeat, hopeful outlook, and I share with others that they can make a positive impact for the world. Perhaps that impact has already been made!

In this book, mental health issues, physical issues, caregiving, and additional stories are sections. Chapters within the sections, with personal stories, are followed by factual and cited information. Within the chapters, websites and miscellaneous information may be included. Information for the book was gathered beginning in 2008 and was updated in 2011. If you are intrigued by the information provided, investigate the websites or additional information. Definitions were usually found through Google searches. Profits from the book will be donated to predetermined charitable organizations. Look for even better books in the future.

DISCLAIMERS

Medical Disclaimer:
The information contained in this book is provided for the reader's general information only. The author does not give medical advice or engage in the practice of medicine or counseling. The author under no circumstances recommends particular treatment for specific individuals and in all cases recommends that readers consult their physician or local treatment center before pursuing any course of treatment.

Trademark Disclaimer:
Product names, logos, brands, and other trademarks featured or referred to within this book are the property of their respective trademark holders. These trademark holders are not affiliated with this book. They do not sponsor or endorse this book.

Permission has been obtained to use stories.

DEDICATION

To Jan and S.W.R., thanks for your inspiration,
your diligence, and your laughter

SECTION A:
MENTAL HEALTH ISSUES

Mental illness is nothing to be ashamed of, but stigma and bias shame us all.

Bill Clinton

Famous People Who Have Had Mental Illness

Hans Christian Anderson, Ludwig von Beethoven, Winston Churchill, Kurt Cobain, Charles Darwin, Emily Dickinson, Thomas Edison, F. Scott Fitzgerald, Betty Ford, Paul Gauguin, King George III, Johan Goethe, Ernest Hemingway, Victor Hugo, Ignatius of Loyola, Thomas Jefferson, John Keats, Abraham Lincoln, Martin Luther, Michelangelo, Florence Nightingale, King Saul, Robert Louis Stevenson, Sir Isaac Newton, and Howie Mandel

Author's Note:

The following stories convey the contributor's personal experiences. In that vein, as people read on they may see some unusual words or spellings.

Chapter 1
ANXIETY DISORDERS

WHAT IS GENERALIZED ANXIETY DISORDER (GAD)?

Bruce

It's been fortunate that I have a very caring family. My parents work hard, and as I was growing up, my siblings and I had interests other than sports. However, as I aged, I did participate in wrestling, running, tennis, and was on the swim team in high school. I became popular, "played the game," and had long-term relationships with females. But I knew I was a homosexual in a small Midwestern town. Are alarm bells sounding in your head? They screamed in mine! High school was a confusing time, because I was trying to figure things out. Self-esteem became an issue because I started thinking other students knew I was different. I believed they were thinking "faggot" when they looked at me or thought I was so gay that I "swished" when I walked. Leaving home to attend a university in another city was a good choice and has proven to be a significant factor in shaping my life.

In this new city, I graduated from the university, I was always a good student, found professional employment, and met my lifetime partner. We have been together now twenty-one years. Long-term relationships seem to be my forté! I found work at a large institution, and I was extremely good at my job. Even though tolerance of gays was apparent in the city, comments made from time to time by others touched my nerves in a harmful way. My upbringing dictated I endure such thoughtless remarks, and this was additionally detrimental to me. At work, I would talk of my roommate instead of saying my partner's name, because I thought I would sound effeminate otherwise. I either avoided answering the phone or lowered my voice when I did. Eventually, I became comfortable enough with coworkers that I started coming out to them. It was a slow process and spanned ten years.

After a decade in this section, it was time to think about different work opportunities. I chose to change jobs at the institution. Switching has proven to be a mixed blessing and a definitive decision for me. Because the environment at my new location seemed so forbidding, from management to employees, my nerves were stretched tight at all times. Old fears and thoughts came back to haunt me, so I was speaking again of my roommate instead of naming my partner and again began to lower my voice when answering the phone. After acclimating to the new environment, I found that one coworker had a gay brother and another had a gay brother-in law. This helped me feel much more comfortable. After working at this job for another ten years, downsizing came along. Decades seem to be turning points for me. I was being pressured to take on a new role and to accept increasing amounts of responsibility. My already taut nerves were stretched yet more thinly. I had "outbursts" from time to time, which did not endear me to management, and the icing on the cake was when a female coworker accused me of sexual harassment. Hah!

Yet more pressure, depressing thoughts, and bouts of uncontrollable crying during trips to the restroom finally led to a mistake in my work. Its' discovery provided an excuse for management to push me out. These events, combined with thoughts of suicide, one day helped me choose to enter the Psych Clinic instead of walking past. This led to a stay in the hospital and my parents visited me. I was pleased when my father hugged me and said he loved me. This was a wholly different situation than I was used to. I knew then that we were important to each other! It was a seismic shift in attitude and was pivotal for me. My partner and I are now accepted as a couple and we are supported by my family.

After leaving the hospital, I visited a local free clinic. I still felt out of control because I relived—and still do—the unpleasant times, and I continue to need medication and therapy. The doctor at the free clinic, upon seeing my face, gave me tests and quickly diagnosed generalized anxiety disorder. After talking some, depression was also diagnosed. The doctor explained the two frequently go together. I currently receive long-term disability benefits, as I await a determination about my grievances with the institution. The whole work scenario has been upsetting and leaves me feeling angry, treated unfairly, abused, and violated. These emotions are deeply felt indeed.

As I look back, I am quite proud of the positives in my life. I have a caring family; a monogamous, loving, twenty-one-year relationship; I was successful at my job; and I have created a lovely backyard. People have said it looks like a park. Also, I purchased and paid for the house before the age of forty. I am a perfectionist sometimes, but I have learned it is sometimes acceptable to be "satisfactory."

Now I keep busy. Otherwise, I get bored, tired, and unwelcome thoughts intrude. I would much rather work than be idle, so I have many irons in the fire. I volunteer as a tutor at a local community college, and I enjoy teaching very much. I find myself re-learning skills unneeded for many years, and it captivates me. Often I think of taking courses to become a teacher and then I recall that as a child, I enjoyed playing this role immensely. I think to myself that further education could be a good thing. I deliver meals on wheels, volunteer at the local NAMI chapter, and work on commission creating stained glass windows. For that, perfection is definitely needed. I enjoy cooking, landscaping, know my way around my computer, and make a mean ice cream. I have also had thoughts of opening a gelato shop, though that is far in the future. I am a just a fountain of exciting future possibilities!

At this time, I am enjoying my life and feel better now than I ever have. I believe we all have trials to endure. Mine revealed that I have more strength and resilience than I ever thought possible. The trials also demonstrate my talents and my determined attitude to succeed. Hey, I am okay!

GAD

– Is/Cause

A) The National Institutes of Health (NIH)-Pub Med Health explains GAD is a pattern of frequent, constant, worry over many different activities and events – http://www.ncbi.nlm.nih.gov/pubmedhealth/PMH0001915/.

B) The Mayo Clinic states GAD is present when ongoing anxiety interferes with every day activities and relationships, it might even be making life hard to enjoy – http://www.mayoclinic.com/health/generalized-anxiety-disorder/DS00502.

– Symptoms

A) The National Institutes of Mental Health (NIMH) explains people with GAD can have physical symptoms along with the worry, such as fatigue, headaches, and muscle aches – http://www.nimh.nih.gov/health/topics/generalized-anxiety-disorder-gad/index.shtml.

B) The Mayo Clinic tells us symptoms might be trembling or feeling itchy, sweating, nausea, and diarrhea – http://www.mayoclinic.com/health/generalized-anxiety-disorder/DS00502/DSECTION=symptoms http://www.mayoclinic.com.

– Tips

A) The Mayo Clinic informs us the two main treatments for GAD are medication and psychotherapy. The most benefit might be derived from a combination of the two – http://www.mayoclinic.com/health/generalized-anxiety-disorder/DS00502/DSECTION=treatments-and-drugs.

B) The Anxiety Disorders Association of America has many suggestions for treatment; conventional and alternative. Conventional treatments could be several medications and/or many different therapies. Alternative ideas are Kava, acupuncture, and yoga, along with other suggestions ~ http://www.adaa.org/finding-help/treatment/complementary-alternative-treatment.

Step 1. Consult a professional.

What Is Paranoid Personality Disorder (PPD)?

Jerome

Spending much of my time visiting various websites implies it is my favorite activity. It's true. Different Internet sites teach a lot about technical topics such as science, civil defense, and telecommunications. Science interests me very much, and I can spend hours reading online. I could read books or go to a museum, but it is very convenient to sit at my computer screen, have the information at my fingertips, and remain in my home. There are several music websites I visit. The songs appeal to me and relax me at the same time. Relaxation has become a huge part of my life.

The northern region of North America is where I live; I have been diagnosed with paranoid personality disorder. That is the reason I spend so much time on the computer. Websites on the Internet allow me to connect with other people on YouTube, Myspace, and Facebook, so I am less isolated. In the past, when I wanted to escape my reality, I would go to a site with personal information and blogs. I read about the difficulties of others and have come to recognize that I could actually be one of their group. This has been a tremendous comfort to me and helped me to get through some pretty tough times. Meeting people face to face is a somewhat unnerving situation for me, so this works out much better. Also, the Internet connects me worldwide.

Another site, called Skinhead Moonstomp, I enjoyed for the music I could hear there. The site was taken down. Though I am not a skinhead, nor desire to be, I found that I connected with the music emotionally. I feel that Oil, a punk rock variation, and Ska, reggae with jazz and/or blues, freed me from myself and empowered me to be comfortable with my place in society. I am a son, a brother, a friend, and in a way, I am an explorer. That is my life now.

What led up to these circumstances? When I was thirteen, I was walking with a friend. Just sauntering along, when I was suddenly surprised that my legs were less flexible than before. It was like they would still move, but locked up a little with each step. My young brain was having trouble taking in this unexpected change, when I started panting and sweating as well. I felt like screaming; what I did was keep walking and then rested when I got home. When I woke up, I felt even worse than before. I was stunned these things were happening to me, a teenager, but still the symptoms remained. I was truly baffled. What could this be? The first people I relayed the information to were my parents. Their answer was less than satisfying: "It's part of puberty." As far as I knew, my friends didn't have to deal with this in their lives! It seemed, or so I thought, I would just have to go it alone.

As I got older, those anxious feelings continued. Finally, it became so bad I was almost afraid to leave my home! Three years after the first symptoms, I went to see a psychiatrist. This first doctor teased me, refused to make eye contact, and made me so mad I snapped and started yelling. Needless to say, there were no further visits to that doctor. I felt quite vulnerable when I saw the second doctor, who did many, many tests and offered little help. Again, there was no relief. Another three years passed, and I was more determined than ever to find help. Then I went to a third psychiatrist, who asked if I ever felt anxious for no reason. *Yes.* We did more tests and he eventually assessed paranoid personality disorder. Medication was prescribed, and he referred me to group therapy. Well, I was fearful of meeting new people, but I was resolute in my purpose. I was tired of being afraid! I realized upon arriving at group that I had company; there were others with similar feelings. I had friends again and the third time had been my lucky charm.

The first medication I used gave me blinding headaches, enough so I had trouble seeing straight. When I went to see yet another psychiatrist, the doctor changed the medication, and now I am able to use that one without side effects. I'm very glad those terrible headaches are gone!

Since diagnosis and therapy, I have done much soul-searching. I realize now that I used to hide myself away in a corner to protect myself. I wanted to avoid the judgment of others; I could just see it in their eyes. After seeing this look enough times, I was extremely sensitive to it. There was plenty of hostility on my part, responding to the hostility of others. That was my defense: anger. Group therapy helped me to know that there is less to fear and that people other than my family can be trusted. I now feel freed from the fear.

These days, I am more confident and assertive. I have chosen goals and would like to go to a trade school, perhaps to learn telecommunications engineering. I am also very interested in design and feel I would be quite successful at repair. It has been an eventful, but worthwhile, journey. Now I am focused on my career path and am ready to set things in motion to move forward. Currently, I listen to music and fantasize to relax. I think about what others' lives might be like. Knowing myself as I do now, and knowing what I want, helps me when people judge. They have made comments like, "I wish you would die," and have made fun of the way I walk. How crummy is that? I can now walk more freely than at first, but not as freely as I could originally. I do have tools though, and I can deal with the walking and the comments.

I enjoy my life. My friends and I have good times and I make sure the friends I do have fulfill my needs. Another thing, I am persistent in working toward having my needs met. I like to be around people with disabilities; they are hindered by their situations, as I am. There are times I would like for things to be different. I see others functioning in normal ways, and I'm jealous. Then again, I recognize the love and sacrifice of my hardworking parents and younger brothers, and I am grateful to them. I am very fortunate to have love and, with medication, a stable life. I am a man on the brink, who needs only a bit of momentum to advance. That momentum will certainly be found, and I am ready to move ahead with confidence and optimism.

PPD

– Is/Cause

A) The HIV-Pub Med Health states that PPD is a psychiatric condition evidenced by long-term distrust and suspicion of others, but is different from a fully developed psychiatric disorder like schizophrenia – http://www.ncbi.nlm.nih.gov/pubmedhealth/PMH0001934/.

B) According to the Cleveland Clinic, the PPD personality tends to be paranoid when there is no reason to be suspicious. Also, PPD usually begins in young adulthood and people with PPD are more commonly men than women – http://my.clevelandclinic.org/disorders/personality_disorders/hic_paranoid_personality_disorder.aspx.

– Symptoms

A) Medlineplus describes an inability to work with others, social isolation, and hostility as some symptoms of PPD – http://www.nlm.nih.gov/medlineplus/ency/article/000938.htm.

B) Psych Central explains that people with PPD can read hidden threatening meanings into benign remarks or events – http://psychcentral.com/disorders/sx37.htm.

– Tips

A) Ehow explains ways to treat people with PPD. Among them are individualized, group, and self-help therapy – http://www.ehow.com/how_2088467_treat-paranoid-personality-disorder.html.

B) The Cleveland Clinic states people with PPD usually do not seek treatment on their own because they don't see themselves as having a problem. When treatment is sought, it usually focuses on increasing social interaction, communication, and self-esteem. – http://my.clevelandclinic.org/disorders/personality_disorders/hic_paranoid_personality_disorder.aspx.

Step 1. Consult a professional.

Chapter 2.
BIPOLAR DISORDER

WHAT IS BIPOLAR DISORDER (BD)?

Amanda

As a child, I always felt different from those around me. Though I could *almost* identify why it was so, the mystery remained. There were times when I could clearly see that I was depressed, which made me feel even further removed from my young classmates. I kept to myself, becoming more and more withdrawn, and by age eleven, I was all too familiar with the feeling of melancholy.

After a major surgery to correct severe scoliosis at age twelve, I felt even more changes than I would have liked. I spent the next seven months recovering and during that time, I experienced an inability to sleep. My mind would begin to race so quickly it was impossible to keep up. As the months passed, that flurry of rapid thought continued, my ability to concentrate dwindled, and I slept less and less. There were nights when sleep would totally elude me, because I was consumed by a need for movement, creativity, and productivity. Four nights without slumber were common, so I remained unconcerned. I figured this was normal.

As quickly as I would feel the first desperate need for continuous motion, this mind-set melted away into an overwhelming sadness that consumed me. Motivation would be scarce and I wanted nothing to do with the world around me. Turning to drugs, which removed me from an intolerable reality, I spent several months in a perpetual haze of pot, pills, and anything that would make me forget how utterly miserable I was. It flung me deep into a hole from which I had neither the will nor the tools to climb out. It seemed that the light which appeared above me slowly began to dissolve and with every passing second that light was moving further and further away from my reach. At seventeen, I found myself still within the hole, and the light above me was but a sliver of fading hope. I attempted suicide, downing twenty-four Darvocet over the course of two hours. Fortunately, my attempt was discovered.

As the weeks wore on, my need to abuse drugs decreased, and that tiny light at the other end of my prison gradually grew larger and larger. Suddenly, it burst into a brilliant fire, a beautiful, radiant glow directly over my head. This incredible starburst flooded me with a frenzy of artistic inspiration and that old familiar need for constant motion. I created some of my most memorable art pieces during this time; one idea following another. Actually, there were so many ideas that they were tripping over each other! I was overflowing with creativity, happiness, and confidence. What anyone thought of me didn't matter. I cared only about these fabulous feelings and my newly found artistry. This was a state in which I hoped I'd remain forever. But along with those beautiful, cherished feelings came other elements of mania. My irritability and agitation spilled over, making me snap randomly at those I loved. The inspiration I had felt turned into a non-stop flow of intrusive thoughts, ideas, and anger. I was barely sleeping; I was barely hanging onto my sanity, but would eventually regain my footing.

That was a turning point for me, and I decided that I needed to contain both my depression and my worsening mania. It was hard to admit that I needed help, but I felt I had little recourse. I chose to see a therapist to help me sort through the thoughts in my head, and I selected a psychiatrist to begin a regimen of medication. My psychiatrist diagnosed bipolar disorder and urged me to find more information on this illness. That way, I could understand what I go through a little better. It was the first step of many to reclaim my sanity.

To tell the truth, this has been by far the hardest path to follow. I have taken many, many psychiatric medications, and I've had to switch meds on a regular basis. They would either stop working or would exacerbate my depression or my mania. Finding the right cocktail is incredibly tough; truthfully, it's a pain in the ass, but it is something that I learned was crucial when managing my bipolar symptoms.

A cure for bipolar disorder has yet to be discovered. Medication is a means to minimize symptoms and to manage them better. I still go through manic episodes, just as I go through depressive episodes and mixed episodes. My medications need to be monitored just as closely as my behaviors. After years of learning how to identify and manage my symptoms, I have been able to catch myself as I shift episodes, so they may be treated by adjusting my medication dosage. Also, I can tell if I need hospitalization, which helps me stay safe.

While it's likely different for every bipolar patient, I know that in order to lead a productive and stable life, I will probably always be on medication. I've come to a point where I have accepted this. I would urge anyone who is experiencing symptoms similar to mine to see a doctor and give medication a try. This may be the key to managing your symptoms and could allow you to live a life free of ever-shifting moods. It's a hard pill to swallow, literally and figuratively, but because I have chosen to swallow that pill every day, I have chosen to give myself a chance at a more stable existence. With medication, the light above my head is neither a fading ember nor a blinding vision. I have found the way out of the hole. With my experiences, I am ready, even eager, to take on the role of a valuable contributor of knowledge!

Chrisandra

Since experiencing my struggles and being diagnosed with bipolar illness, I have learned of similar mental illness on both sides of my family. It's almost as if I was destined to be a part of this group. I am aware of several individuals in my extended family that clearly self-medicate with alcohol to deal with what I can now recognize as bipolar symptoms. As far as I know, only two family members currently receive help for those mental illness symptoms. Thankfully I do.

After the birth of my son in May of 1999, within days of arriving home, I first noticed symptoms of bipolar illness. I was a young, first-time mother with unusual circumstances. Back then, I thought these indications were normal for just having a baby, and it would pass. I do recognize that caring for a baby is life changing, but I also had increased energy, did not need much sleep or food, I had racing thoughts, and generally my moods were very different. I now know that I was experiencing mania, which continued for about three months. Then I crashed and experienced a deep depression. When the blow of depression came, I would feel incapacitated and flat. These are frequently bipolar experiences.

During a manic period, I would know extreme highs, with heightened sensations such as sight, especially colors. Sounds were amplified, tastes were exceptional, and my sense of touch was enhanced. I felt grandiose, like I could do and be anything. I also knew tremendous loss as the result of behaviors during the manic period.

At this time I was divorced. I fought for custody of my child, lost a job, lost my car; I had debts resulting in bankruptcy, criminal charges, a loss of self-esteem and goals, etc. I also had almost an obsession with religion and a sense that some things were within my reach, which was mostly untrue. I was confused by the symptoms I was having and felt that I was totally alone, without anyone to turn to or trust. It seemed that I was at the bottom of a deep pit and could not climb out or even see the light as a guide to get there.

The thought kept coming back, *How did things get so bad, so fast?* I also thought that my life was basically over and that I would never be able to get back on my feet to enjoy time with my son. I feared the future, what my family and friends would think of me, and how I would deal with the stigma of mental illness.

The future is where I focused my thoughts. The main objective for me was to get better, so I could return to my young son's life. I also realized that my experience was something I could reflect on, and that maybe I could help others in the same situation by offering support and guidance.

This was also a time of struggling with medications, testing which were the right ones, and staying medicated rather than thinking I was cured and could move on. I had to think about therapy, hospitalizations, and applying for Social Security Disability. I also read and absorbed as much information as possible on bipolar illness. On a positive note, I do enjoy helping others to get help. I use my communication degree to speak to people about bipolar illness.

Humor is not a part of the bipolar story, but there can be acceptance. I have come to realize there are a number of people around me, that I thought I knew so well, and have since found that they share the bipolar diagnosis. It's fascinating. When I can talk with someone and they say, "Oh, it sounds like you are telling me about my own life," it's also comforting. It is such a humbling and down to earth moment! Everything changes at that point. In accepting my diagnosis, I continue to see a therapist, because life is stressful in general and talking helps.

I encourage the positive relationships in my life and continue to meet and talk with new people. I keep a close eye on myself daily to see how I am feeling and what might be triggering my mood: whether it is chemical or situational. I maintain my medications, sleep, diet, etc., as best as I can. I continue to read and learn about bipolar illness. I strive to take time for me; that is very important overall.

Recovering has been a long road, plus I have learned a lot about myself and others as I have experienced my illness. I am thankful that I am at the point where I can embrace the diagnosis rather than fear it or be ashamed by it. I am looking forward to doing something positive now so that I may help others and continue to grow personally. When I explain about bipolar illness to someone for the first time, I tell them that it is a lot like diabetes. I have found that people are more apt to visualize a physical illness than a mental illness. I have learned that bipolar illness is something that must be managed, much like diabetes. It's important to educate oneself and reach out to those who are there to help.

My son and my husband, Brendan, who I've been married to for five years, are my inspiration. Realizing that I can contribute to society, even though I have bipolar illness, is inspirational. Being passionate about life is fantastic. Fortunately, I have the initiative and desire to read and learn as much as I possibly can about being bipolar. I have spent many hours in the library and at the local bookstores absorbing information. I took responsibility for my illness early on. I cleaved to my doctor, therapist, church, and the friends and loved ones that cared enough to listen and accept me for me. I am a bipolar individual. It has made me who I am today. As a result of the struggles and strife in earlier years, I am truly a stronger person now. I have become educated, which benefits me personally and allows me the opportunity to help and guide others. At one time I said, "Why me?" Now I say, "I have bipolar illness, it doesn't have me. So what can I do with it to make a difference out there?"

Seven years ago, as a result of a horrible manic episode, I pretty much lost my life over a three-month period. Since then, I have had the chance to regain it. I have remarried; I now have a supportive, loving, and encouraging husband, who has helped me get to this better place. My relationship with my son is strong, and I have achieved time with him after several custody battles. I have earned back good financial standing and have fulfilled my debts and obligations to society. I am now organizing a non-profit group to nurture the arts and culture in my town, as I run a local art gallery. I am enjoying a sense of balance after regaining my self-esteem and am finding one of the largest missing pieces in my life: my faith. Accepting my diagnosis, I am moving on and am actually, finally, embracing it. I have created a Facebook page called Bipolar Artist. It helps me to connect with others and also helps to express my own feelings. I usually spend three days a week at my art gallery, and there I also have the opportunity to interact with a wide variety of people.

I look forward to making the most of the knowledge and experience I have to share regarding bipolar illness. I would like to continue to reach out to others on a one-to-one level, as well as with public speaking. It is a goal of mine to work through my church and provide outreach and support to those struggling and coping with bipolar illness. I would one day like to be able to offer something in written form about my experiences.

I have come to realize that the little things in life really mean the most. Waking up each day, starting fresh, and experiencing the beauty of nature is something that drives my attitude and outlook. I have found the idea of, "one day at a time," pretty much applies to all of life, and I remind myself of that often. I truly believe that the idea, "less is more," is very healthy and that reaching out to others is rewarding on so many levels. Learning from life's experiences and then applying them to the future benefit of the individual, as well as others, is fulfilling. I have learned it is important to be positive, even when it is a challenge to do so.

My husband and son give me the greatest sense of pride, happiness, and support. My parents are both living, are in their late seventies, and struggle with health problems. Health issues are sometimes a challenge to manage mentally, physically, and emotionally. I have a brother who is ten years older than I am. He has come to accept my illness and supports my accomplishments. My younger niece and I are eighteen years apart, but have always been close. She was diagnosed a few years ago with depression and anxiety issues, and I have been able to be there for her to offer support, guidance, and information. Being able to bring beauty and help to others has become my life's work. I have more to do yet and will enjoy every moment!

BD

Bipolar disorder falls into the category of mood disorders in the DSM-IV.

— *Definition*

Manic—condition involving highly energized mood, unusual thoughts, and possibly erratic actions.
Depression—feelings of prolonged sadness, pessimism, guilt, and hopelessness.

— *Is/Cause*

A) The NIH-Pub Med Health tells us that bipolar disorder involves periods of elevated or irritable mood which alternate with periods of depression. The mood swings can be abrupt - http://www.ncbi.nlm.nih.gov/pubmedhealth/PMH0001924/.

B) The NIMH says bipolar often develops in late teens or early adulthood with most cases starting before twenty-five - http://www.nimh.nih.gov/health/publications/bipolar-disorder/complete-index.shtml.

– Symptoms

A) The Mayo Clinic says bipolar disorder is sometimes described as manic-depressive disorder and ranges from the lows of depression to the highs of mania – http://www.mayoclinic.com/health/bipolar-disorder/DS00356.

B) The National Alliance on Mental Illness (NAMI) states symptoms can range from mania—racing thoughts and flight of ideas or increased talking/rapid speech to depression—loss of energy and feelings of hopelessness and guilt – http://www.nami.org//Template.cfm?Section=By_Illness&Template=/TaggedPage/TaggedPageDisplay.cfm&TPLID=54&ContentID=23037.

– Tips

A) The NIMH explains that several medications, beginning with mood stabilizers, can be helpful along with psychotherapy – http://www.nimh.nih.gov/health/publications/bipolar-disorder/complete-index.shtml#pub8.

B) Helpguide.org says more than medication is needed and a combination of things is most successful. Education about the situation, communication with doctors and therapists, a strong support system, making healthy lifestyle choices, and staying with the treatment plan is best – http://www.helpguide.org/mental/bipolar_disorder_diagnosis_treatment.htm.

Author's Note—A movie called My Friend Paul tells the story of a person who has bipolar disorder – http://www.imdb.com/title/tt0183548/.

Step 1. Consult a professional.

Chapter 3.
EATING DISORDERS

WHAT ARE EATING DISORDERS (ED)?

Christina

One day when I was eleven, I remember crying hysterically in my bedroom, because I was too large to fit into my size sixteen children's jeans. I had reached puberty. I thought my life was nearly over because of a pair of denim pants! As I look back, it is evident how ridiculous that was, but at eleven years old, my world was crashing over me; it smothered me with a blanket of self-hatred and insecurity. So, I did what I thought was the right thing and cut back on the amount of food I was eating. It seemed a simple solution.

The following year, three weeks after my 12th birthday, I had major surgery. That day changed my life and my perception of myself forever. Recovery from the surgery was frightening and disastrous for the young person I was. Many complications caused me to lose a massive amount of weight and a month of down time. For a while after the surgery, the subject of weight was avoided by everyone around me. But I wanted to know! Because the squeaky wheel gets the grease, I kept pestering the nurses to let me see what I looked like. Finally, the day arrived, and I was led to a mirror. Through a morphine-induced haze I could see an emaciated image staring back at me. I wanted to look like that forever, so I worked to keep myself thin, very thin.

Many years later, when I began college, I had already been diagnosed with bipolar disorder. I was still learning about that illness; it was a bitter pill to swallow at such an impressionable age. The regimen of pills each day kept me balanced, but also caused me to gain weight. Are you seeing warning signs? Over time I began to feel the same smothering effects I felt at age eleven; dealing with my expanding body became intolerable. I decided to start restricting my food intake in the hope of removing the excess weight and the feelings of inadequacy consuming my thoughts. I began cutting out many foods that I normally ate, exercising as often as I could, and dreamed about losing enough weight to feel okay with myself. I did lose weight, though I felt it should be more. The warning signs were flashing wildly!

Surfing on the Internet, I eventually found a community of bloggers. Beware of the people conversing about eating disorders on the blog website Livejournal. This site covers many topics, so the people I'm speaking of were discussing weight loss and wanting to be thin. It is young girls and young women supporting what, at first, seems to be a beneficial site. I came to know differently. Some in this small community had eating disorders; some were looking to acquire them. All those bloggers belonged to the pro-ana (anorexia) community.

I knew there were others who could relate to my situation, and so there were. Unfortunately, the vast majority of that group of people were turning eating disorders into a game, a trend, a badge of honor. Most promoted the idea that all eating disorders are lifestyles as opposed to serious mental illnesses. They would add "ana" or "mia" to their screen names ("ana" meaning they had anorexia, "mia" meaning they had bulimia), and by adding those little pet names to their name would automatically give them that eating disorder. They would end their blog posts with, "Think thin!" or, "Those who skip dinner end up thinner!" They would tell each other to, "Starve on." They would also create groups dedicated to seeing who could lose the most weight in a certain amount of time, or to see who could liquid fast the longest. Perhaps the most appalling of all, to keep themselves motivated, people would post "thinspiration" at the end of their message, using images of models and actresses who were thin, or even others who were emaciated. Since that time in 2003/2004, the number of those sites promoting eating disorders has grown exponentially. The sites recruit younger and younger members who want to acquire eating disorders. Anorexia, bulimia and ED-NOS (eating disorder not otherwise specified) are dangerous and life-threatening illnesses. They are not a game, cute, or funny!

In reality, eating disorders rob people of their livelihood, their sanity, and a lot more. I found that out for myself as time passed. At one point in 2003, a few of my friends, my sister, and my fiancé at the time held an impromptu intervention for me. Those caring people expressed their concerns over my extreme weight loss and my withering appearance. I listened, I contemplated, and I lied. I said I would seek treatment, knowing I wasn't ready to give up my eating disorder. By the time September of 2004 rolled around, I was so consumed by not eating that the only thing that mattered to me was maintaining my low weight. As a result, I lost many of my friends, because I kept myself isolated, I had to drop out of college because of my declining physical and mental health, I lost my job, and worst of all, I lost my fiancé. At the time, I saw these events as a free pass to continue slowly killing myself. However, I eventually got to a point where any activity was impossible. I finally decided I really did need help and sought treatment. I received inpatient treatment at the Renfrew Center. It helped a great deal with numerous misperceptions and thoughts, and I was recovering.

But soon after discharge, I relapsed—and hard! For me, the moment of clarity came when my sister harshly declared, "There is no point; it won't help." She was speaking about treatment, of course. Right then and there I decided to prove her wrong. As I pulled myself out of the relapse, over the course of two years, I slipped and fell along the way, but always kept in mind how far I had come. It was one of the hardest things I have ever had to do. By 2006, I experienced a period of partial recovery, and it was a very happy time in my life. I was balanced, able to hold a job again, and things were good.

At this time, I have relapsed once again, and the happy place is non-existent. However, I do have hope. Even though some days follow the old familiar pattern, there are also good days. Just as with any illness, we learn. I know now that recovery from an eating disorder is a lengthy and ongoing process. I know I am a good person. I know I have talents; I am an artist and a writer. I know I have a support system. I know I have strength and courage; I have faced many issues. Most of all, after many years and stumbles, I know that I can and will recover fully!

Jess

— *Pre-Bulimia*

Twenty years ago, I was sixteen. I was average height, weight, and shape. Though I had always thought I had thunder thighs, weight issues were an uncommon thought. I ate a good, varied diet, and the only problem, or so my dad thought, was that I wanted to be veggie. I hated meat, so I ate a lot of cheese for protein. My dad regularly voiced the concerns that it was really bad for my cholesterol and was fattening. He said, "As a young lady you need to be careful." At the same time, I was just starting in a new relationship with my childhood sweetheart. I was really happy, but what I didn't know was that my boyfriend's mother really wasn't. On Thursday nights I became a regular visitor to his house for tea. After eating, his mum and I would clear the table, do the pots, and she'd explain to me how bad an influence I was on her son. She would tell me it was my fault he did/didn't do something. She would tell me I was the cause of things I had no way to know. I felt so bad! Good heavens, I was so young, naïve, and impressionable, I began to think perhaps there was some truth to what she was saying!

I always apologised, though it was never enough, and I started to feel very guilty. At that time, Princess Diana was in the news about her bulimia. Whilst I never really understood, I did get the part about her making herself sick. Being sick to my stomach was something I'd hated since being a child. I'd rather have any illness other than that. Then the idea struck my brain; I needed to be punished. Maybe bulimia would help me stop upsetting his mother, and it would stop me from getting fat, like my dad worried about. I thought it would be the best thing all around. This thinking set my feet firmly on a path which soon went through a long, dark tunnel. I became a person with bulimia. It sounds bizarre now, but at the time, I felt so bad that I can sincerely remember believing it to be the answer to my problems.

— *Bulimia*

In the early stages, I was just entering this gloomy tunnel and could still see light from outside. I would be sick weekly when I went for tea. Occasionally, I would make myself sick when my dad got onto me about the cheese. I had no binging episodes at all in the beginning. As time went by, I started to become more sensitive and had started worrying a lot more about my weight. By now, the tunnel was getting pretty dark, and being sick became a form of punishment for many things going on in my life. Throwing up was a regular thing: three times a week, sometimes more. As I went forward, light was absent in the tunnel; I couldn't see. I became unhappy because of the bulimia. Little comments that had never bothered me before suddenly did, and talk of people's body shape or weight, as we were in our young adult stage, upset me. I always thought these comments were a dig at me. I was really low, the bulimia turned, and I started to binge. Not hugely to start with, but enough to make me feel guilty and to go be sick.

I had started the vicious cycle. I began to wonder where the bulimia tunnel led; I couldn't see and had to feel my way. I ate when I felt down, was sick because I'd overeaten, then felt down again. Over the next four years, the frequency of overeating increased to me being sick daily, and quite regularly, twice a day. My symptoms eventually became induced vomiting once or twice daily and binge eating large amounts, approximately four or five times weekly. There were constant worries about my weight, and I had feelings of inadequacy, guilt, shame, and fear of being found out. I also suffered depression and an inability to control myself or the feelings that consumed me. All of this was cause for and caused by the bulimia. I was in the heart of the tunnel, and it seemed endless.

At the time, I felt like a really bad person. The way my future mother-in-law treated me made me feel like it had to be my fault. It never occurred to me she wanted to hurt me because she didn't want me around her son. Perhaps she was angry with him and taking it out on me. Maybe she thought I was too good for him, could that be it? What I knew was that she was the adult, and I believed whatever she said was true. The more I thought this, the more the feelings intensified, and so did my punishment. Being sick and making myself feel horrid, emotionally and physically, helped, though of course, it didn't take anything away. The bulimia was never-ending! I felt I was paying slightly for my behavior and was trying to rectify the weight problem. I didn't suppose that the vomiting was making me have weight changes then, but the feeling of putting on a pound was huge. I also felt I had to do something quickly to appease my father. I couldn't seem to please anyone!

What was a typical day like as a person with bulimia? Food was always in my thoughts. At its worst, I would worry straight away how I would get through the day. For breakfast, Mum would ask what I wanted to eat, and I'd have trouble choosing between toast or cereal. Which had more calories? Which would fill me? Mum would get really annoyed with me, as I couldn't make up my mind. Eventually I'd say, "Just tea, Mum." She would say, "You need to eat. You can't work all day on just a drink. Now, what do you want, or I'll just fix it for you."

After I ate whatever she'd fixed, I'd think, *That's not good.* I'd go to work feeling bloated and full. I'd hope I'd be on one of the vigorous jobs to burn some calories. When lunchtime came, I'd need to go buy something, and I'd think, *Oh goodness, where shall I go? I'm so hungry and it's been such a long morning, maybe I'll go to Thurston's. I'll just have to be sick afterward. I'm on lunch alone, so no one will know.* Off I would go and take away a lovely vegetable pasty. Looking over other available items, I'd think, *That rum truffle with a cornflakes bun also looks delicious.* Then, additionally, I would decide to get some chips, scraps, and peas. Then, just one more stop for pop and chocolate to eat at home. Lunch would be so tasty, eaten alone, with the door locked. I had time now to relax. I can't remember any thoughts I had. After eating I would need to be sick. Once the acid hit I would be sick. I'd be sure to give it one more try, because I couldn't afford those few extra calories. Then I'd get some milk to rinse my mouth. I'd be fine after that; I'd just drink loads of tea to fill my tummy, so I wouldn't feel hungry. The afternoon and well into the night would be busy. I would finally finish at ten.

After arriving home, I would be too tired and couldn't be bothered to cook, so I'd get takeaway again. I'd think, *Bella is so nice, and they do make the best fries when I ring them.* It would be a half an hour to wait, and because I'd be starving, I'd think, *Maybe I'll have one of those chocolate bars to put me on until it's time.* Then the doorbell would ring. *It's here!* I'd think. And the food would be good as ever. But then I'd think, *I'll save some for tomorrow.* Soon I'd have more food-related thoughts and think, *Well, okay, I'll have only one slice of pizza left, but at least I saved some.* After that, I'd need to go to bed thinking, *I'm so tired!* In bed, I couldn't settle my stomach, because it would be far too full. I'd look at my tummy in the mirror and think, *I'm fat, look at how far it sticks out. It's no good!* I'd have to be sick again to help me feel better. Damn the acid taste and heartburn. I'd think, *Now I will never sleep because I feel so washed out, and yet my heart is racing.* Thank goodness, I would be alone; I did so hate myself. I'd wish for just one day off. Maybe tomorrow, please let it be so.

Over the years, my weight changed more, due to my work and the long hours spent on call. Cooking wasn't always an option, so it had to be takeaway on those days. I dreaded and loved it all in one. The food tasted so good, but always led to vomiting. It created huge guilt trips and struggles within my mind. The guilt, pain, and depression weighed on me heavily. The binging got even worse. I look back now and wonder how I could have been so incredibly naïve. The reasons don't make much sense with study, but I know how intense they were at the time. I wish I could go back to change things.

The most overriding feeling, every time I binged and purged, was guilt. It felt so good when I was eating, then so good purging. Afterward, I would think about any little bit of weight gain and know that I had caused it. Guilty. When I felt ill because of the bulimia, family and friends would feel sorry for me and I'd feel bad about that. Guilty. I was deceiving them and I felt bad about that. Guilty. At the same time, other feelings I had were sadness and loneliness. I spoke to no one about the bulimia, even though it had become such a big part of my life. It isolated me and made me lonely. Through it all, I made plans to get married to my boyfriend.

With the wedding fast approaching, my future mother-in-law was openly nasty to me and about me to anyone who would listen. Was I really so bad? I have learned that it wasn't me who was bad; twenty years and much hindsight are great enlightenment!

— *The Accident*

In December 1995, I had an accident at work. I was a senior veterinary nurse and head of weekends. It was a profession I had always wanted. I loved my work! It was a Sunday, and I was moving trays of twelve to twenty-four cans of pet food. It was time-consuming and hard work, with heavy lifting involved. When I had finished, there was a bit of an ache in my back, but who wouldn't have it? Forty-eight hours later, I had been rushed into hospital and was paralysed from the waist down. I didn't know what was happening. After surgery, I had months of rehabilitation. I can now walk small distances around the house, etc. Outside, I can do short distances with my crutches, but any further, and I need to use my wheelchair. I am lucky; I could have had to use a wheelchair for any mobility. I know I could have been much worse, and I would love to be better than I am now, but I am grateful for the abilities I have.

The accident changed so much and made me realise that whilst I couldn't change certain aspects of my life, I really needed to have control over the things I could change. I also realised a good support network is critical. When I first wanted to deal with the bulimia, I had to tell someone, and that was my then best friend. She was a person I trusted and we had a heart to heart. She encouraged me to tell my fiancé and then, in time, the doctor. She knew he was what I really needed. It was the best decision I ever made.

The accident has impacted my life hugely, as prior to the event, I would go camping, walking, play squash, swimming, and many other sports. Since then, I can't do any physical activities. I have also lost many friends, as, basically, they didn't have time for me anymore. In May 1997, I had the daunting prospect of facing my previous employer in a legal battle. It was a harrowing time, having so many people against me, including my best friend. In the end, she would not give in court the supporting evidence she originally gave my solicitor. It was awful, and she had to be subpoenaed. That hurt so much! The last time I saw her was outside the courtroom, where she couldn't even look at me. The pain I felt in losing her after all we had been through was unbearable. I lost the court case on a technicality. Coming out of the courtroom, I had to endure the laughing of my previous coworkers; they were people I had worked alongside for years. In that moment, I felt the loss of my friends, my job, and to a large degree, my life.

– First Husband

Just ten days after the court decision, my husband of nine months went out one night clubbing, got drunk, picked someone up, and was unfaithful. When I asked, "Why," he said it was my fault, as I'd lost the court case. He wouldn't have "his" half a million to spend, so he had to cheer himself up! It was such a betrayal, and for me, I knew it to be the end of my marriage. Unfortunately, with everything that had happened, I'd lost all my confidence, and I didn't have the strength to leave. So, outwardly everything was okay, but inwardly I was desperately unhappy. He kept on cheating, was uncaring of my feelings, and I made the decision to remain childless. I always wanted kids, but I couldn't have them with a person who cared so little about others. It was one more terrible, painful blow.

– Light!

On the positive side, after so many miserable, lonely years, an old school friend came back into my life in a huge way. He was living on the streets, having been evicted by his ex at the time, so my husband offered him a room. I think he saw my friend as someone to keep me company whilst he was out, now four to five times a week. The good thing was that you can put on a show for a few hours whilst visiting people, but you can't pretend twenty-four hours a day. My friend soon saw what the situation was like for me. He finally helped me realise the situation, then gave me the courage and confidence to leave my husband and my sham of a marriage. A knight in shining armour had come to my rescue! The day I split was like dawn breaking for the very first time. It was the first glimmer of hope in my life! The weight of the world was lifted from my shoulders, and I felt free enough to fly.

– Treatment

I'd seen many doctors related to the accident, and eventually, I went for help with the bulimia; my inspiration to go was my life. I wanted one; I wanted mine back. I was a person I didn't recognise. I had lost my confidence and become quiet and insular. I didn't want to go out, never saw friends, was snappy and irritable, depressed, and out of control. The bulimia ruled every part of my life. I wanted "me" back, fun-loving "me." I wanted to be the happy-go-lucky person who enjoyed going out with friends, enjoyed sports, and enjoyed food or an occasional pudding guiltlessly. To be normal again and to have my life: that was my inspiration and what kept me going.

My treatment brought forth an emotional roller coaster! When I went to the doctor's office, I chose to go into group therapy. It's odd for me as, being shy like I was, I usually ran from groups. On the first day I went to join the group, I was terrified. I was frightened of the unknown, of being judged, of being treated like a freak, of having to say what my day was like, and ultimately, of them being unable to help me. It was actually very different, because everyone was kind and understanding. When the staff first sat me down and explained about the way I was, it was amazing to me that they understood. That was the second time I saw a bit of hope. Even after people knew about the illness, I still couldn't talk about it except in group therapy. I hoped and desperately wanted to be normal again and to have my life back!

Learning about bulimia has been an experience in itself. None of us knew anything then, beyond the binge and sick circle. When we learnt the dangers of what we were doing to our bodies, we did all vow to change. I had finally found a match that would dispel some of the darkness of the tunnel for a moment; it was enough to give me some bearing and spur me onward.

Bulimia, no matter how severe or mild, creates an imbalance within the body. If left untreated, the imbalance can lead to other illnesses. The stomach is filled with acid to break food down. The wall of the stomach is designed to be able to cope with this, where the rest of the body is not. So the constant vomiting can damage the fingers and hand, mouth, throat, epiglottis, esophagus, and the stomach muscles. Bleeding occurs as linings are lost. Ulcers can form, or worse, a rupture to allow the acid into other parts of the body. This can kill exceedingly quickly and without warning. Vomiting itself can cause choking and suffocation if fragments are inhaled into the lungs. The constant vomiting can lead to bad breath, mouth ulcers, swelling of the tongue, headaches, cramps, pulled muscles, and dental decay and rotting. If the sufferer is young when he or she starts, it can cause growth stunting or deformities. In older people, it can cause period fertility problems and complete infertility. This can happen to both male and female sufferers. Modifying one's actions becomes crucial.

Let there be little doubt, treatment for eating disorders is harder than for many illnesses, as the physical and mental have to be treated together. Huge amounts of willpower are the only way to come out the other end of the tunnel. Bulimia feels like a shameful issue, which is sadly why many sufferers don't get the treatment they need. They need help quickly to reduce the effects of bulimia. Worldwide, eating disorders are played down and, to a degree, swept under the carpet. They might instead be explained for the danger an eating disorder is, for females *and* males. This way, people might not end up with the guilty, shameful, and secret illness society has made eating disorders. The illness needs to be *highlighted*.

Social problems are easily recognizable. These include mood swings, snappiness, anger, fear, paranoia, delusions, secretive behavior unrelated or related to the bulimia, depression, shame, guilt, becoming insular, and pushing friends and family away. Relationships are also affected. Single people can't cope and find it too difficult to start relationships. For those in relationships/marriage, maintaining them can be hard, and many times, divorce occurs. The stigmas create such problems that many sufferers can't confide in their partners. It can also cause monetary problems for some sufferers. Binging on food can bring about debt and its own problems. It's such a sad, complicated, serious illness, with so many side affects, most of which people don't know until it's too late. In particular, *bulimia can cause death.*

In treatment, we wrote weekly diaries of everything we consumed, our thoughts, and why we felt that way. Then we had to say if we were sick or not. It was so hard to face my fear and read about myself. For many weeks, it brought feelings of total shame and guilt, though at the same time, it also brought progress. It was good when the diaries started to show signs and triggers, real reasons that gave the staff ways to help us. I was moving ahead, my footing was more firm, and my steps were more confident. I would reach the end of this blasted tunnel, because things were continually getting lighter!

At the end of the course, I felt elation. I had far to go before I was cured, but even I could see and feel the changes. I realised how lucky I was to have found my path to recovery. It is a chance everyone should have. It is possible to reach the light!

When I started on the road to recovery, I still had binging and purging thoughts, but as I started to have even slight improvements, I also started to really have hope. The more improved I was, the more hope I had, and so it went. As weeks of improvements occurred, I started to believe in myself again and in the fact that I could actually recover. I was always realistic, which helped me to keep going. The longer I went to therapy, the happier I felt. I was also healthier, more confident, and more normal. I could go out and enjoy myself without a struggle in my head. It was freeing and wonderful! I still look on recovery today as such an achievement!

I also found that recovery in itself spurred me on. It's like going on a diet. When I started, I would think, *I'll never reach my goal.* Then, every time I lost a couple of pounds, I'd get excited and want to try harder for the next weigh-in, and the next, and so on. I was incredibly proud the first time I went a week without vomiting. I was elated when I could go out, have a small dessert, and I didn't rush to the toilet afterward. I think because bulimia is such a secret illness, only people with the bulimia can spur themselves on. Trying to change because someone says it's the thing to do puts more pressure on the person trying to change. It makes things so much harder! Now my family helps me keep going. I don't ever want to go back to the way I was. I'm happy, healthy, loved, happy with what I look like, and what I've become. I can't imagine, and wouldn't want, my family to go through the pain and heartache I did. I also have two sons, nieces, and since Christmas, a goddaughter. I don't want them to see or be exposed to bulimia. Peer pressure can create much hardship, and they will have enough to deal with. My past will remain in the past. To think about the traumatic episode takes some effort, but I'm willing to do it if others can be helped.

– I Have a Life!

As I look backward, I can see myself trudging through the tunnel, sightless as I was, always compelled to keep moving forward toward the light I knew I could find. When I looked forward, I could see myself counseling others. I'm a Guide Leader now, and the girls I see at ages eleven to fifteen are so impressionable! I always listen to their concerns. I try to help steer them to make wise choices. If weight issues come up, I try to help them look at things in a different and positive way. I am incredibly aware now and really want to help people choose, or get back on, the right track. Now when I hear the awful and sad stories of what bulimia can do, I know I'm very lucky.

As to my knight in shining armour, he's now my wonderful husband. In July 2003, the first of my longed-for sons was born. In February 2008, we welcomed our second son. I told my second husband about the bulimia right at the beginning. He was so supportive; I always knew I could talk to him and he would do whatever I needed to help. So, though it was still very, very hard, I did have the challenge eased by a good support network. You just cannot go through, or get through, recovery alone. You need to speak to at least one other person you trust, or as many people as possible. Ask them to help you every step of the way. I will always be grateful to the friends who helped and shared my pain, the hospital group, my best friend, and my new husband.

As people grow, they might never think about life experience, what they want to be, or where they want to go. Experiences are so influential. My life has had the bad, the average, and the good. Whilst I can't change what I have done, I can certainly learn, change, and adapt toward a better future. I'm a mother, wife, daughter, sister, auntie, friend, and Guide Leader. I truly believe my experiences can have an impact in many of these areas. At the times they were happening, I thought bulimia episodes were the worst things that could happen. Now I know better.

What do I look forward to? Easy: my life. I love my family and friends dearly. I only could have gotten through all my problems with their support. I'm looking forward to all our sons' milestones and achievements. My family is there, no matter what. They may have trouble understanding, coping, or agreeing with what we do, but I know if I pick up a phone and say, "Help!" they will be there in the blink of an eye, as I would be for them. In the same manner, I would lay down my life for my two boys.

My life's theme has to be family, in particular, my immediate family. My husband is the second, but boy, what a difference from the first! After marriage to a man who was abusive, took my money, had countless affairs, and cared nothing about me, Dunk was a miracle worker. Whilst I was first married, my confidence was shot, and I didn't have the strength to fight my ex-husband. Dunk helped me to believe in myself, see what was happening, and become aware of how ill I was. It took a long time, but I found the strength to leave my ex-husband. Now, I'm loved unconditionally and deeply. I feel safe and happy. Dunk totally turned me around and I will always thank him; hopefully it is enough.

People I thought I would never have in my life are my two amazing boys. Kieran was first. Finding out I was pregnant was just the most joyous feeling in the world. Brandon is our second son. Again, he was a dream come true, and everyone was thrilled. He's also loved so very, very much. My parents worship the boys, as they never thought they would have grandkids. My brother also dotes on them; he doesn't have children of his own. We are totally blessed with our sons; they make Dunk and me complete. Life is great!

My family is foremost in my life. There is my husband Dunk, my two sons, my mother, father, and brother, my auntie in Australia, and my ninety-year-old grandmother. I would lay down my life for any of them, just as they have always been there to support me. My parents are wonderful. They are still together and have just celebrated their ruby wedding anniversary. They are always there to help and guide me when I need it. They try not to interfere, but let us know they are a phone call or a ten-minute drive away, day or night.

My brother and I couldn't be closer, and we are very alike. He's kind, caring, funny, and a fantastic handyman. He does tremendous charity work and was rewarded this year by being invited to the Queen's garden party for her thanks. We are all so proud of him. I have an auntie I'm very close to. Sadly, she has now moved to Australia, though she is very involved in what we are doing. She is due to get married next year, and I'm so sorry we'll miss her special day. I also have a grandma, another auntie, cousin, and the most gorgeous half-cousin, for whom we have been waiting twenty years!

Now I have the ability to help other people to achieve, and hopefully, this will continue. My success is definitely having my life back and being in control. I now feel normal because, instead of the other way around, I can manage what I eat. I tell bulimia what to do. It's huge to be able to look at food and wonder whether to eat it, decide not, and that ends it. Fights within my head and not giving in are non-existent. When eating, there is only moving on. I can have a treat like chocolate, chips, anything, as I know that's all it is; a treat. I can make food decisions rationally and easily, the same as most others. Yes, after my accident and the damage my ex-husband and his mother did, I put on seven stone.

I then dieted in the form of cutting down. I still eat this, that, or the other, which has allowed me to lose more than the seven stone. When I go out, I will sometimes have chips or pudding, and boy, do I enjoy them! I gained knowledge and fought back! I feel fantastically proud for cracking my demon! My success has restored my confidence, which is why I want to share my experiences. I hope to help many other people to know, "Success is possible!"

ED

Author's Note—The DSM-IV says an eating disorder may be evidenced by a tremendous disturbance in eating behavior. How does this happen? Possibly because we are often told that we have to be thin to look good. It could follow then that perception of oneself might help create a disturbance. We can look good, eat healthy, and comfortably. Moderation may be our key.

— Is/Cause

A) The National Eating Disorders Association (NEDA) states that while eating disorders might begin with preoccupation on food and weight, they very probably are about much more. People are encouraged to investigate, a phone number is available ~ http://www.nationaleatingdisorders.org/information-resources/general-information.php#causes-eating-disorders.

B) The Something Fishy website explains that the most common element inherent among all eating disorders is low self-esteem ~ http://www.something-fishy.org/whatarethey/edordiet.php.

— Symptoms

A) Women's Health explains that eating disorders frequently develop in adolescence or early adulthood, but can occur anytime. Females are more likely to develop eating disorders than males ~ http://www.womenshealth.gov/bodyimage/eatingdisorders/.

B) The National Association for Males with Eating Disorders, Inc. separates symptoms into different categories. Among Observable Physical Symptoms are Anorexia-feeling cold even when temperature is normal, Bulimia-dry skin and bloating, Binge eaters-bloating and swollen hands and feet ~ http://www.namedinc.org/symptoms.asp.

– Tips

A) The NEDA explains that seeking help might be a frightening thought, but gaining support from a trusted friend, family member, or school counselor might be the first step on the road to recovery ~ http://www.helpguide.org/mental/eating_disorder_treatment.htm.

B) The Something Fishy Organization states that the person with eating disorder has to find something that works for them. It might be one-on-one therapy, support groups, clinics which may be inpatient or out-patient, art therapy, church groups, a combination of any, or none of the above but something completely different ... there are many options out there ~ http://www.something-fishy.org/helping/whatyoucando.php..

Author's Note—A moderate and balanced (a serving at each meal) diet of protein, vegetables, fruit, dairy, and carbohydrates can help the feeling of being full and may also help maintain health as well as a comfortable weight.

Examples of food choices include:

Proteins = 4-6 oz. (women) or 6-8 oz. (men) fish, turkey and chicken, soy, eggs, or beans

Vegetables = broccoli, carrots, green pepper, celery

Fruits = apples, oranges, grapes, strawberries

Dairy = milk, yogurt, small amounts of cheese

Complex carbohydrates = whole-wheat bread, rice, noodles.

Simple carbohydrate = sugar, it is a source of energy and can be a large contributor to health issues. Sucrose, high fructose corn syrup, and corn syrup are examples of sugars. Moderation and avoiding snacking is important.

Author's Note—An Internet article describes healthy weight loss - http://fitbie.msn.com/lose-weight/she-lost-110-pounds-and-training-marathon?gt1=50014.

Step 1. Consult a professional.

Chapter 4.
SUBSTANCE ABUSE

WHAT IS SUBSTANCE ABUSE/DEPENDENCE?

Candy

— *Childhood*

The day I was born, my daddy held me, shed a loving tear or two, and named me Candy. On the spot, he wrote two lines of a song about me; he was a very talented man. That night, he had my name tattooed on his arm. From the time I was very young, he and I had to keep our relationship secret, because I was forbidden to see him. Sure, as if that was going to happen! I often stayed with my grammy, the mother's mother, and she would take me to see Daddy without the mother knowing. He taught me about music and singing. At six, I wrote my first song. To him it was the best ever written. I was so proud! Daddy blessed me with musical talent and another, less fortunate "gift." More on that later. Daddy died when he was a young man. While he was alive, I felt loved. For the first twelve years of my life, I also felt somewhat protected. I say that because my life had always been filled with horrible physical, psychological, emotional, and sexual abuse. Blessedly, I don't remember some of the worst of it. I left home when I was fifteen. First, the mother abused me and then it was her and her second husband. They gave me no reason to ever claim them as mine, so I won't. I was treated as an intruder into their lives until the day I left that gruesome existence. I am incredibly thankful to have had the ability to leave and survive. I am successful in spite of all of their efforts, thanks to the strength passed to me by my daddy!

Before talking about any abuse inflicted upon me, I must mention the abuse I was inflicting upon myself. I was a full-blown drug addict at twelve. Crack cocaine was my drug of choice to deal with the painful death of my father and the miserable reality of my life. Crack was perfect for me, because it is odorless, colorless, and can be transported easily. Daddy's death created loneliness, fear, confusion, and sadness in me, so how do you think I dealt with it whenever those feelings were present? Crack, of course. Drugs were also the cause of his death. At my tender age, I didn't know there were other ways to cope with so much awful pain. The mother resented me, the eventual husband of the mother took his cue from the mother, and neither knew that I needed help; they wouldn't have helped me anyway. So the death of my father went unresolved, and the abuse persisted. Because crack cocaine was always my solution, at least I could escape temporarily.

Three years later, I was reacquainted with death. I had two best friends, Faith and Emily. We were called the three musketeers, because we did everything together. We decided one day to go to an all-night skate that night. Faith chose to walk alone and meet Emily and me at the rink. We wanted to pick her up, to take her with us, but it was Faith's choice to walk. She never showed up at the roller-skating rink. We didn't know why. We were to learn that a child molester, just released from prison, dragged Faith into his car, and either she tried to get out or fought with him and was pushed out. However it happened, my friend ended up landing on the windshield of an oncoming car, with a devastating result.

— Abuse

We lived in a rural area, where horses were ridden frequently; I had three of my own as pets. The morning after the skate, some different friends rode over on their horses. Dramatically, they gave me the news.

Faith was dead. Nooooo! It couldn't be true! I screamed and cried. The husband came running and heard me repeatedly saying, "Faith is dead." Having delivered their message, my riding friends left. The icing on the cake was when the husband said, "It probably was for the best, because Faith was a troublemaker who was expelled from school." As if that mattered to me! I knew what word I would like to call him—if I dared!

The mother wouldn't believe Faith was dead until she read it in the newspaper. When she did, she cut out the article, put it on the refrigerator, called me down to the kitchen, and made me read it out loud, while Faith's picture stared back at me. The mother made sure I could see and hear her laughter as this took place. I wanted to yell, "What do you two think you're doing? You're both disgusting!" But, I had learned a lot and knew it was better to keep my thoughts to myself. I went to my room, without comfort, to console myself.

Talking about the abuse, it's amazing to me that I can be where I am today. I hope others can also survive and succeed. More details of my abuse include beatings with a two-by-four, being made to drink from a stream on my hands and knees, told I was an animal, being punched in the face, and being beaten so I was unconscious from the first blow and could barely walk the next day. After that one, the mother told me I would be staying home from school for a few days. Hah! She didn't want anyone to clearly see the evidence of abuse!

I was a voice and business major in high school. Music is what interested me most, and was also a calming influence. The music class assignments were the only ones I completed. One time, the mother tore apart my precious music and trashed my room. I told her I needed the ripped-up work for class. She said, "You didn't write that. You're too stupid to write something like that. Who'd you copy it from?" I screamed, which I knew not to do, that she had destroyed all of my music! So she called her husband and whined to him. He would often say to me, "You're whale shit, because nothing sinks lower!" When he came home that day, the mother carefully told him, "Don't kill her." Uh oh, I knew what would happen but was learning not to care.

The mother tried to get me to commit suicide twice, that way she and her husband couldn't be accused of murder. What she didn't know was that I had been praying God would kill them! She was successful in breaking my nose three times. I had to reset it myself, and that was not a pretty sight to witness or to feel! The third time was the last time—for everything. She screamed that I was a loser and worthless like my daddy. I believe she was secretly jealous of us, because I was told his name was never to be spoken again. That did it! I put some personal items in a bag, and when I left, she warned that she would shoot me if I ever came back. I screamed the words I had wanted to say my whole life, "I Fucking Hate You!" There was only silence as I walked out. Hmmm, I was fifteen, and I had finally had the last word! The results of my young life were multiple.

— Addiction

After leaving home, I was able to stay with a friend and her mom for a while. I had to keep going to school and no drugs were allowed. Finally, there was someone to call "Mom," and I still do. Being an addict like I was, trying to avoid crack was a tough rule to follow, so I kept using. When I couldn't locate cocaine, acid would do. I couldn't concentrate and kept losing track of my school assignments, but I managed to graduate at the bottom of my class. I think the school pushed me through so I would be out of there. They wanted no part of a drug-abusing, physically abused student!

Then, my friend's mom caught me when I had a bad acid trip. Busted! She had warned me, and out I went.

At first, I had my car and a part-time job, but the car broke down, and I lost the job. So the streets were now my home. I slept in abandoned buildings, on park benches, under a bridge, and my life was all about getting high. I lived on the East Coast and sometimes would start the day in one state and end up in another. I wouldn't know where I was or how I got there. Whatever happened in my life is a foggy memory. One day, I was at a fast-food place and just sat at a table. There was a man at another table, studying me. Fortunately, he was really a decent guy. After a while, he came over and asked if I was hungry. When I said I was, he bought me food and offered to let me shower at his house. A shower sounded heavenly to me! After his girlfriend came to his house, they dropped me off, and I was on my own again. It was nice while it lasted! It would be a long, hard road to travel before recovery happened, but happen it did.

− *Recovery*

As I said, getting high was my reason for living, and I was always on the lookout for my next fix. I did whatever it took to make that happen. I was living on the streets when I turned eighteen. One day, I was walking along the sidewalk, high as a kite, and passed a hospital. What happened next was an act of God, because addicts just don't do this. I walked into the hospital ER and said, "I'm a drug addict and if I don't get help, I'm going die." They first tested my blood to verify the truth of my statement. I was told that, with the drugs in my system, I was lucky to be alive. So I was right!

The detox period at the hospital was three days, although I think it's longer now, as it should be. I couldn't eat or drink anything with caffeine. Withdrawal set in quickly. I shared a room with another girl, but then my main concern was getting high again. I remember sitting in the corner, knees drawn up to my chest and arms wrapped around them, rocking back and forth, and crying. I remember lying or kneeling on the floor and vomiting, because there was no time to get to the bathroom. It was unbelievable how much I wanted to leave and use again! It was extremely painful, physically and mentally! Three days later, I was asked if I wanted to continue treatment in a rehabilitation program. They had to ask? At that point, I knew three things: I had just detoxed, I wasn't doing it again, and my life was still on the line. So I went.

There were group sessions, recovering addicts as speakers, and private sessions with the doctor. All of these were very helpful, and one thing was crystal clear to me. We don't choose addiction: it chooses us. Thinking back through my family history almost predicted my addiction. Today, I am an addict who chooses to not use. In the beginning, I was a poor patient, and that's putting it mildly! We had different chores to do every day and a certain time we had to be in bed. Some of the people in there had at least a decent childhood; some did not. I didn't want do chores or make my bed every day! I had to, literally, learn how to live a normal life, because I'd never had one. I could have left at any time; attendance was voluntary. Believe me, there were times I wanted to walk out the door, but I always stayed. Fortunately, I was given the strength, courage, and wisdom to know that I needed it.

The worst days were visiting days, when people were allowed to have visitors. I was the lone stand-out, because there was no one to visit me. No one knew I was still alive! It meant a lot to me that a counselor noticed and would take me to another room just to have a conversation. She knew how things were for me, because she was also a recovering addict. The adage holds true: "It takes an addict to cure an addict." On the day of my release from the recovery program, I had to see the doctor one last time. He summed things up very simply for me. I will remember what he said forever: "If you go back to using, you'll end up in the hospital again. This time, you will be rolled into the morgue on a gurney instead of walking into detox." That stark statement had impact enough to erase any possible return to drug-seeking behavior. It still influences me to this day.

– *Living Life, Part I*

When I walked out of rehab for the last time, I had nowhere to go. I was street smart and knew what I could do. That led to thoughts of crack, which immediately led to an alternative—prayer. I kept asking God to please show me the way, and I soon had my answer. I found myself standing in front of a rescue mission. I walked through the doors and told a person working there that I was homeless. The first question I was asked was, "Why are you homeless?"

"Because no one wants me," I replied. From the look on her face, I saw that this answer was unexpected. It seemed she couldn't believe something like that could happen. She went on to explain the rules of the mission to me and gave me a piece of paper with more rules. I was very familiar with rules by now!

We were allowed to have visitors, so I got in touch with my friend and her mom. They were so proud of me and came to see me at the mission. It was a tearful reunion filled with love. It was at the mission that I met my future husband, Michael. After he had asked me to marry him and I had accepted, Mom begged me not to do this. She said I was way too young, I had been recovering only three months, and Michael was a recovering alcoholic and addict who chose to stay away from rehab. Two months later, we were married and moved from the mission to the apartment. With my newfound freedom from everything, of course I knew best. I wanted everyone to know I had gotten my life together. Mom pleaded with me, even on the day of the wedding, to not get married. The wedding was small, with about ten people there. Then the rape happened.

— Rape

We had been married two weeks, I was eighteen, and we were both newly released from rehab. Michael and I had very little. The rescue mission helped us to get a small apartment, so we bought two chairs and a coffee table from the thrift shop. That was what we had for furniture, and there was no phone. We were living in a very bad part of town. One warm evening, my husband and I decided to take a walk. We were close to home when we were stopped by three men. Two of them engaged Michael in conversation, while the ringleader drew me away from the group. Fear was my immediate reaction when he pulled out a knife and held it to my throat. I wanted to scream, cry, or do something, but I didn't dare. The ringleader said to my husband, "What are you going to do now?" My husband's first thought was to get help, and to my disbelief, he walked away. He didn't care enough to fight for me! When Michael turned the corner, he sprinted to the nearest telephone and dialed 911. It didn't matter to the ringleader what my husband did; he knew what he wanted. I sure wasn't thinking as I was dragged over to a building and had my head bashed against the brick wall, I don't know how many times. Unconscious and bloody, I was being raped when emergency vehicles came.

The rapist ringleader was caught, jailed, prosecuted, and found *not guilty*, even with the testimony of his two friends! When we were leaving the courtroom, the rapist came right up behind me and whispered, "I'm not done with you yet you bitch." Yes, I was scared to death!

— Living Life, Part 2

About a month after the rape, I found out that I was pregnant. The pregnancy was thrilling to me and I knew from the timing it was my husband's child. Whew! I kept it to myself for a while. Shortly after that, Michael had to go to jail for three or four months. I was trying to get used to being alone in the apartment and to being an expectant mother. I was so happy to be carrying a child of my own. This baby would never know the pain a hand could deliver or the sting of degrading language.

He would know true love! I would hold him over and over during the day. I would play games with him. I would tell him how much I loved him. I could be the mommy I wished I had. My future was really looking bright!

Mom begged me again, like she had about the wedding, to leave Michael in the dark about the pregnancy. But, I felt he had to know; that telling him was the right thing to do. Mom had a bad feeling about Michael and she was right. After his release, he started drinking again, very heavily. Both of us were unemployed. Because I was considered high risk, I was ordered to stay in bed for the first five months of the pregnancy. Then, when he was drunk, which was all the time, Michael started abusing me. It was a walk in the park compared to what I had been through, but now I was carrying another life! Even after he punched me in the stomach, I stayed with him until the baby was born. Then the baby and I were out the door! Michael and I were really just friends anyway—and not even that friendly. I went back to the only real home I'd known: I moved in with my best friend and her mom. Michael and I had joint custody of our son, until the boy started telling me about disturbing things happening when he went to visit his dad. After my son told me, "Dad asked me if I ever speak to you about the bad stuff he does, and he told me he'd kill me if I did," neither of us saw Michael again. He was out of the picture in a flash and forever!

My son and I grew up together. I was blessed with the best child I could ask for and I learned the skills of being a parent. Raising him has been the most rewarding and wonderful accomplishment of my life. At first, we barely scraped by, but I always told my son that we are the richest people in the world because we have so much love. That makes all the hardship worth it. The Salvation Army, Toys for Tots, and the Red Cross are awesome charitable organizations that really helped us through that time. As my child was growing, I got better-paying singing jobs and I formed my own band. I stayed with my son as long as I could on the nights we performed, then left him with a sitter. We even tried Nashville for a while, but things didn't work out, mostly because finding a trustworthy person to leave my son with was impossible.

We moved back. I formed another band and loved it. Financially, things were good and getting better. We had both been through so much; I knew there was a reason.

– *PTSD*

Though I didn't know what it was, I began noticing in grade school that I would jump out of my skin when loud noises would happen. The ringing bell for a fire drill would send the hairs on the back of my neck straight up, and I felt like jumping to the ceiling! It scared me to death! I would cringe at the barking of a dog and cover my ears. I still do. People will stare at me when I do this; I get embarrassed and have to leave. Balloons have the same effect, because I know they'll pop eventually. I'll jump and people stare because they don't understand how terribly this affects me. I also found that some smells will stop me in my tracks and send me into flashback. Murphy's Oil Soap is one of those smells. When I lived at home, we had hardwood floors washed with Murphy's.

When I was thirty and began counseling, I learned this actually had a name. It was called post-traumatic stress disorder, or PTSD. My counselor would try different ways to lessen the effect of a loud noise. She asked me to remember ten things and then, as I was thinking about them, she moved behind me and clapped her hands. I almost flew off my chair! Once, when we were talking, she stopped, leaned very close, and snapped her fingers. I was startled. If someone behind me touches my shoulder, I am jolted. Firecrackers make me totally panicked. All of these things have always alarmed me, and still do to this day. For panic attacks, I take medication, which really doesn't do much for me. I just think, *I've been through worse!* So I keep going.

– *Depression*

You may wonder how all of these events affected me. The darkest times I can remember were when I suffered from clinical depression. It was awful, terrible, very deep depression. Often, it would last a few days up to a few months. The thoughts I had are hard to explain, but I'll try. I felt like I was a burden on the world; I hated myself. I would just lie on the sofa and cry or rock myself and pray to God to go to sleep. I have always had trouble sleeping. One time someone asked me what it felt like to be depressed. I told her it felt like I was walking down a pitch-black alley, and there was only despair and sadness surrounding me. Then the grim reaper took my hand and pulled me even further down. It was a most frightening feeling! Very scary indeed!

— *I Made It!*

Things started to improve when I finally sought help from a psychiatrist. It was a long process of finding the right medications for me. I still go every three to four months; the doctor just wants to make sure I'm still doing well. I always have been, since we found the right meds. I take anti-depressants and anti-anxiety medications for PTSD every day. I'm so thankful the right meds were figured out for me, because now I'm happy, happy, happy! Sometimes I have a low, underlying depression, but it's nothing like before. I just have to stay unstressed on those days, and I like to be alone. Mostly, that's all in the past.

It was tough for me to understand the loss of daddy and Faith, but I know they are with me in spirit. I can feel it, and I think Daddy would be very proud of me. What I have found is that I can't be afraid for the rest of my life. If I am, I'll never experience life. I'm proud to look in the mirror and say out loud, "I'm a survivor!"

Now, a big part of my life is being a humanitarian. I want to give to others what I have been given, and more. I work with many charities and organizations. I want to help others rehab and stay off drugs. I want to help stop abuse of any kind. When I am unsuccessful in helping someone, or in what I have set out to do, it hurts my heart and drives me to work harder.

When one walks down the street, or into the office, smiling at everyone is a good thing to do. So is giving someone a hug. It's unbelievable what a small, kind gesture like that can do! Forget about handshakes with me; you're getting a hug! At Christmastime, dropping that little bit of change into the Salvation Army pot will help someone. If you go ahead and make eye contact with the person ringing the bell, they will appreciate the recognition that they're out there because they want to make a difference. You might try donating a toy to Toys for Tots, no matter how small or inexpensive it is. You'll help to make a child, who may not get anything else, very happy. If you know of, or even suspect a child is being abused, please do something about it. Calling the police or social services anonymously is a possibility. It just might save a life and keep the child safe. Donating food to your local food bank or blood to the blood bank are other ways to help. It's up to everyone, all of us, to make change happen. We can stand united and make this a better and safer world!

Michael Jackson's song Man in the Mirror rings so true for me that I listen to it often. Something else that rings true is, "What doesn't kill you makes you stronger," and I'm certainly living proof! It's so true for many of us. And finally, my experiences allow me to joyously say, "Here's to wishing you love, peace, wisdom, and strength."

Andrea

Sobriety is an excellent choice! Though it was hidden for a while, my true personality is happy and joyful. My knowledge of our family history begins with my grandfather. Since then, substances have always been our escape. Grandpa would come home drunk every night, and one of those nights, he raped my grandmother. That's when my mother was conceived. Fortunately, this harsh beginning still allowed my mother to be the happy person she is. My parents divorced when I was in fourth grade, and when I was about thirteen, my oldest brother sexually assaulted me. Then, my own addiction to alcohol began. I had to mask the pain, shame, and suppress my emotions somehow!

This brother also assaulted one of two older sisters. He has since committed suicide. The other sister slipped into drug and alcohol addiction and died of an overdose. One of my two younger brothers is a pot smoker; one is an alcoholic. I am the survivor who has broken the mold! I am in recovery, have gone a different route, and I work full time, while I set a good example for my three beautiful children. Why am I telling this story? Now I know that *secrets kill*, because the only way for me to get better is to share.

Living in different states has helped me get DUIs in each. I am fifty-one now and have been sober almost five years. You could be asking, "How did it happen?" One year, on Halloween, my kids were going out trick-or-treating. I drank a little before they went, and while they were going from house to house in the neighborhood, I drove along with them. Why did I drive? That way I could drink from the big jug of wine I made sure was in the car! Think about it: on this particular night, kids were running and walking everywhere while I drove under the influence!

Then it struck me what I had done. I was finally ashamed of myself. I wanted so badly to die. I couldn't even look at myself in the mirror; I hated who I was! That night was my last DUI; I began rehabilitation even before going to court. I had put my own and other's children at risk. I deserved better, and so did my kids! I was in the rehab program for six months total, with extra time added. I thank my counselor for helping me know that I needed that additional time. While in rehab, I asked for literature on forgiveness. That's how I got the help I needed. I had to forgive myself first before forgiving anyone else.

Before going to rehab, I knew that I was in a bad way. I had moved from just drinking to also using drugs to get the same high that alcohol used to do by itself. I told my daughter once that smoking pot was my medication. It was a way to numb myself. Since reading the literature, I have done some tough soul-searching. I forgave myself for nothing and everything, my brother for the assault, and my mother for letting the assault happen. I have learned it's not my fault! To help me heal, I have taught religious education classes and worked at a day care. While working these jobs, I tried to let children know that some things are okay, like a hug, while a trusted adult needs to be told when someone touches them in ways that make them feel uncomfortable. The idea was not to frighten them but to help them be more alert.

As I continue in my sobriety, I have trouble recognizing the old me. The recovery program led me to faith in God, and I use that faith as inspiration every day. I worked the Alcoholics Anonymous (AA) and Narcotics Anonymous (NA) programs until I felt strong; every day their readings inspire me. My children inspire me, because I want to be the mother they deserve. My job is stable, and I love waiting tables. Meeting new people is a joy. I like being friendly with customers and they seem to respond. The familiar customers have gotten to know me well, and the restaurant even took up a collection for me when I was in the hospital for twenty-one days. How much more could a person ask?

Given the circumstances, my children and I live in the same house, but it's in bad shape, so my youngest daughter spends nights with her father. He has been living at his parents' condo. The parents are snowbirds and come down during the winter months. My son sleeps here on the couch. My ex-husband and I have been divorced two years, because I couldn't deal with his alcoholism anymore. That man is an alcoholic in denial! After finishing the rehab program, I tried to stay in my marriage of nineteen years for the kids' sake. I went to Al-Anon, but I could see that staying in the marriage was doing more damage to the children and me than it was helping.

Our fourteen-year-old daughter and seventeen-year-old son live just ten minutes away, but my ex chooses to drink instead of seeing the children. As a matter of fact, the drinking is much more important to him than any relationship. My oldest daughter is in college, her third year, and I worry about her. I worry about her drinking, because her dad lets her drink and get drunk with him at his place when her fourteen-year-old sister is there. All three children see how I have turned my life around, and the youngest two wish their father and sister would do the same.

I believe God has helped me to learn some tough lessons and to face what seemed to be impossible problems. I pray morning and night on my special pillow with a happy face smile. My daily readings are *Twenty-Four Hours a Day,* by Hazelden Clinic; *Just for Today,* which is an NA daily meditation; *Time for Joy … Daily Affirmations,* by Ruth Fishel; *The Language of Letting Go … Daily Meditations for Codependents,* by Melody Beattie; and *One Minute Devotions for Girls,* by Carolyn Larsen.

These readings I try to do in the morning; they help me stay focused on who I am throughout the day. Whatever the situation, I know I can give it to God; He will handle it. Then I can say, "Thank you, God, thank you, Jesus." I believe my children see my unshakeable faith, and it gives them a sense of security. My youngest loves animals and works at the wild bird center near here. Both of the younger children have been in the Workforce Treatment Program of South Florida. My son has earned his GED and is waiting to get into college.

Many things are on the horizon for me and for my family. We will soon be able to move into a Habitat for Humanity home. Those construction delays are frustrating! I look forward to meeting a man who is in recovery and knows what I've been through. We will share each other's company, joy, and he will be a man of character! I also look forward to living my own life in recovery. I must concentrate, every day, to be the dependable person I want and need to be. Most of all, I must keep on using my resources wisely for God. The way to be happy is to do God's will. Everything is about love: sharing God's love. I am a productive member of society today because of my program and my faith in God. Working His will is a very big part of my program. I also say the third step and seventh step prayers every morning. My favorite King James edition bible verse is Philippians 4:13: "I can do all things through Christ who strengthens me." It's all about staying above the influence!

Substance Abuse/Dependence

Author's Note—Drawing on numerous experiences, the author knows how tremendously hard cessation of substances can be. The author also knows how difficult it is to understand behavior resulting from substance abuse. The author further believes people have the ability, strength, and courage to accomplish their goal!

– *Definitions*

Substance Abuse—continued non-directed use of any substance for the purpose of its altering effect to the mind or body; the substance is often drugs or alcohol.

Substance Dependence—The DSM-IV describes a pattern of harmful substance use that leads to life impairment from one or more of the following in at least a twelve-month period:

- Failure to attend to obligations at work, home, or school, such as poor work performance, neglect of children, or school suspensions
- Continued substance use in hazardous situations, such as driving
- Continued substance related involvement with the legal system, such as arrests
- Continued substance use despite recurring difficult social or personal interactions, such as fights or spousal arguments

Tolerance—The body's ability to become less responsive to a substance with repeated use. As a result, it takes more substance to create the same effect.

Withdrawal—The group of possible symptoms experienced with the abrupt termination of substance use. Withdrawal may be experienced from smoking, drinking alcohol, or an administered drug.

– Is/Cause

A) Emedicine explains that abused substances produce some form of intoxication that alters judgment, perception, attention, or physical control. - http://www.emedicinehealth.com/substance_abuse/article_em.htm.

B) Emedicine also states, factors within a family that influence a child's early development may relate to increased risk of drug abuse. Some are a chaotic home environment and ineffective parenting - http://www.emedicinehealth.com/substance_abuse/article_em.htm.

– Symptoms

A) The American Council for Drug Education states there are indications when a young person may be using substances. The key is change; it is important to watch for any significant changes in your child's physical appearance, personality, attitude, or behavior - http://www.acde.org/parent/signs.htm.

B) Although the symptoms of alcohol use depend greatly on many factors—such as age, gender, or weight—Penn State University explains people with alcohol dependence eventually build up a tolerance - http://www.hmc.psu.edu.

– Tips

A) The National Institute on Drug Abuse (NIDA) explains scientific studies demonstrate that treatment employing key principles can help people recover their lives. Some of these are, no single treatment is appropriate for everyone and treatment needs to be readily available - http://www.drugabuse.gov/infofacts/treatmeth.html.

B) Substance Abuse and Mental Health Services Administration (SAMSHA) has a treatment center locator ~ http://findtreatment. samhsa.gov/.

Author's Note—The author has had many informative occurrences with alcohol abuse and dependence. It is possible drug use is similar. Here are some learned tips:

- Al-Anon can help a person dealing with an alcohol abuser; Narc-Anon can help those with friends or relatives using drugs.
- Truth from the person abusing substances can be unlikely.
- Some awful, unbelievable behavior may result from substance use.
- Relating to others with similar issues can be important for the person using substances, also for interested parties.
- The partner/family/employer cannot make recovery happen, but it can be influenced.
- Identify whether the user is being enabled and how. Does the user need shelter, money, someone to excuse him/her, or someone to take the verbal/mental/physical abuse? Enabling will likely encourage the abusive behavior.
- Pre-rehabilitation, one-on-one talking with the person with substance abuse issues will likely not be effective. The person is probably not thinking clearly even though it seems he/she is.
- Ultimately the person, alone, must choose non-drug-seeking behavior or sobriety. The person recovering from substance abuse/dependence will have to address it every day, one day at a time.
- To be successful, it is often necessary to remove the person from familiar locations, situations, and people.
- Plan ahead! If the person chooses to accept help seek professional aid immediately (now, not later). If you wait until later the person will likely change his or her mind.

Step 1. Consult a professional.

SECTION B:
PHYSICAL ISSUES

All that is valuable in human society depends upon the opportunity for development accorded the individual.

Albert Einstein

By the author: Contending with any kind of illness is, at the very least, a nuisance. As you read on, you might be able to recognize the courage and commitment needed to face one's challenges.

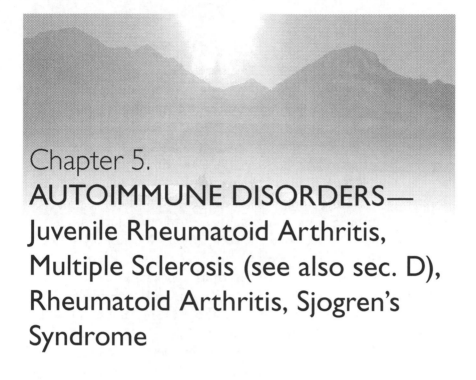

Chapter 5.
AUTOIMMUNE DISORDERS—
Juvenile Rheumatoid Arthritis,
Multiple Sclerosis (see also sec. D),
Rheumatoid Arthritis, Sjogren's
Syndrome

WHAT IS JUVENILE RHEUMATOID ARTHRITIS (JRA)?

Kay

Growing up in the warm climate of the western U.S. was terrific weatherwise. I also had many caring relatives with whom to interact, and that was great. Other aspects of my young life were less desirable. I had symptoms indicating to my parents that there was trouble early on. When I was three, the doctors started testing for juvenile rheumatoid arthritis (JRA), because I was in constant pain, had frequent fevers, and inflamed red and swollen joints. When I was seven a definitive diagnosis of JRA was made, though to me, it was inconsequential. What I knew was ever-present pain. I understand symptoms may go away or last only a few months. I have the type that lasts a lifetime. Added to this, the year of my diagnosis, my dad passed away, so you might say the year was a bit bumpy. The superhuman efforts of my mom were helpful at calming any fears and filling the void for my sister and me. From an early age, I learned to endure, move forward with purpose, and to have a positive attitude. At this, I have become quite talented.

Even as a child, somehow I knew that doing things for myself was very important. Family was always there any time I needed help, but I always did what I could. As I grew, I felt the world was a quicksand of emotional and physical pain. Did I rebel? You bet! The physical manifestations of JRA were unrequested, unwanted, unrelenting, and would definitely be my constant companion. Why me? For added measure, I thought romance was an unattainable dream, because who would want someone with deformities? There were surely those. Eventually, I came to understand that JRA was my divine gift. I realized I was special to be singled out, so I chose to love myself. That has allowed me to love others in greater measure.

It has also helped me to be a more confident person, knowing I can tackle whatever challenges come my way. One of those challenges is social. I would have liked to know sooner, however, I have come to realize that if others are bothered by my appearance, it is out of my control. I can only control my response, so I invite questions about JRA. My acquired self-confidence has become a definitive goal for me. I am unquestionably victorious in reaching this goal and have achieved my objective: to live happily.

Meeting my future spouse was a fun and exciting day. We each had agreed to visit a theme park with a mutual friend. We enjoyed the hours together, hit it off, and have been together ever since. I was most impressed with my husband's accepting attitude and kind ways. He is in the armed service and we now have two beautiful children. They miss their dad when he's away and the kids enjoy the time when he's home, as do I. My husband and I share household chores; I do what I can, and his concern for my health is always evident. We both like to cook and tease each other good-naturedly over who will fix meals. Many times we eventually work together to complete preparations.

Our daughter is an angel sent to be the kindest helper imaginable. She learned how to clean the house at four and how to cook at five. Pretty amazing! My son is younger yet, but helps when he can. Both children are quite aware and concerned for people with health challenges. I am disappointed that they have had to grow up more quickly than others their age. I do believe they will be more sensitive people as they grow, and will be better for having firsthand knowledge. This will give them an enhanced perspective, different from many other children. What a thrill it is to be their mother and a part of such a fantastic family! We get along pretty well!

When I rise in the morning, moving can be difficult, because my joints have stiffened overnight. I have learned to ignore the pain and press on, unless and until the daily meds I take fail to provide relief. When I experience this excruciating, incredible pain, I have to visit the hospital, so away we go to the emergency room for aid. Another development now has to be added to my ever-blossoming list of ailments: a stomach ulcer from so much pain medication. And my blessings continue …

As mentioned previously, I have deformities. When I was seven, my feet were interesting enough that one of my doctors wanted to write about them for a book. My feet are already published, and now the rest of me will be as well! You might see others with RA whose fingers are quite crooked, as mine are. Also, I have recently been diagnosed with osteoarthritis (OA), which means joint degeneration. It has been happening to me since my teens, according to the doctor. By telling my story, I hope I can help people understand that arthritis happens to young people as well as those older. Also, I wish to help people know how one might accomplish certain tasks. One example would be turning a doorknob. It is an everyday occurrence to most; however, for those with arthritis, this can be a dreaded necessity. I have learned to put the knob between my middle and ring fingers, so I can use more arm motion than painful wrist action to turn. I am extremely willing to share information with newcomers to the world of arthritis. Anything I can do to help make life easier.

I view life positively and see my family as a constant wonder. I love my husband, my children, and myself. In the future, I hope my spouse will travel safely, and I wish continued good health for my little ones. So far, JRA symptoms are non-manifest in them, and though JRA and OA may be an issue in the future, I hope it is avoided! I believe my children will be wonderful contributors to society and help others know that which has become so familiar to them. I have little doubt that my kids will be successful in their future endeavors, and I believe their growth will include love of selves, love for others, and love of God. Already they are little miracles!

Sandy

My journey has been bumpy, but I have survived successfully and look forward to more successes. We lived in the Northeast when I was growing up. There were five of us: my parents, brother, sister, and me. When I was eleven or twelve, uncomfortable and painful symptoms started to appear, though I didn't know they were symptoms. I couldn't understand why I was always tired, why my joints hurt, and why they had a strange redness. Naturally, my folks took me to see a doctor, and after many tests, junior rheumatoid arthritis (JRA) and anemia were diagnosed. For an active pre-teen, this was quite limiting! My friends didn't understand how painful it was for me to move; my aunts, uncles, and cousins sure didn't know how to react to my difficulties; and I felt different, like a social outcast or a lone eagle. To the doubters I said nothing, because I was so young, and these feelings were extremely alien to me. My family has always been supportive. It still has taken a while to become happy with who I have become.

As I've gotten older JRA symptoms have lessened, but residual challenges have cropped up. I became a nurse and practiced that honorable profession for several years. When nursing, I enjoyed offering kindness to patients who had no one else to visit them. I liked helping people. I found that the patients responded when an interest was shown and when I offered comfort. It worked out well. When I couldn't work anymore, I bowed out reluctantly and gracefully. Some of the subsequent health issues that have developed are Crohn's disease and ankylosing spondylitis, a chronic, inflammatory arthritis of the veterbrae. The diagnoses made me feel helpless. Being in control is important to me, as it is for most people.

Being judged because of my invisible circumstances is an isolating experience! It is difficult to explain how incredibly weary I have become with all of it. With the Crohn's, there are days when trips to the bathroom are necessary every few minutes. Sometimes I feel like I need to have a toilet close by, wherever I am. Maybe I could put a T.V. in the bathroom! For some, diet makes a difference, but for me, that is ineffective; if I eat, it's an issue. I saw a gastroenterologist, who increased medication and helped me learn some new information. Then, when I investigate something else, another doctor will scold me. Well that's too bad, because I always hope to be better. God and prayer help me look for the good.

To de-stress, I often write poetry and love to listen to music. My faith is strong, and God has been my inspiration throughout my life. On a warm night, I go to the beach, listen to the waves, look up at the stars, and feel closer to Him. Some days, I just lie in the sun or mold sand. Perhaps that sounds a bit odd for an adult, but the warmth of the sand and movement of molding loosens my joints. Pain meds alleviate little, so warm sand feels wonderful!

Once, I became infected with something which I apparently picked up by walking barefoot on my beloved beach. I was in the hospital for a time, had a 104 degree temperature, my leg swelled to elephantine size, and I almost died. Wanting to avoid that happening again, now I wear something on my feet so I stay healthy. I'll leave the little buggers in the sand!

Would I like things to be different? Certainly, but I laugh a lot. Laughing is important to keep up my spirits. I'm in my forties and have two daughters. My ex-husband and I are friendly for the sake of our children. The younger girl lives with me, is now in her teens, and is a lovely, sweet person. The older daughter still lives in the Northeast and has blessed us with a grandson. I have moved to a warmer climate because it suits my bones much better! My folks are here, so I have a support system in place, and my family is really terrific. They understand my situation, because autoimmune disorders seem to run in the genes; many relatives have a similar diagnosis. I have avid curiosity and frequently seek out information on the Internet, so I have much knowledge stored in my head. As a matter of fact, I understand there is research suggesting a link between up to thirty auto-immune disorders. If that link could be found, who knows how far it could take people experiencing the disorders.

My belief is that awareness and resources are much-needed factors with RA. Conveying to others how many joints we have in our bodies and what it feels like when they all hurt is difficult. More research is needed! Sometimes I think, *Why me?* Just RA might be manageable, but the numerous additional issues are almost too much for me to bear. Then I think, *There are many other people who have challenges worse than mine.* I try to focus on the positives. God, prayer, counseling, and continually thinking, *Others are worse than me,* all help. If I refocus, I feel like a *Wizard of Oz* character; I can recognize the many tools I have within me and concentrate on them!

My first daughter was diagnosed with Asperger's syndrome and has difficulties, but is very determined, smart, and has a good heart. When my second daughter was born, she looked up at me with clear eyes and such trust it was overwhelming. I knew then that she would be okay. It was a pivotal moment.

Living with pain has made me appreciate life in all ways possible. RA has taught me to be non-judgmental, open, empathetic, and understanding. Denial is, many times, a part of health challenges, and I have often said, "Denial is not a river in Egypt." I took on my own willingness to deny and have worked through it. Giving in is different than acceptance, and while I would like my health situation to be different, I do accept it. I look forward to times when I can relax on the beach, talk with friends with RA, laugh, and re-invent myself.

In many ways, I still think of myself as a teenager. I like to have fun, enjoy life, and keep it lighthearted. I recognize that stress makes a person even more sick and that good times are to be enjoyed to the fullest. I believe we ought to live each day as though it's our last, because one day we'll be right! As my philosophy I choose, *Carpe diem.* The Latin poet Horace uses the words to mean more than, "Seize the day," but also to, "Enjoy or make use of the day." That is my goal!

JRA

— Is/Cause

A) Kids Health states that JRA is an autoimmune disease. For some reason the body can't tell the difference between healthy cells and invaders. It releases chemicals to hurt the invaders, but is actually hurting healthy cells ~ http://kidshealth.org/parent/medical/arthritis/jra.html

B) JRA typically appears between six months and sixteen years of age ~ http://kidshealth.org/parent/medical/arthritis/jra.html

— Symptoms

A) Medicinet states that there are three types of JRA, pauciarticular, polyarticular, and systemic onset ~ http://www.medicinenet.com/juvenile_arthritis/page5.htm.

B) For more information, links are provided ~ http://www.medicinenet.com/juvenile_arthritis/page5.htm

— Tips

A) Emedicine health explains that medical treatment is trying to stop or slow the progress of JRA inflammation and to relieve inflammation. Self care is not recommended with JRA ~ http://www.emedicinehealth.com/juvenile_rheumatoid_arthritis/page8_em.htm

B) WebMD states that physical exercise and medicine are the basis of treatment. The treatment is determined by the type and severity of JRA ~ http://www.webmd.com/rheumatoid-arthritis/tc/juvenile-rheumatoid-arthritis-treatment-overview

Step 1. Consult a professional.

What Is Multiple Sclerosis (MS)?

Cora

Starting life in a rural area near a small river town of the Midwest was ideal for a child. However, it has taken some time to realize how impoverished we were. We always had food to eat, though I can remember rivers of potato soup, and I do enjoy homegrown veggies! Moving to a more urban setting helped to improve family circumstances by allowing more employment, educational, and social opportunities. Our clan consisted of two parents, two brothers, and me, the tomboy. Besides participating in numerous sports when I was younger, I could throw with the best of 'em, I would read libraries of books that took me many places. I loved it! I learned about other cultures and dreamed of living different kinds of lives. I also remember constantly stubbing my toe, which may have been a precursor of things to come, or maybe it's just that I was clumsy. As I got older, I thought educating young people would be my profession.

When a person reaches her teenage years, it can be difficult to predict what choices she will make. When I was a senior in high school, my parents were in the beginning stages of divorce; the timing was less than ideal, and my "dark ages" began. I could deal with divorce, but then I learned I had to decide with whom I would live. I was thrown into in a tailspin! I've been described as a "peacemaker," so maybe it's understandable how this decision was incomprehensible to me. What did I actually do? I looked for a way out. I made procrastination into an art form, attended a local college for a year, and then, much to my parents' dismay, chose to marry. Marriage proved to be a mix of negatives and positives, as many decisions are. My husband and I lived a while in Germany and became homeowners upon our return to the United States. Painting and sprucing up followed.

After a while I remember thinking how terribly clumsy I had gotten; what in the world could this be? Eventually, a misperception issue caused me to drive an ATC, the predecessor to the ATV, into a fencepost, and the result was seventeen stitches in my leg. This was definitive for me because it might have been caused by MS, or maybe it was the beginning, but after healing I began to notice symptoms.

When I was in my mid-twenties, these strange symptoms started with the feeling of numbness in my legs and with double vision. Always being active, I was riding my bike at the time of this numb feeling, and a few weeks later, a terrible headache preceded double vision. I thought, *What is happening? I am not imagining these things!* A trip to the chiropractor proved I thought I was numb but could feel a pinprick. A trip to the optometrist sent me to an ophthalmologist and then on to a neurologist, who referred me to state university hospital. Good grief! The numbness disappeared, but the double vision remains, corrected by glasses.

Over the years subsequent symptoms have been plentiful and somewhat sporadic. Among those are weakness, imbalance, incontinence, and spasms. Combined with other symptoms and numerous tests I was eventually diagnosed with MS. My immediate reaction to this diagnosis was *tremendous relief,* because there was a name for the strange things happening to me. At first I acted as if there were nothing wrong. What else could I do but wait to see what would transpire? With only experimental medications at the time, still being tested, the minimally helpful neurologist explained there was little to be done. What was the reason I continued to see him? Darned if I know!

The aforementioned incontinence has plagued me from the beginning. It started out sporadically, because it didn't matter where I was, I always looked for a bathroom. The trouble eventually became more of an issue. Finally, I was compelled to have a major surgery. It might have worked better, but not for me, of course! Two minor surgeries and another major surgery were required to correct the first. Thankfully, all has been resolved at this time.

MS progression has been very slow for me, and new medications have been developed since my diagnosis. The recommendation for MS meds is to begin med therapy soon after diagnosis, and that already leaves me out. Maybe I could have asked more questions at the time of diagnosis, but being a fatalist then, I thought this was just the way it was. Passing years have brought sorrow and joy in equal measure. I've have had my share of drama. For example, I've experienced divorce and marriage, rented an apartment, owned a home, not worked, and worked, and I've also been diagnosed with osteoporosis. I've had falls when I stayed down until someone helped me up, and those when I could help myself up. I really wish only to explain that I have had my share of fatigue and stress. Both are to be avoided to the utmost when one has MS. Oops! I also had the emotional issues of dealing with MS and life in general. Back then I would get rid of stress by reading or exercising, often by walking.

The slow progression of MS might have been aided by my reluctance to have it consume my life. Besides walking, I would also ride my bike. Walking up to the corner and back on my lunch hour, or at the mall on the weekends, were frequent excursions. I once did an extended bike ride; even so, 150 miles was a large bite to chew. Later, I even crawled around on the floor, until I started falling over! But I still do stretching and physical therapy with physical therapy (PT) students from the university. Actually, they do the work now.

Accepting help was the most difficult of all the transitions I've had to make. When functional, I was very independent. Now I need help transferring from recliner to wheelchair, vice versa, and with most other things. At this time, I have much for which to be thankful. Would I choose to walk again? Absolutely, only now I am armed with an enormous awareness to the difficulties of others.

Going back to when I was still able, when I divorced I realized I was truly on my own. I didn't want to be alone, even as I knew it was necessary. Emotionally I wallowed in sadness, almost depression, and thought life was no longer worth living. One day I opened the mailbox to find a cheerful card from my mother. I knew it was a sign! Bless the mothers of the world and especially mine. From that point on I have looked forward.

At mid-life plus, experiences I have had with MS and osteoporosis are many and varied. As you may be aware, accidents happen in a heartbeat. Once, I was in the bathroom of my apartment and missed the chair as I tried to transfer. I tried mightily, but it was impossible to lift myself high enough to sit down on the chair seat. Because I always held onto something I could lower myself to the floor without bone breakage. I had to rest a while after this fiasco, and I thought, *Now what am I going to do? The phone is in the living room and I'm in the bathroom, on the floor. Damn!*

After I had collected my wits, I thought, *Well, it's been a few years, but I used to crawl. Maybe I still have some ability.* I sat where I was and unlocked the chair to bring it to me. After getting it situated, I was able to lock it and pull myself to my knees, facing the seat. Pushing the chair, and guiding it by leaning on the seat, I was able to move one knee an inch, then lock the chair so I could bring my knees even, and not lose the chair. It worked!

Inch by inch, locking and unlocking, I left the bathroom, and moved down the short hall. At this point I had reached the living room. I took stock of my situation; the room looked as wide as the Mississippi! By this time, my knees were v-e-r-y sore, and I was tired to the point of exhaustion. I thought, *I can't go on!* Then I thought, *But, what else can I do?* I realized no one knew there was anything wrong. If someone telephoned, I couldn't answer, and it would be some days before anyone came looking. So I forged ahead, moved out across the living room, until finally I reached the phone and could call 911. Success! Rescuers came, and after some questions, I was placed gently in the recliner. It felt so good after such an ordeal. Please believe me when I tell you I felt it the next day!

Another time, using the electric wheelchair, I broke my leg and had to wear a cast for six weeks. How does that happen? Suffice it to say that I have been, and still am, fortunate to know intelligent, caring people. My P.A. had warned me both times, once to always have the phone with me and once to slow down! He did come to live with me and has rescued me a couple of times since then. I looked forward to better experiences.

I knew that if I still wanted to teach I needed to move to another city. A very wise person helped me know that furthering my education was the only way to realize my goal, so away I went. Thus began "The Enlightenment." I quickly recognized that the "fit" in the region where I had lived was uncomfortable for me, though I was totally unaware of it until I actually moved. This new location has become my home. Following my divorce, I went back to undergraduate studies, advanced to graduate school, and graduated with a master's degree. Until recently, I was teaching at a not-for-profit agency, helping people know how best to aid those with disabilities. With my talents it was the perfect job for me. I fulfilled my desire to teach, wished it had happened sooner, and that it had lasted longer, because I really enjoyed being an instructor. I found I had a knack for teaching! However, I needed lots of help to get there. From birth on, help from innumerable parties has been evident.

My family has been amazingly supportive during my transition from walking to needing an assistant. Health challenges happen not only to one person, but to all members of the family. Actually, others have accepted my circumstances more easily than I have. My P.A. is now part of my family. You get quite cozy, and know a person extremely well, when you work and play together so closely. Tremendous enjoyment and respect represent our countless experiences together. Love and gratitude are my overwhelming response to the generosity of others.

Looking back, whether my education was informal or formal, negative or positive, one learns from one's experiences. Learning from, and sharing with others has been a hallmark throughout my life, so I guess I may have always taught, in my own way. The last several years, I believe affirmation and positive thinking can sustain and encourage a person. I have learned that I enjoy helping others and can teach in a positive way. It is a win for them and a win for me! What joy!

Alex

Reaching midlife has been a fascinating passage for me. I was born in Sweden, with many animals as friends, and I immigrated with my mom to the United States when I was ten. The hugeness of this country has left a lasting, but positive impression. After all, here I remain. Having resided in the West, the East eventually became my home.

I entered college in 1975, at age seventeen, as part of the Early Admission Program. I returned for my high school graduation after my first year in college. I thought art would be my major course of study, but what is that saying? "If you want to hear God laugh, tell Him your plans."

Art was my major at Temple University in Philadelphia, and an art gallery was interested in doing a show of my work. I was very excited! They wanted a few more pieces, which I had planned, but then the MS hit hard and fast. I was seeing double (diplopia), and my eyes hurt terribly (optic neuritis), along with coordination problems. The show never happened, and I had to change majors just when I almost had enough credits for my B.A. degree! Because of the difficulties I was experiencing, I went to see a doctor. I was diagnosed with MS, which progressed quite rapidly. The artwork I had been doing required delicate coordination, and naturally, it was no longer among my abilities. At the same time I was experiencing gait and balance problems. As a young person, with a promising future in jeopardy and one who had life-changing circumstances and decisions all at once, I was completely overwhelmed!

Severe disappointment, depression, and anger followed. The rapid progression of the MS—I went from no symptoms (asymptomatic) to not walking (paraplegic) in five years—may have been assisted by my own thoughts. I worked at a teaching hospital with an excellent medical library, so when I was diagnosed, I used the library to learn about MS. Then, I mistakenly took what *might* happen to be what *would* happen. It seems to have been a self-fulfilling prophecy. Three things took place to help me recover from the downward spiral and put me back on course.

Firstly, I had success with newly found efforts to be creative through writing. Secondly, I developed my disABILITY resource website, which helped me gain positive, appreciative feedback that also caused me to think. Most importantly, a relationship developed with a nurse at the hospital. We started as platonic roommates, because she needed to share expenses, and to get away from her previous bad roommate situation. She gave me a kick in the butt when we became involved. She told me bluntly, "I won't feel sorry for you, because you're already doing that!" It was a much-needed wake-up call.

Writing was something I had been dabbling in, so I really focused on writing professionally. Apparently it was meant to be because my books were also being published. All right! I also changed majors from art to psychology at school. When I began attending classes again, I went part time. I lost most of my hard-earned credits, but I went to school days and worked full-time nights. My job required little mobility, which was great, because I was using a wheelchair full time. An added benefit of the job was that with my laptop I could write during quiet times at work.

My schooling went well and I was elected vice president of the university's chapter of Psi Chi, the National Honor Society of Psychology.

In addition, I was accepted to an honors research program and, at the same time, I started and did much of the work for a university reference newsletter. Talk about stressful! Inching agonizingly toward my goal, which was college graduation too many years and dollars away, something told me I needed to write more. So I dropped out of school altogether to focus only on work and writing. Writing in both disability-related nonfiction and fiction, sometimes using disABLED characters, was fun, therapeutic, and provided some needed money on the side. After many submissions to publishers, I was also fortunate enough to have three books published.

Along with writing books, I have written many magazine novelettes and short stories, and nonfiction magazine and newspaper articles. I have done work for many disability volunteer organizations as well as sit on their boards. I have participated in numerous forums and created about fifty websites, starting at disabilityhelper.org and branching out from there. I tell you of my accomplishments to emphasize the *abilities* of countless people with challenges, no matter their situation.

Now we come to my feelings about MS. The diagnosis of multiple sclerosis has been a combination of curses and blessings. Sometimes I am angry and depressed about being as dependent as I am, but I have MS to thank for learning about myself. I will not finish college, but I have discovered writing as a new profession. While several loving relationships have also not worked out as I hoped, I remain close friends with each person. For five wonderful years I was married to a fantastic wheeling lady, also with MS. Since our divorce, we have a somewhat different relationship. I still share a home with this lady, even as she has remarried her first husband, who lives with us and works part time helping to care for me. Oh well, it works for us.

Having previously been mortified about public speaking, being in disability forums, speaking at writer's conventions, and to disability groups has increased my confidence significantly. If I could magically walk again, would I? I believe I would not if I would lose what I have learned, but MS research is advancing so rapidly, who knows what will happen in the future? I also believe I have been quite fortunate to experience life with and without certain abilities. MS allows me to think and learn about new and different ways to accomplish tasks. All in all, MS is not bad; it's all about thinking and doing differently!

Peter

By the time I was thirteen, my younger brother and I were orphans. My mother had passed away with breast cancer, my father a few years later from unknown causes. Until that time, we had lived an ideal, stimulating, musical life in a Midwest city. My father was a pharmacist who owned a drugstore, while my mother taught music in public school. We enjoyed much company; people were always coming and going as my mother gave piano lessons in our home. When our mother became ill with cancer, our grandmother paused her own life and came to the rescue. She stayed on after our father died and raised us in our home so that uprooting our young lives was unnecessary, thank goodness. What an incredibly selfless act! I eventually entered the business world fairly close to home, while my brother lives in a nearby state and is in the legal profession. It was during my time at the local college, and my brother's at a distant university, we made the decision to sell our family home. Our grandmother had resumed her life after we were both away at school, and our house was lonely for occupants. Now I have a marvelous wife, Peg, and we have seven offspring; five girls and two boys.

At middle age and working, one time I flew to Florida to give marketing presentations throughout the state. I know it seems a cliché, but during the trip my luggage was lost. Naturally, I needed clothes and other items, and as I was shopping at the mall, I became aware of a tingling sensation down my spine when I walked. It was the strangest feeling, and I was curious what it might be. Because I ran regularly, my immediate thought was that I had pulled a muscle. The next instance of tingling was when I had been sitting for some time. This time the tingling was traveling up my left arm, so it made me think I was having a heart attack.

Speaking of these happenings with Peg, a nurse, I was firmly and caringly encouraged to see a doctor. Now when I am "firmly encouraged" by my wife, I know it is definitely something to be checked. Upon seeing the doctor and explaining this odd symptom, I said I thought I had pulled a muscle. After a preliminary examination, the doctor took me at my word and prescribed muscle relaxants. They were ineffective. On my next visit to the physician, X-rays were taken, and he referred me to a neurologist, who told me I had either MS or a post-viral infection.

The next day, after the MRI and a spinal tap showed plaques on my spine and my brain, the neurologist diagnosed MS. Thinking back, I remembered a time, months before, when I was in a Thanksgiving run and my legs felt like I was running in wet cement. It must have been an early indication of MS. I knew little about this illness, but I was relieved when the words "cancer" and "Lou Gehrig's disease" were not suggested for the diagnosis. I dreaded both of them! The diagnosis of MS was unquestionably life-changing for me. I felt I had the choice to accept it, deal with it, and keep going, or let it define the person I was. I decided my life was good, I was happy, and nothing would change!

Telling Peg about the MS diagnosis was terribly difficult, to say the least. At the time, she was caring for her father, who had mesothelioma. In her state of concern for her father, hearing my diagnosis was too much to bear. She and I were newly married, and life was good to us. This was not the time for bumps in the road, but then, is it ever? Peg was angry with the news of an MS diagnosis, because as a nurse, she had seen its effects when ministering to others. This time it was my turn to minister to her. Fortunately, I was able to get a chuckle by telling her, "Look at it this way, at least it isn't cancer or Lou Gehrig's disease." We always *try* to look on the bright side. Actually, I thought about two things: past difficulties and how I got through them, and the abundance of blessings I have. Then I knew that I would succeed. Additional assistance came from my faith in God and from the beautiful people in my life—my wife, family, and great friends.

Starting medication early seemed to be beneficial for me, and it typically relieved my symptoms. As the MS has progressed, I have tried different methods of treatment. Currently, each month I receive Tysabri infusions, which seem to be helpful. My right leg was first affected, and at this time, the same leg is largely unresponsive. Because of this, we built a fully accessible ranch home with all necessary items on the first floor, which my wife also enjoys. I have two walkers with a seat; one is in the house, and one travels with me. I use crutches to get around if I need them, and hand controls on our handicapped accessible van so I can drive to get out and about. I do exercises in our home every day, which include walking up and down the flight of stairs between our first floor and the basement ten times. Whew!

When the first exacerbation happened, I found myself dragging my right leg, and I had no strength in my right hand. Shaving or holding forks or spoons was impossible. One time, my sons were outside in the driveway playing basketball. I went out to join them, thinking I could put the ball in the hoop like I always had. Hah! Do you think my body was going to respond? When I tried to shoot the ball, I had no strength in my right arm, there was no force when the ball left my hand, and it dribbled off my fingers like rain off of plastic. Play stopped instantly; we all were convulsed with laughter at the sight! The next day, I went on a business trip in a private plane to Missouri. When my colleague and I first saw each other at the airport, he was surprised to see me dragging my leg. I said, "If it doesn't bother you to be seen with someone dragging a leg and eating with their off-hand, I'm okay."

It was okay with him, so we took off for our meeting. The next day, Peg called the neurologist to tell the doctor what was going on, and the doctor said, "I want to see Peter right away!" When the doctor heard, "Peter is out of town on a business trip," he was floored. It was unbelievable to him. Already alarmed at hearing my symptoms, the incredulous doctor said, *"What?!"*

Another funny event happened when I was dancing with my walker and our daughter Meggan at her wedding reception. We were having a great time doing the Macarena, and were energetically dancing up a storm. Totally enjoying myself, I forgot to remember I was a bit unsteady on my feet. What do you think happened next? I made one of the moves a tad too vigorously, and ended up throwing myself to the floor! My daughter felt horrible and thought it was somehow her fault. To give her a reprieve I said, "It's no big deal; I'm just falling for you." After all, it was a time to be lighthearted!

When I think about uplifting times, I realize my life has always been full of variety, which in itself inspires me. I try to see the glass as half full. Peg and I have a partnership, because we are best friends and our faith is strong. We are also active in our church and, until recently, I spent many years leading the high school youth group for the church. Filling that role provided me with incredible experiences. I have been blessed with many circumstances, which I feel have made me a better person. After a successful life in the business world, I found an opportunity that was so fulfilling. For many of the working years, I had yearned for further meaning in my life; I was looking for fulfillment. The opening for youth leader at our church was just the right position at just the right time.

Working with the kids was a passion of mine, and this has helped keep my mind active. I know that God has been, and always will be with me, leading me through difficult times. Thankfully, I have enough energy for the activities I enjoy. During a support group meeting years ago, I heard about a retired coach in a nearby community who speaks about having coached athletics from a wheelchair. What an inspiration! When I feel the need for some additional stretching exercises to keep loose, I request of my neurologist, "Would you send me to more physical therapy sessions?" Last session, I was told I was the poster boy for the value of doing regular exercise. Hearing something like that is inspirational in itself!

Among the highs I have known, the pinnacle was being honored with the youth ministry adult award. I received it during my last year, in front of eight hundred people; it was attended by all ages. I have enjoyed the last eleven years, the opportunities I have had, and how much I have grown. I look forward to many new opportunities. Among those opportunities will be spending more time with Peg, spending time with our children and grandchildren, and spending time with friends. I also look forward to getting involved with the next thing God has planned for me. I have great doctors, good health plans, and I am married to a person who is a nurse and fabulous companion. I will live life to the fullest and have faith that I will be directed to the next successful experience. I'll leave worrying about the unknown to others.

Since the diagnosis, I have given much thought to how MS has impacted me as a person. I no longer take my days for granted, so I make an effort to improve the value of my time. I am truly blessed, and the challenges of MS have given me courage and power. I have several noteworthy indications my life has been successful up to now. I am proud of our children, who are good mothers and fathers to our grandchildren. My faith has always been a large part of my life, and I am proud Peg and I share a life worshipping together. Our partnership has grown the past four years with our participation in study programs of our faith community. I am proud of my commitment and involvement on several boards in the local community and their appreciation for my contributions. I am proud of the opportunities to work with young people, and to make a difference in their lives. I am also proud of the good friends I have and of my spouse. We get along well.

My daily activities are enhanced because I use a CPAP machine when I sleep. It has made a big difference in quality sleep time and waking up well rested. Fortunately, I'm not affected, as many people with MS are, by fatigue during the day. Right now, throughout the week, I spend time on the computer, helping to promote faith activities by sending e-mails to my distribution list of four hundred-plus people. I worship about twice a week for a couple of hours, facilitate faith study with my wife one morning per week, participate in a men's weekly prayer group for an hour, and do household chores that are possible. My specialties are doing dishes and emptying wastebaskets. I also do daily exercises and go to movies with Peg. In the future, my enjoyment will mostly be found in being a better person, enjoying and spending time with family and friends, and finding and doing things that make a difference in the lives of others.

My philosophy, or philosophies you might say, tell me life experiences are what they are. The idea is to make those experiences as favorable as possible. I have heard the difference between being bitter and better is "i." How true it is! It is up to me, so I choose to be better. As you might be aware, I have a positive outlook, and I believe the Nike commercial says it all for me; "Just do it!"

MS

Author's note—This portion of the chapter draws on the experiences of the author. Other information is from cited sources.

— Is/Cause

A) Effectively what happens with MS is demyelination, which can expose nerves. Compare a nerve to an electrical cord. Think of the copper wire, which conducts electricity, as the nerve and the insulation of the cord over the copper as the myelin. When the copper of the cord is exposed, bad things can happen. A similar situation may occur in the body when nerves are exposed, or nerves may not conduct impulses effectively.

B) The cause or cure for MS is unknown

— Symptoms

A) The Mayo Clinic says symptoms can include numbness, diplopia or double vision, difficulty walking, balance and coordination issues, and spasticity ~ http://www.mayoclinic.com/health /multiple-sclerosis/DS00188/DSECTION=symptoms.

B) According to the magazine of the NMSS, sleep disturbances can be fatiguing for people. Those with MS may rise frequently in the night to use the bathroom (nocturia) or be awakened by restless leg syndrome and periodic limb movements. Suggestions are also offered ~ Momentum. NMSS, Winter 2009–2010.

Author's Note—It is the understanding of the author that spasticity and spasms are both uncontrolled muscle contractions. The difference is in speed of movement; fast equals spasticity.

– **Tips**

A) Treatment suggestions for MS have consisted mainly of medication. The neurology channel suggests treatment's purpose is to relieve symptoms, slow the course of the disease, and to provide psychological support – http://www.healthcommunities.com/multiple-sclerosis/treatment.shtml.

B) The NMSS has suggestions about how to live with MS from those newly diagnosed to those with advanced MS and how to accomplish it in a healthy way – http://www.nationalmssociety.org/living-with-multiple-sclerosis/index.aspx.

Step 1. See "Movement, ALS" and "Movement, Paralysis" this book.

Step 2. Consult a professional.

WHAT IS RHEUMATOID ARTHRITIS (RA)?

Scott Harvey

New Zealand has always been my home. Eight years following employment at Burger King, and about six years ago, I was diagnosed with rheumatoid arthritis (RA). Later, I went into remission and had an opportunity to farm. So, in February of 2007, Shelly and I decided to move from Tauranga to the New Zealand back blocks. We lived on a milking farm, and looked forward to a better life for ourselves and our four children. Shelly had two kids from a previous partner, and we had two of our own. Living there was great! It was a job that dreams are made from, and we loved it. The girls really enjoyed a school with fewer students, and Shelly was able to be a home mum, which she loved. I helped her learn to drive, which was fun and brought us closer together. I had four a.m. starts, which I loved, and this was a place I could be at one with myself. Then, in August of 2007, I picked up a septicaemia G virus from a cow, which affects only people with RA.

What did I notice? Well, my hands, neck, knees, ankles, and shoulder joints were even more sore and swollen than before. Getting on and off the farm bike, turning hoses on, getting off the tractor, and lifting the cups onto the cow for milking were normally simple things to do, but now were incredibly difficult. It was intensely painful. Tasks that usually would take twenty minutes took over an hour. When I saw the doctor, he prescribed high doses of prednisone, which scrambled my brain but worked wonders for the pain. Two weeks later, I crashed big time and spent two weeks in the hospital, recovering. I also got baker's cysts in both my knees and learned that they are sometimes a symptom of the RA. After this spell of hospital rest, I seemed to be better. Soon after going home, I had chores to do and I went to work. After only an hour, I could hardly move! Back to the hospital I went for another three weeks. Well, my employer needed someone to take care of the job full time, which I understood, but it disappointed me tremendously. We had to leave our idyllic life, and we moved back to Tauranga. The day I left the farm, some of my heart stayed.

We were back in Tauranga for only three days when my body crashed again. The baker's cysts in my knees popped, and it was like someone had shoved a hot poker in them then left it there. The specialist prescribed an I.V. drug called methylprednisolone. I was given three doses over three days. Though I wasn't told of the side effects, it made me feel like Superman within four hours! I was sent home after the three days. That night, my head felt like I had smoked a bag of pot, which I dealt with okay. The problem was, a side effect of methylprednisolone is steroid-induced psychosis. That is a loss of contact with reality. The psychosis caused me to do really dangerous things—like drive. Looking back, this was the worst moment of my life.

Because I didn't realize the drug had caused psychosis, I had my two children with me as I drove. I knew I was hungry, so I went though the drive-through at McDonald's. Thinking I was still in the lounge, I asked the person whose voice came over the speaker box to change the TV channel. I remember the kids were crying. At home, I sat outside in the car to eat my food and didn't know where I was. Then I took the kids into the house. Levi, my son, was just three months old at the time, and though it's now unbelievable to me, when I looked at him

I thought, *Who are you?* I didn't know why this strange child was in my arms! Shelly came home and asked, "How is Levi?" As an answer, I started crying. When she asked, "What is wrong?" I said, "Nothing, I'm fine." Then I handed our son to her, left the house, and went walking—alone.

That night I slept under a tree in Gate Pa Park and talked to old Maori warriors. There has been no further methylprednisolone treatment for me! I have since learned it can take up to two years to clear steroids from the body. They're gone, and I am currently doing well.

After five months of medical issues, I had to declare bankruptcy; I was unemployed and unemployable for the time being. The strain also created partnership problems, which are always troubling, and I became depressed and anxious. Looking back, I see how these circumstances caused me to go up to a hill and take the two hundred fifty 10 mg prednisone tablets I had been collecting. I quickly learned that with prednisone overdose, one remains alive, just becomes high. I was at another very low point and thinking of other ways to do what I came here to do. Just then, a mate of mine sent a picture of my daughter to my phone. It was like a bolt of lightning! I started thinking about my children, decided I wanted to live for them, and went to my car. I drove myself to the hospital, though it was a very interesting trip considering the situation! At first, the hospital was going to let me go after checking me over, but I said I would cause myself harm if they did. I was admitted and stayed there for a week of intense therapy.

Somehow, I knew there was help. I don't know if I would be alive today if it weren't for Queen Elizabeth Hospital in Rotorua, a rheumatology hospital. I walked in there so depressed I could hardly move. After a program of recovery and rehabilitation, I walked out a completely different man. I was confident and capable. Counselling a couple of times a week, physiotherapy a couple of times a week, hot pools, spa messages every day, wax therapy, and some amazing therapists worked wonders. As I tell people, I lost Scott over a year ago and then discovered him again!

There are some days when the hours are terribly long and hard because of my sore joints. Those are the days I find happiness by looking to the future. I live in a rented house now, and I'm working toward having shared custody of my children. I also study. I am on the first year of my bachelor's degree in social work. A master's degree in social work is what I strive for. My eventual goal is to help men who have lost everything due to disabilities. Now that I have walked the walk, I can talk the talk!

My mother also has RA and is totally disabled. She has been all my life, so I have always known her as disabled. She has an amazing mind and has passed along her love of learning to us. Several other family members live with RA, like my cousin, my mum's older sister, and a great aunty had it. But throughout the family, my mum is the most disabled and yet the most learned!

We all have challenges; it's what we do with them that demonstrates our mettle. Going to Queen Elizabeth Hospital and living with my mother helped me to know how to demonstrate mine. The way I view it, RA is only a disability; it is not my life. There is so much more!

RA

— Is/Cause

A) The Arthritis Foundation tells us RA is chronic inflammation of the lining of the joints ~ http://community.arthritis.org/community/raconnect.htm.

B) Medicinet explains the cause of RA is unknown. Viruses, bacteria, and fungi are suspected, but unproven ~ http://www.medicinenet.com/rheumatoid_arthritis/page2.htm.

— Symptoms

A) The Mayo Clinic lists several symptoms, among them are fatigue, fever, and weight loss ~ http://www.mayoclinic.com/health/rheumatoid-arthritis/DS00020/DSECTION=symptoms.

B) Family Doctors.org tells us that hands, wrists, feet, and knees are commonly the first joints affected, often several joints at once ~ http://familydoctor.org/online/famdocen/home/common/autoimmune/disorders/876.printerview.htmlThe University of Maryland Medical.

– Tips

A) The Johns Hopkins Arthritis Center tells us there is no known cure for RA and the desired outcome is the lowest possible RA activity; remission if possible – http://www.hopkins-arthritis.org.

B) WebMD explains treatment often includes physical therapy; sometimes surgery is necessary – http://www.webmd.com.

Step 1. Consult a professional.

WHAT IS SJÖGREN'S SYNDROME (SS)?

Ellie

Living in the western part of the United States has been educational and interesting. Now it's also our home. I grew up in the Midwest, so after moving, I learned lots of things and about different terrain, weather, and plant life. Recently, I have been the fortunate recipient of some of the fruits of those plants: huckleberries to make jam. Huckleberries are considered a "bite of heaven" in these parts. They taste much like blueberries, though they are smaller and grow only in the mountains. It is impossible to duplicate ideal growing conditions for huckleberries in one's garden. Though that makes collecting them an effort, we are inordinately grateful to have the opportunity. Bears also consider huckleberries a delicacy, so it takes a brave soul to do the collecting! Making jam takes many berries and lots of preparation time, but the result is well worth it!

I have lived my life positively and happily. The past is unchangeable, so I am always looking forward. My husband and I have been married thirty-three fabulous years, and we have a thirty-one-year-old son, who keeps me laughing. My husband and I met when we were in the Air Force and married after a year. Together, we knew we had the love, discipline, and dedication needed for whatever would happen. We settled in Idaho, after being stationed in Washington, and raised our son. I was a working mother, a legal assistant, and I was healthy and joyful until about midlife. We had just taken a dream vacation to Hawaii when upon returning home, I experienced symptoms like a gallbladder attack. I went to see the doctor, and a CT scan revealed a mass on my kidney. The words, "You have cancer," were an incredible, unbelievable shock to me. I was home alone and received this news over the telephone. "No!" This was impossible, but there it was! My wonderful husband came home from work, took one look at me, and knew immediately there was something terribly wrong! I tearfully gave him the awful news. He comforted me, has always been supportive, and I knew that together we would weather this storm.

Surgery to remove a kidney was swiftly deemed necessary, after which there was extended recovery time with excruciating pain. I had recovered only a few months from this challenging situation when I began having aching pain in my remaining kidney. I was immediately alarmed and thought, *What can this mean?* I also had other symptoms: my mouth was as dry as the Sahara, which made it terribly difficult to swallow; my eyes were dry, but then it's always dry where we live; and my back hurt dreadfully. Unless you've had back pain, it's hard to describe just how debilitating it is! In addition to all of that, I was continually losing weight. My darkest moment came when I stepped on the scale at the doctor's office and weighed only 105 pounds. That's skin and bones for me, and I knew if I kept losing, I was not long for this world! I had many questions with few answers. Had the cancer returned? Was it ever gone? What would my future be like? Just what was this?

The doctor prescribed a narcotic pain reliever to help me while the testing process began. I was proactive in my treatment and pushed for a diagnosis. After months of testing for everything else, and all tests came back negative, I suggested an autoimmune disorder. Well, the tests finally came back positive. Just as I was becoming crazed with pain and unable to swallow, the doctor diagnosed Sjögren's (pronounced show-grin) syndrome. Huh??? I have since learned that, taken together, my symptoms are a form of lupus. The chronic pain in my back remains, though it is now controlled. I have also learned the syndrome can mean dry eyes, muscle pain, arthritis, and a whole host of other symptoms, many of which I have experienced. Thankfully I was diagnosed, because I wasn't ever going to give up on searching for answers. I knew I had much more to do with this life!

Through all of the trials, my family and friends have sustained me with their love and caring; however, the most steadfast of all has been my husband. He has supported me throughout the many ups-and-downs and on the days I thought survival was unlikely. When the pain medication would cause me to do or say something I thought was silly, my husband would quickly add, "Those must be really good drugs you are taking!" Five years of living with prescription narcotics, weight gain, and fighting constantly with the insurance company has made me extremely aware of the many difficulties people with health issues have. I think my continuing and constant insurance battles, finally convinced the insurance company to approve a spinal stimulator implant in my back. With it and the medication, thankfully, the need for steroids has been eliminated. I am now able to function normally, most of the time. On the bad days, getting out of bed is a struggle; on the good days, I can live my life. When an attack happens, every part of me aches. It feels like I have been thrown down a long flight of stairs, and I don't want to move. So when I feel an attack coming, I know to limit my activities. How fascinating it is that one can become so attuned to one's body. Having mostly good days now is wonderful.

Receiving assistance from the insurance company—Does that sound like an oxymoron?—has helped me become a better person, more confident, and more proactive in my own care. I guess being successful in my effort to reduce chronic pain has had some benefits. I'm smiling! I have also come to relate to others having health challenges, though it is easier to understand a person's situation when that challenge is visible. Seeing my neighbor, a polio survivor, walk down the street and bent over, is an inspiration to me. Things could be very different!

My issues are less visible, which can be difficult for me. Questions and understanding from others can be elusive and frustrating. The questions can range from unexpressed, leading to people's continued ignorance, to overabundant, which leads to invasion of my privacy. I have come to accept that I will live with my disability the rest of my life. Also, I know my situation could develop into full-blown lupus; that possibility is always there. I will overcome whatever develops, just as others must deal with their situations. I am grateful for my abilities, and when I see individuals functioning as normally as their capabilities allow, I make an effort to be kinder to them— and to myself.

When my mood becomes exceptionally gloomy, I have only to talk to my husband or son. A conversation with either of them can lift my spirits and get me laughing. A shot of laughter is wonderful medicine!

SS

— *Definition*

Chronic—ongoing.

— *Is/Cause*

A) The Sjögren's Syndrome Foundation explains that it is a chronic autoimmune disease in which a person's white blood cells attach to the moisture producing glands ~ http://www.sjogrens.org/.

B) The Mayo Clinic gives us additional information. SS is usually characterized by dry eyes and mouth, and usually affects people over forty ~ http://www.mayoclinic.com/health/sjogrens-syndrome/DS00147.

— *Symptoms*

A) The University of Washington tells of SS symptoms other than those listed above, such as swollen salivary glands, dryness of the vagina, and fatigue ~ http://www.orthop.washington.edu/PatientCare/OurServices/Arthritis/Articles/SjogrensSyndrome.aspx.

B) Johns Hopkins Medicine mentions burning and numbness of the extremities and anemia, or low white blood count, as possible symptoms ~ http://www.hopkinssjogrens.org/disease-information/sjogrens-syndrome/.

– *Tips*

A) Medicinenet states that treatment is usually directed to the particular area of the body affected and that artificial tears can help with dry eyes. Humidifying can help with dry mouth. Keeping the mouth moist will also help prevent dental decay – http://www.medicinenet.com/sjogrens_syndrome/page4.htm.

B) WebMD suggests treatments like easing fatigue by balancing rest and exercise, and using medications – http://www.webmd.com/rheumatoid-arthritis/arthritis-sjogrens-syndrome?page=2.

Step 1. Consult a professional.

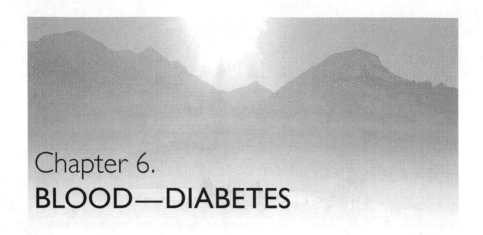

Chapter 6.
BLOOD—DIABETES

WHAT IS DIABETES?

Edward

It was a sunny day three years ago. I was doing some errands near my home in the bustling city of Kolkata, India. I suddenly experienced excessive thirst; it was like I could drink more than all the fluids available to drink! At the same time, I was confused, disoriented, and was unsure where I was. An observer might have thought differently, but I knew there was an extraordinary cause for these unusual circumstances. I was able to make my way home and I found I was fatigued beyond belief. However, when I lay down, sleep eluded me. Did this combination of events make me anxious? Absolutely! Never having been in this situation before, I was unprepared to know what to do. Well, I thought my best option was to visit a doctor, so I did.

When I saw the doctor, he told me, after blood tests, that I had diabetes type II. He optimistically added that I did not require immediate medication and put me on a diet. Well, this might have seemed usual to the doctor, but I was a bit panicked. Then I thought about it, and knew this was a situation I could deal with. Eating differently would take effort, thought, and dedication, but I was certainly capable. It seems that seeking out a knowledgeable expert has been a wise course of action. I followed the regimen and my "new" lifestyle helped me to rise above the diabetes. I found that the more I practised restraint, the stronger I became mentally and physically; this served to spur me on. Further encouragement came from the support of family and friends. The ultimate assistance was delivered by my faith in God. With so much aid, I could only succeed!

Now, the diet has become natural for me. It consists of vegetables such as salad with lettuce, cucumber, onion, radish, and tomatoes. Fruits such as grapes, pineapple, and bananas are disallowed, while bitter melon, watermelon, apple, and citrus fruits are allowed. Mango and guava are also allowed, when in season. Grains can be whole wheat bread, rice, or pulse. Protein sources can be chicken, fish, goat, mutton, and small amounts of lean beef. Some nuts and cheeses are also allowed in very small quantities. Sugar, candies, chocolate, and pork meat products are taboo.

What was most important for me was spacing and reduced quantity. When I eat several small meals, rather than three heavy, large meals, it works out much better.

After following this diet a while, my friends remarked how much younger and more fit I looked. Even though I felt good about this weight loss, I was worried. Was it a bad sign or a good one? I lost about 10 to 15 kg, which helped me a lot. I felt better, my blood sugar levels soon became normal, and all of the excessive thirst and craving for food was gone. It sure seems it was a good regimen to practice. I followed the doctor's instructions very thoroughly and additionally started doing yoga. I maintained this strict diet, using sugar-free sweeteners, and I had only occasional soft drinks. I am nicotine and alcohol free and have maintained the weight loss. Superb!

I certainly felt, and feel, better after the modifications than I did before. I studied about diabetes from information found on the Internet and learned that my system was producing insulin, which was being used incorrectly. Vitamins and minerals prescribed by the doctor also helped me tremendously. Soon, I was back to normal. Having diabetes type II is a life-changing situation that is a surmountable challenge. It's only a bit different than usual, and when this challenge is monitored, it is manageable.

From the Internet, I learned there are three steps to carry out when living with diabetes type II. The first is to have knowledge of the disease, its symptoms, and its possible cure. The second is to contact a good doctor and follow his advice faithfully. He knows about treating your illness. The third step is to avoid alcohol, drugs, fads, and negative thoughts. One thing I can assuredly say is I never doubted that I could be cured of diabetes, as long as I wanted to be free from this disease.

I have received support from many sources: my doctor, my children, and a deep faith in God. They have all helped me maintain health, hope, and an optimistic attitude. I am a born-again Christian. My son has steadfastly said, "Dad, you can overcome this pesky disease with your faith and willpower. I am sure of this," and so I have. Diabetes has helped make me a stronger, better, happier human being in the sight of God and man. Perhaps my experience can help people with pre-diabetes to be cured before it actually develops into diabetes. Perhaps those with diabetes can become active participants, be hopeful, and keep believing that, with God, everything is possible.

Each morning, I have a simple breakfast of fruit and whole wheat bread, read my mail, check the news on the television and spend time with my grandchildren. Then I go to my laptop, access the Internet, and enjoy myself doing what I like best: connecting with other people. After lunch, I rest by reading, watching TV, and then have a short nap. Later in the evening I take a brisk, thirty-minute walk. I see and chat with friends and neighbours before it's time to go back home. For dinner, I have white meat or fish then I watch the FIFA soccer World Cup, cricket, a movie on TV, or the news. Then I read my Bible and ask myself, "Today, what I could have done to be better in God's sight?" At eleven or twelve p.m., it's off to bed and sleep.

A good family background prepares one for many challenges in life. My grandfather was an Englishman who married an Indian lady, and our family still belongs to the community of Anglo-Indians found in many large cities in India. The marriage took place during British rule, and we continue to flourish. When India became an independent nation, my parents decided to remain settled in India, while continuing our British ancestry and way of life. Today, we are pleased to have the best of both worlds: English and Asian. My children are well educated, are happily married, and have lived abroad in the USA.

Education helps a person to understand and prepares one for gainful employment. The children have all decided to come back to India and are living and working here. My lovely wife passed away in 1986, at forty years old. I have no doubt she would be as delighted as I am.

My family comes first with me, and I look forward to spending time with my children, grandchildren, and catching up with my friends on Facebook, and My Opera. I have found that life must be taken as it is dished out to us. We can control certain things, but I have found there are many things beyond our control. So, it seems best to be philosophical about life, and to enjoy doing what is right. The main belief I utilize is to live a life without causing hurt or pain to those around us. That includes society, family, and country. Most important is to be acceptable to God.

Lindsey

They've come on gradually, these health issues I have. The word I might use is "insidious." I grew up in a part of the country where crops grow easily, given the right conditions, and I have always enjoyed eating. Fixed a certain way, food just tastes good to me and I like tasting it. Possibly, that explains why I have been overweight most of my life. Before now, it has been little more than an irritant. However, when I was in my forties, I started showing signs of arthritis in my knees. But wait, there's more! The main issue has become a definite health risk, even life-threatening. Diabetes is my nemesis.

My husband and I have lived in several states, but after our last move, I went to a new doctor for a checkup. She did an A1C test, which confirmed a diagnosis of diabetes. What indicated to her she should check? Well, as it started, I was always hot and sweaty, from the time I stepped out of the shower until I went to sleep at night. Then it developed that I was always hot, sweaty, and thirsty. I also had hot flashes. Even then, I didn't think anything was seriously wrong. After I was diagnosed, I understood all the signs, and I thought, *This is not a fun thing to have happen!*

I must be constantly aware of what I eat, and that's hard for me. As mentioned, I take pleasure in eating food. Unfortunately, most things I like are missing from the suggested diet. Because I have retired, I have much time to think about food. Because I think about food, I think of the really good things that I know are tasty. Because of that, I succumb to the temptation to fix those tasty meals. Oh, they're so good! Then I feel bad, because I know I could have eaten better, and I believe I will eat better next time. I do crafts and have found that it's something I'm good at, so that helps me avoid hunger pangs sometimes.

From the time of diagnosis, I was in denial, and it might sound ridiculous but I still am, to a point. Back then my thoughts were only, *I don't want to have to monitor my food, my blood sugars, etc. I really don't like sticking myself half a dozen times a day. This diabetes is a very controlling disease!* It was to the point that diabetes was controlling me instead of the other way around.

Diabetes affects a lot of things, like circulation, eyesight, blood pressure, and the heart. My circulation, from about half way down my leg to my toes, is deteriorating; actually there is no feeling. My blood pressure is elevated, but with medications, it is in check. I do have the onset of heart disease, but I'm not taking any medication at this point. I'm supposed to keep my blood pressure in line to help with the heart problem. But, being an excitable person, that's easy to say and hard to do!

My focus has been to get back on the Weight Watchers plan, because I have seen results from staying with that for several months. I believe I will feel better when I do it. You see, a couple of years ago, I was inspired to go to Weight Watcher meetings. I lost forty pounds, and my blood sugar came back into the desirable range. As an added bonus, my knees, legs, and feet didn't hurt. Intellectual knowledge and actually practicing that knowledge are two very different things. Now, I try to do what needs to be done and to follow the plan, but it seems impossible to regain my past footing. The forty-pound weight loss took effort, learning a few things, and changing a few things. I am exceedingly proud of that accomplishment!

Not long after reaching my goal, I had hernia surgery. After recovering, I started gaining again. Why? Because I was able to eat again without getting sick. Also, I thought I could follow the plan on my own; I had it memorized, didn't I? Wrong! I was steadily gaining back what I had lost when I was diagnosed with cancer. I was severely stressed now! On top of just plain liking food, I'm definitely an emotional eater, so having the Big C didn't help. The doctor had recommended Weight Watchers in the first place, so maybe I will do it again.

Though I can only change the present, what I suggest to those younger than me is, "Start at an early age and watch what you eat. Eat healthier, because for many diseases, it's the key. By weighing less, the chances are better you will not have to deal with arthritis and other ailments." It is possible others who are overweight may avoid these complications, but it is unlikely. Arthritis can be debilitating in a lot of ways, and the longer it goes on, the worse it gets. I have "Arthur" in my knees and now in my hands. Thankfully, rheumatoid arthritis was not diagnosed! As a bonus, I have a degenerative disc disease in my neck and lower back. Ouch! With less weight to work with, it might be alleviated. We will see.

I'll just end this by saying that, as a whole, life is good. I do what has to be done. It's when I analyze everything that I say to myself, "Wow!" I have family; my husband says I'm the toughest person he knows and helps me get through the worst days. We have wonderful children and grandchildren, so we are proud of them. I am fortunate to still be mobile. There are challenges, like when I go the mall or when I have to park out very far. Then I use a cane, and I may get a scooter at some point; there's some time before that happens. In the future, bad things indeed can happen, such as loss of limbs or eyesight, due to diabetes. Those are a big concern, and the complications go on from there. I will continue to try the best that I can do what needs to be done. Who knows, maybe I'll lose the weight again and more, start walking, and become a healthier person. I will never give up!

P.S.

I had the courage to go back to Weight Watchers several months ago, and I am getting better! My regimen has become quite simple. I take no more pills, and I'm on a different insulin, which I take only at night. We're still in the testing stages, so it may change if my morning blood sugars stay high. This is much more manageable for me. How about that: I am doing it!

Tamara

Diabetes is a part of me, and I am a part of diabetes. We are one because I was diagnosed at three years of age with type I. That means I make less insulin than I need to survive and have always required injections.

When a person is taught to be careful from such a young age, the situation is very manageable. Taking care of oneself and planning are involved in the course of a day, but I do quite nicely.

According to family lore, my parents became alarmed when I was drinking many litres of fluid and constantly using the toilet. Though it seems uncommon, and could be a strange symptom, the back of my hand also went blue. After I was diagnosed with diabetes, everyone in my family was shocked, as there is no one else with this condition among us. For all we knew, I was the first ever!

Forty years full of experiences with diabetes leave a lot of possibilities to discuss. I have been cautious to avoid being in diabetic shock and close to coma. Being careful to balance my insulin intake with my energy output keeps me healthy. I have dealt with the grief of losing my mum, who provided much of my care; I have gone through pregnancy and had a baby. Being a mum myself, I have known incredible rewards. I now understand how my own mum could care so well for me, and I am grateful.

Humour is a part of my life every day. I am a happy person, who always finds something to make me chortle. Thanks go to my family for creating an atmosphere in which I could flourish. I continue that atmosphere for my own child. My mum was an extraordinary person. Once she learned about diabetes, she took care to make sure I knew what had to be done. I can remember times when she would teach by example. At parties, she would put together a plate of food meant specifically for me. I wasn't allowed to pick at the other food that was there, even though it sure was tempting! It was quite strict, I know, but that example continues to serve me well. I am glad to say that my diet, weight, and health remain carefully monitored yet today.

Every day is interesting, has new challenges, and offers different opportunities. I know that people with diabetes have many concerns, not the least of which is dental hygiene. Maintaining excellent oral health is crucial. Another thing to think about is heart disease, so I always stay active. After forty years of living, I wouldn't change a thing. I love my family, my child, and my life! A diabetes diagnosis isn't the end of the world; it seems to me that the best way to view the condition is that it must be treated with respect. It is my belief that if you respect your body and look after it, your body will respond. After all, one is all we have! Forty years of diabetes encompasses lots of memorable events, too many for my "young" mind to recount. As with any other challenge in life, one must do one's best, and one will come out the other end. When we do that, we are stronger than before.

Every day is a success to me! Currently, I have just started on an insulin pump and, touch wood, it's going really well. I am more than a little bit excited, and I'm keeping the pump! By far, it is the most efficient way to deliver insulin, though I must keep in mind to regulate it. I find it fits quite smoothly into my lifestyle.

My experiences may seem usual, but each day is unique to me. I eat, sleep, work, and deal with whatever comes my way. I look forward, as mums are wont to do, to my son doing well. In years to come, I'm looking ahead to the grandkids! Life experiences affect everyone, with or without a long-term medical condition. My belief is that life is what the individual wants to make of it. I am an average person, just a little bit different, and I enjoy every minute of every day. Happiness is what my life is about!

Diabetes

– Definitions

Insulin—the hormone that controls the amount of glucose in the blood. Blood transports glucose to the cells of the body for use as energy.

Glucose—a simple sugar that is a source of energy for living organisms. Fruits and honey are among the things that contain the carbohydrate.

Type I Diabetes—When the body fails to produce the hormone insulin, glucose cannot be converted to a usable form of energy. Insulin input is required for type I ~ http://www.diabetes.org.

Type II Diabetes—A condition in which the body does not produce enough insulin, or it is ignored. www.diabetes.org.

Gestational Diabetes—When a pregnant woman, who may not have had diabetes before, has a high glucose level during pregnancy - http://www.diabetes.org.

– Is/Cause

A) Medicinenet explains that diabetes is caused by insufficient production of insulin. The production can be absolutely missing or too little for the body's needs - http://www.medicinenet.com/diabetes_mellitus/page2.htm.

B) The Department of Health and Human Services suggests ways for people to manage their diabetes - http://www.hhs.gov/news/factsheet/diabetes.html.

– Symptoms

A) The American Diabetes Association lists frequent urination, great thirst and extreme hunger as possible signs of type I diabetes. Type II indications may be any of those from type I or blurred vision and/or tingling in the hands or feet - http://www.diabetes.org/diabetes-basics/symptoms/.

B) The Medicinenet website has a separate link for symptoms of men and those for women - http://www.medicinenet.com/symptoms_and_signs/article.htm.

– Tips

A) The Medicinenet website focuses on the goal of treatment, which is to moderate the level of insulin in the blood. The treatments for type I diabetes are insulin, exercise, and diabetic diet. For type II diabetes, concentration is first on losing weight and then on exercise and diet - http://www.medicinenet.com/diabetes_treatment/index.htm.

B) The Emedicine health website explains how important it is to eat a healthy diet to control diabetes complications and has several suggestions to keep blood sugar at a healthy level. Among them are to eat about the same amount of food each day and to eat meals or snacks at about the same times each day - http://www.emedicinehealth.com.

Author's Note—Counting carbohydrates might work for some. Education about it is recommended.

Author's Note—An insulin pump could be considered as an insulin delivery system - http://www.diabetes.org/living-with-diabetes/treatment-and-care/medication/insulin/insulin-pumps.html.

Step 1. See "Mental Health, Eating Disorders," "Muscles, Heart Disease," and "Senses, Blindness," this book.

Step 2. Consult a professional.

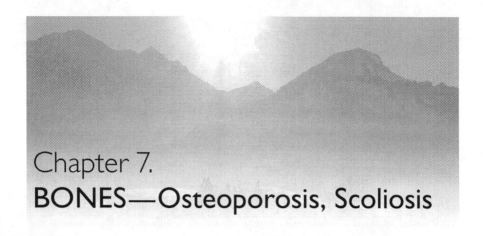

Chapter 7.
BONES—Osteoporosis, Scoliosis

What Is Osteoporosis?

Summer

It is great to help others learn about health issues with something as subtle as osteoporosis. Because my side of the family has a history of dreaded cancer, I would get checked every year as advised. Cancer: just the thought is terrifying! I was extremely faithful in seeing the doctor, and all seemed to be going well with the cancer checkups. However, one time when test results came back, we found I had low estrogen. So I was treated for menopause. Well, I could live with this without a problem, right? Then I started to have back pains, and my estrogen level was still low. Now I was starting to wonder what was up. I was a young woman in my early thirties. I had an active family to raise, and I was always tired. Why? Added to this, my back still hurt, my hair was falling out, and I would frequently spasm (involuntary muscle contraction). Was this pleasant? Hardly! The thing that seemed to help was a very strong injection; I still have them occasionally for bone pain and spasms. What was next? Well, that step was to have a hysterectomy, which catapulted me directly into menopause. I was only thirty-two! What might my life be like now if medicine to boost my estrogen had been prescribed immediately after the surgery? We'll never know. Of course, as all of this was taking place, I went on raising my family in South Africa and smiling.

Fast-forward ten years. I am in my forties, and the cancer results are always favorable. That's good! My doctor was still concerned, because menopause tends to lower estrogen levels, which can affect bone density. Bone density: what is that? It is a term I was unfamiliar with, and it is the amount of matter making up the bone. After the doctor explained it to me and suggested a test, I thought there could be little problem with my bones. After all, low bone density was something for people who were much older than I. Surely I wouldn't have old age sickness, so I breezed in and took the test. The results? I was horrified and shocked to learn I have the bones of a seventy-two-year-old woman, and it was permanent! What? I am still young! With my bones in such bad shape, it was little wonder I was unable to do what I had always done! Now what am I to do?

The thought of living, being sick, and taking medication every day caused me to be inconsolable. I was at ground zero. I fell into a deep, dark well of despair and even thought of ending my own life. Then, a lifeline appeared, and I was saved! My world began to lighten when my children and grandchildren told me they believed in me. My husband said, "You're a strong woman, and we will get through this together." What a wonderful family I have! I went to see a psychologist, and she helped me to cope with my thoughts. It was only with the help of all of these caring people that I survived.

The doctor informed me that osteoporosis progression could be slowed with medication, which was good news. Working toward that goal, I started to take calcium, vitamin D, and Osteobon. I could, and have thought, *Why me?* and, *Life is so unfair*. Well, I could also sit in a corner and cry. So my thoughts have become, *How do I want people to see me?* The answer comes to me and directs my actions. I prefer achievement, so I stand up and do my best.

My lifestyle has changed drastically, diet first. Calcium is a major concern, so I have lots of milk products, like milk, cheese, and yogurt, with an egg each day. I eat green leafy vegetables, like broccoli and spinach. Fish is almost a daily staple, while coffee, salt, and salty foods are avoided. I searched the Internet for additional osteoporosis assistance and found some exercises to do. Exercising depends on how my day is going. Because I continue to have considerable back pain, many days any exercise is difficult to impossible. Added to that, my wrists are becoming quite brittle so that even a handshake can cause a bone break. Struggling with the results of osteoporosis has been depressing, so I have been to see a sociologist to help me cope. Though I have to say there are residual days of low mood, I do well by focusing on my family and smiling.

My husband and I have been married thirty years, and we have our four lovely daughters to think about. Keeping them safe is a major concern. Instead of letting dire thoughts ferment like wine, I think about my children or grandson; that always brings a smile, and so does all the positive steps I am taking. My life has been a series of challenges, as most are. Whatever the challenge that comes along, I fix whatever needs fixing. I have always been strong, and whatever needs changing, I make an attempt. Because of my difficulties, I have found something that needs fixing. As is my way, I searched the Internet and learned of a doctor who has osteoporosis. He is studying it, and he sounds great. I trust he will make new discoveries.

As I said, my lifestyle has changed, starting with diet. I have completed that portion of the recommendations. Exercises also can help, which I have also mentioned. A third segment is attitude. I stay positive, have faith, and believe God will decide my future. What might be suggestions to others? I would say, anyone can have osteoporosis, so ask the doctor about a bone density test, along with other regular checks. People sometimes ask me for tips, and I enjoy helping them; it helps me to feel better. Also, I believe miracles can and do happen!

I used to love to pick up my three-year-old grandson and cuddle with him. He lights up my life and brings me joy. A while back, he reached for me to continue our closeness. It is now impossible for me to pick up his weight, so I had to explain to him what was happening with Grandma. I told him that my back hurts, and I have to drink medicine every day to try to make it better. He understands pain and is such a sweetheart. Whenever I see him now, he rubs my back and asks how I'm feeling today. We love each other, and he believes I will get better. Isn't that the way things should be? Yes, of course. I continue to believe miracles happen, and I plan to stay around a while to find out. In the meantime, I will continue to enjoy my friends, myself, and my family with a smile!

Osteoporosis

– Is/Cause

A) According to the Mayo Clinic, scientists aren't sure what causes osteoporosis, but says the normal bone replenishing process is interrupted – http://www.mayoclinic.com/health/osteoporosis/DS00128/DSECTION=causes.

B) The National Osteoporosis Foundation (NOF) states there are osteoporosis risk factors. Family history and previously broken bones cannot be changed, but can be mediated – http://www.nof.org/aboutosteoporosis/bonebasics/riskfactors.

– Symptoms

A) The NIH Osteoporosis and Related Bone Diseases explains that anorexia nervosa, insufficient calcium and vitamin D, lack of exercise, smoking, and drinking can all lead to osteoporosis – http://www.niams.nih.gov/Health_Info/Bone/Osteoporosis/osteoporosis_ff.asp#cause.

B) The Mayo Clinic states that bone loss in early stages have no symptoms, but once they are weakened, symptoms can be a fracture of the hip or wrist. Possibly one could have a stooped posture – http://www.mayoclinic.com/health/osteoporosis/DS00128/DSECTION=symptoms.

– Tips

A) Women's Health lists many medications for drug therapy. Bisphosphonates, SERMS (commonly referred to as an estrogen receptor modulator), and other treatments are listed as possibilities – http://www.womenshealth.gov/faq/osteoporosis.cfm#i.

B) The NOF lists ways to prevent, slow, or possibly stop osteoporosis. Two of these are to get enough calcium and vitamin D and to engage in appropriate exercise – http://www.nof.org/aboutosteoporosis/managingandtreating/medicinesneedtoknow.

Author's Note—Milk and yogurt consumption may be beneficial.

Step 1. Consult a professional.

WHAT IS SCOLIOSIS?

The Story of Hope

When I was young, moving to a Midwestern city proved to be a fateful decision for my family. Five of us had to survive on a one-parent salary, as the employment of my father vanished soon after our relocation. This caused tremendous turmoil within him, and his easily ignited anger and vindictiveness made for a very dysfunctional family life. In spite of his guns and threats, we all survived, albeit with some emotional scars. Excelling in school was a way to lessen his criticisms, so we did what we could to excel, the luckiest of us with great success. We had an advantage in that my mother was a teacher, who wisely encouraged us to get a college education and be prepared to support ourselves, so that we would not need to be dependent on a spouse for that support. We three daughters have followed in our mother's footsteps, and also have become educators. It is amazing the impact courageous individuals can have on their children!

While in middle school, I first noticed pain while carrying a heavy load of books. What could be the cause? Also, I noticed that shoveling snow was painful, and in the Midwest wintertime, it was often a necessity! In college, I began to notice differences between the right and left sides of my waist. I realized that others also noticed my asymmetry, because a friend walking behind me mentioned that one of my shoulders carried higher than the other. This was very odd! A few years later, I was working in a hospital and decided to have X-rays taken. A radiologist saw me standing erect, viewed the X-ray, and pronounced the diagnosis of scoliosis of the lower back. Finally, at the age of twenty-two, I had irrefutable evidence which explained why no one should think I was exaggerating about my pain! I believe that my scoliosis may be congenital, as I have a number of other asymmetries, including the length of my legs, deviated septum, crooked palate, crooked chin, and more. More recent X-rays have shown osteoarthritis and a chipped vertebra in addition to the scoliosis.

The chipped bone is likely from long ago, when I was violently mugged, and my head was smashed into a frozen parking lot. I was temporarily dazed, and there was lots of blood, as head wounds bleed freely. Nonetheless, exercising questionable judgment, I drove myself to the emergency room, where my head was X-rayed, stitched, and covered with a pressure bandage that circled my head. The attack left me with a fear of strangers, which lasted a very long time. This was not to be the end of the excitement.

During the week following the mugging, I was in another frighteningly close call while at work—with an elevator this time. It crashed into the top of the elevator shaft, and I heard cables breaking and slithering down the sides of the elevator compartment; they fell twenty-one stories to the bottom of the shaft. The floor indicator showed that I had fallen several floors before stopping with a jerk. I pushed the emergency button, quickly explained my predicament, and help was on the way. I thought, *Two such incidents in one week is a bit much!* During the rescue, it took some time for the repairman to finally free me from my confinement between two floors, including a terrifying sudden series of jerks downward, without warning from the man working on the other side of the doors. When they finally opened and with his first glimpse of me, shock registered on the face of my rescuer. He had the strangest look, as if wondering how I was injured and bandaged even before he had freed me!

The scoliosis has been a more chronic issue. Standing or walking for any length of time can be excruciating, so employment or enjoyment involving either is impossible. Some time ago, I purchased a thickly cushioned mat to lessen the pain when standing while cooking in the kitchen. Just prior to that, some of the more effective pain medications were withdrawn from the market, so I was left with pain. I wish I could have the option of reading about the risks of taking these medications, then make my own choice about whether or not it is worth those risks to improve my quality of life. Instead, drug companies are pressured by the threat of lawsuits to withhold treatments that could improve the lot of many sufferers.

At one point, invariably during evenings following a day spent mostly on my feet, I would be walking across a room and suddenly experience an excruciating flash of pain, which would cause me to immediately shift my weight to the opposite foot. I would balance on that foot for as long as it took for me to muster the courage to take another step, knowing that a searing jolt of pain might or might not accompany it. It had gotten to the point where I could no longer put off investigating surgical options for my condition. Once I had met with the orthopedic surgeon at the Mayo Clinic, I learned that there was nothing that could be done for me surgically. Knowing that if my quality of life was to improve, I would have to do the work myself, I went to a physical therapist, and that began the months of recovery that was in my hands alone to achieve. It is not a goal that can be achieved and abandoned, but must be worked at constantly and with diligence. It has become a part of my routine to do my exercises in our Family Y pool, five times a week, in order to strengthen the muscles surrounding my spine. I have been doing this for years now, and have enjoyed significant benefits in terms of being more comfortable for a larger part of every day.

Because of my self-discipline in pursuing the exercise regimen, my quality of life has improved immensely. Additionally, I take an over-the-counter pain medication twice a day. Being in pain is draining, so it is much easier to be happy when one is pain free, and well worth the effort it takes to help that come about.

My family is the primary focus in my life. My husband could be described in many ways, but one of the most invaluable of his traits is patience, which I sought after being raised by a father who had none. Dean and I complement each other's strengths. He can be unconventional in many ways, and that tends to keep life interesting. His choice of a position in the medical field requiring shorter work hours, with commensurate pay, has been good for our whole family. We have always focused on family: from my taking many years of parenting classes, to volunteering in our daughters' classrooms, to Dean coaching Jenny's soccer teams and playing tennis with Becky.

Both of us helped them with homework. I have found motherhood to be a joyful experience—following the pregnancy, that is. I was determined to succeed as a parent, because the tragic contrast between my own parents was so glaring. Both of our children attend college and have chosen professions in the medical field. They have excelled academically, artistically, athletically, and as volunteers in our community and around the world, winning many honors, awards, and distinctions along their way. My beliefs have determined not only my actions, but have also influenced my children's choices. Volunteerism is important to me, because I believe we have a responsibility to others when we live in a community. They grew up seeing that philosophy in action. If there is a need for help, I will do what I am able, as part of an organized group or individually. I sit on the local board of a national non-profit organization, while also regularly volunteering to help others of my acquaintance who need it.

Looking back on my life, I recognize the challenges and good fortune presented to me. I loved teaching. I love helping my husband and my daughters. I love volunteering. I love life and leaving a positive mark on the lives of others. Whatever the circumstances in which I have found myself, I have readily chosen to expend the effort necessary to improve my situation and that of others. Happily, I have also enjoyed the means and opportunity to pursue my own interests and have been able to help my children have incredible opportunities of their own. I have found reading, gardening, quilting, traveling, various art projects, and visiting friends and family to be rewarding experiences. All in all, my quality of life has exponentially surpassed my expectations and I realize that I have truly been blessed!

Scoliosis

– Is/Cause

A) The NIH states that scoliosis is when the spine curves away from the middle ~ http://www.ncbi.nlm.nih.gov/pubmedhealth/PMH0002221/.

B) The Mayo Clinic explains that scoliosis most often happens during the growth spurt before puberty ~ http://www.mayoclinic.com/health/scoliosis/DS00194.

– Symptoms

A) The Mayo Clinic describes symptoms that may include uneven shoulders, an uneven waist, or one hip higher than the other ~ http://www.mayoclinic.com/health/scoliosis/DS00194/DSECTION=symptoms.

B) The Doctors of the University of Southern California also describe chronic back pain and breathing difficulty as possible symptoms - http://www.doctorsofusc.com/condition/document/11573.

– **Tips**

A) The Mayo Clinic suggests a brace or surgery as possible solutions - http://www.mayoclinic.org/scoliosis/?mc_id=comlinkpilot&place ment=bottom.

B) Emedicine.net states there are three main categories of treatment: observation, bracing, and surgery - http://www.medicinenet.com/scoliosis/page3.htm.

Step 1. Consult a professional.

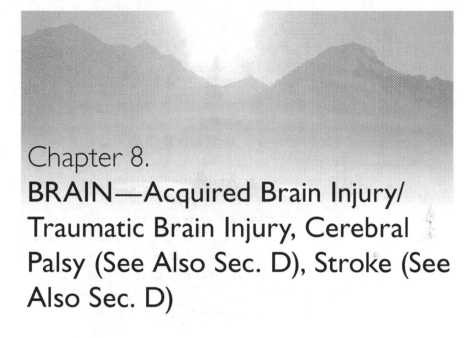

Chapter 8.
BRAIN—Acquired Brain Injury/ Traumatic Brain Injury, Cerebral Palsy (See Also Sec. D), Stroke (See Also Sec. D)

WHAT IS ACQUIRED BRAIN INJURY (ABI)?

ABIs occur after childhood and include TBIs ~ http://www.biausa.org/about-brain-injury.htm#definitions.

Kelli

It has been quite a road for me. Because I was a foster child from birth, I have firsthand knowledge of the foster care system in the United States. I lived in about twelve different foster homes, then aged out. I became too old for the foster care system. A sixth-grade teacher and other positive adults were instrumental in influencing my decision, at eighteen, to choose college over other pursuits. I had plans and wanted to go somewhere in life, so college it was. My DSS (Division of Social Services) person expected to set the bar very low for me. I admired the work she did, but she assumed my aspirations and abilities were unequal to anything more than her predetermined notions. She underestimated me, but I was sure, so I jumped over the bar she set, turned around, and picked it up to set it high over my head. I had a goal and reached it handily!

My focus was social work, and I earned a BSW (bachelor of social work) with an MED (master's of education) in counseling. Until relatively recently, I worked at a local mental health facility, providing counseling. One day early in 2008, I went about my job as usual. The headache I had that morning persisted, but the reason eluded me. I happened to go to the front of the clinic, to the support staff area, where my headache instantly became almost unbearable. Already I was partially unaware of my actions. I went to our nurse's station to take my blood pressure. After doing so, I went back up front and told the staff to call 911 immediately! I don't remember anything beyond the blood pressure check. I have been told that my face was red as a beet; also, I began vomiting and had incredible, constant pain in my head.

Emergency medical services came as soon as they received the call and took me to a small hospital nearby. In performing a CT scan of my head, the doctor could see the hemorrhage in my brain and called another hospital, better equipped to handle my situation. It was all very dramatic, and fortunately, I was unconscious the whole time.

Recovering from acquired brain injury (ABI) is long and difficult, but I know it can be done. Being raised in foster homes engendered survival instincts in me, which have remained active. However, when I was told I wouldn't be able to return to my job, it was the most terrible moment of my life! I began to think, *Oh no, my life is over! What am I going to do if I can't work? I need to get back to my job! I love my job! I was helping people! Why can't I do that again?* Then, that survival instinct took over. There is only movement forward as far as I am concerned. I frequently recall a quote. Paraphrased, the quote is, "The person lacking the courage to start has already finished." I use this to supply momentum at the times I really feel like giving up.

You see, my job was tremendously important to me, with much of my personality wrapped up in it. Being unable to work has made it challenging to maintain my self-esteem, and this has created some identity issues for me. After all, I had done social work for fifteen years. After the ABI, I was basically staying home most of the time. I would only go to my various therapy appointments. During one of my occupational therapy appointments, we talked about the possibility of volunteering. From that point on, I took the attitude that if I couldn't go back to work, I would have to find other ways to help people. I believe God didn't let me live through the brain injury just to sit on my butt! I think my new purpose in life is to use what I have been through to help others.

One day at a time is the way I live now; I avoid planning into the future. Each day is different, and it can be bad or it can be good. On the bad days, I have only to recall how fortunate I am to be alive. Good days are fabulous. I am two years past the ABI incident, and there are moments when I think I should be much farther along than I am. At those times, I remind myself again how far I have come.

For example, I have left side neglect syndrome, though I still feel pain on my left side. This means my brain recognizes only the right side of my body. So, one day I decided to shave my legs. As I was shaving, I continually reminded myself to shave my left leg. By concentrating very hard, I remembered to shave both legs and was quite proud of myself when I finished. Hooray for me! I felt pretty wonderful until my partner pointed out that I had shaved only the right sides of both legs. We burst into laughter and have had many chuckles since!

I have further learned that one needs to be one's own advocate. If I need something, I ask for it. Depending on someone other than myself was a difficult transition for me, having learned early to be extremely independent. I have now created a website, which chronicles my journey, it is Kellithesurvivor.com. You may find it interesting!

Now I have been offered a new opportunity. I have a dog, Kaci, and four cats. Children might have been in my future, though that is now forever out of the question. Even as children might have motivated me, the pets have assumed that role. They keep my mind and body active and keep my focus on them instead of my pain. Kaci and I are being trained so we can volunteer together and do pet therapy. I have seen how helpful this activity can be. It is exciting, because Kaci and I are reinventing ourselves! I am fortunate to have such loving and caring people and pets in my life. Who knows how far we will go? I have started writing a book about living in the foster care system; I began writing before the ABI and now have additional experiences to incorporate. I have many goals yet to be achieved, and I'm very excited about the possibilities!

Jamie (Iron Man) Fairles

Though I am only thirty, I have lived a lifetime in those years, actually more than a lifetime. I love music, mostly rock. I call myself a rawker (rocker). I began playing guitar in ninth grade, when I was fourteen. Now I have four guitars: one bass and three acoustic. Any requests? Movies are another passion of mine, hence my bachelor of arts degree in English and film studies. Would you rather talk movie trivia? In school I played sports. There was football in high school, then rugby my senior year. It seems I needed more of a challenge than football proved to be. I wanted to try everything! One time during a rugby game, my vision lost all color. Now I've watched Dr. Oz, and he says losing color vision is bad. I believe it! When I told the coach, he just said, "You probably hit your head one too many times." Thanks, coach.

Then at eighteen, I "hit the wall." I would get dizzy spells anywhere, at any time, sometimes while I was driving. They were so bad they would nauseate me. I would also get head rushes to the cosmic degree. Though it's not recommended, driving with a head rush like that is some kind of trip! Even as young as I was, I knew something was wrong. When I first went to the doctor I was told I had a cyst on my brain. Okay. I didn't know what to think. The doctor then sent me to the emergency room for an MRI; I had a tumor! What did that mean for my future? Would I survive the surgery to remove it? Until that time, my sister and I loved each other with mostly unspoken emotion. When I was being wheeled into surgery for the operation, my sister shouted out, "Jamie, I love you." I knew then it was time to be very concerned!

Since that day, I have had a total of eight brain operations. I have had three craniotomies, which is surgically opening the skull to access the brain. I have had two internal shunt insertions to drain the cerebrospinal fluid (CSF), which had built up in my brain. This relieves pressure. I have had one external shunt insertion, which creates a passage from one cavity to another. And I have had two ventriculostomies, which is when an opening is created in a ventricle. Ventricles contain CSF. This was done because I had hydrocephalus, an accumulation of CSF in the brain. I have also contracted both bacterial and chemical aseptic meningitis after the first and fifth surgeries, respectively. Infections are a risk with any surgery. I also have left homonymous hemianopsia, which is the loss of half of one's vision. In my case, it is the left field of vision in each eye. This is from the first surgery, because, as the doctors put it, "The optic nerve was assaulted." In reading this recitation, I realize I have had quite a time of it.

After I graduated, I could do everything but drive. This was due to my lack of sight; in fact, the last time I drove gas was only fifty-six cents a litre. A year to the day after my graduation, while in Toronto, I attempted to stop a fight between my half-brother and a stranger. The stranger apparently viewed me as a weaker opponent during the altercation and proceeded to assault *me*. Up to this time, I had six of the operations. When the stranger kept hitting me on the side of my head where the operations had been, I was thinking, *No! Hit me anywhere but there!* Eventually, he wore himself out. However, the damage was done. The repeated blows caused a subarachnoid hemorrhage, which is a form of stroke. I was left struggling to move my left side, which wasn't responding. Imagine my dismay! The darkest moment in my life came when I realized that I was partially paralyzed and had very little balance. Shit! What more could there be? Since then, my mobility has been greatly reduced; I have trouble with walking and with the use of my arm. Well, I did ask the question!

To remain positive and to get through this, I needed to recognize how fortunate I am. I thought, *I have gone through so much, and I still have the cognitive faculties I had before the assault!* I am a much stronger person than the stranger was.

From my view, unless your life has been personally touched by brain injury, or unless one works in the field, sadly, very little is known about this hidden disability. That's why it is one of, if not the, most misunderstood, mislabeled, and misdiagnosed of health challenges! It is my duty to provide comfort to those with a brain injury. To that end, I have created a Facebook group, Supporting A.B.I. (Acquired Brain Injury). The group has over thirty-seven hundred members that span the globe, and many people find it reassuring to know that they are not alone.

Humor is what has helped me all my life, especially after the surgeries. Following my fifth brain surgery, a nerve was touched. It left me with double vision for a period of time. I thought ½ multiplied by 2 = 1, so it seemed to me I should have perfect vision. That's logical, right? Unfortunately, it works only mathematically. Then there was the time when my mom was coaching me to help get my voice back. I had been on a respirator for so long that I lost the ability to talk. Even so, I could hum; verbalization was the issue. I began the effort to talk again by humming and saying words that begin with the letter M. My mother would start by saying an M word, like "Mmmmom," and I'd repeat it. She did that for a while until she said, "Mummmy Mmmmom is beautiful," and I repeated back "Mummy Mmmom is kidding herself!" After that, she knew I was going to be just fine. Through all my trials, my inspiration has been, and continues to be, my mother. She has supported me since the day I had my first migraine. Inspired by my brain injuries, she is the brain injury expert at the Children's Aid Society in London, Ontario. It seems we inspire each other!

After being through so much at such a young age, I choose to give back to those less fortunate. The assault is what led me to become a volunteer at the Brain Injury Association of London & Region. Consequently, that has inspired me to pursue a university education. I may one day have a career counselling others with brain injuries and other brain trauma. My way of accomplishing this mission is to sit on the boards of both the Brain Injury Association of London & Region, which covers five counties, and the Brain Injury Association of Ontario. I am also the peer support coordinator for London and the surrounding area, and it is my duty to match people impacted by brain injuries with others in a similar situation. I encourage them to talk to and support each other, which can be tremendously helpful.

My firm belief is that everything in life has a purpose, and having gone through it all, I decided to obtain my bachelor of social work and eventually my master's of social work degrees. That way, someday, I will be able to work in a hospital, counselling people affected by brain injuries and other brain trauma. I have walked the walk; now it's time to walk *and* talk! I believe the purpose of having to endure my challenges is so I can share my story with others. I would like to inspire and instill hope in people, because there is so much in life to enjoy.

I was just recently accepted into the University of Manitoba's distance delivery bachelor of social work program. It is the only Canadian university offering a BSW program online. I am all about thinking and living positively. The book _The Secret_ states that living positively and thinking positive thoughts will allow good things to come to you. It is what I have found to be true! I think our own life experiences shape us into the people we become, so living a positive life would seem to be advantageous. Would I like my life to have been different? Sure, but I think I would be a different person if I had other experiences than I did. The challenges have made me a much stronger individual and have taught me things that only personal experience could have. I am most proud of being named the Ontario Brain Injury Association's Volunteer of the year for 2008. One of my favorite things to tell myself is, *Negativity is like a soup spoon with holes, useless and pointless.* Yes, it's true. Think positively!

ABI

Author's Note: For the purposes of this book, ABI and TBI are separated.

— Is/Cause

A) The Brain Injury Network explains ABI can be any brain injury after birth, excluding Alzheimer's and Parkinson's – http://www.braininjurynetwork.org/thesurvivorsviewpoint/definitionofabiandtbi.html.

B) The Brain Injury Association states that an ABI can affect the way a person thinks, acts, feels, or moves their body. Internal body functions may also change such as regulation of body temperature, blood pressure, and bowel/bladder control – http://www.biausa.org/living-with-brain-injury.htm.

— Symptoms

A) The Frasier Valley Brain Injury Association states immediate symptoms can vary from none to a mild bleed at the point of injury. Loss of consciousness, nausea, seizures, and confusion are in need of medical attention – http://www.fvbia.org/acquired-brain-injury.html.

B) Brain and Spinal Cord.org informs us that ABI and TBI symptoms are very similar, but are sometimes experienced more severely or frequently with ABI ~ http://www.brainandspinalcord.org/brain-injury/signs-brain-injury/index.html.

— Tips

A) All About Acquired Brain Injury has information which could be helpful to young people and teens with brain injury ~ http://www.aboutbraininjury.org.uk/living_with_your_parents.aspx

B) The Family Caregiver Alliance states that aids can be as simple as crutches or a cane and as complex as a voice-activated computer system or a mechanical hoist to lift someone ~ http://www.caregiver.org/caregiver/jsp/content_node.jsp?nodeid=141.

Step 1. Consult a professional.

WHAT IS TRAUMATIC BRAIN INJURY (TBI)?

Donald

Magic has been my passion from a young age. Most of my life, I have developed my prestidigitation talent and have utilized it to enhance my livelihood with speaking engagements. Motivational speaking, that is. At the highest level, I earned over $100,000 a year. Truly, magic has been good to me.

I became fascinated with the art of magic at nine years old; I am self-taught. I learned from magic sets (a group of tricks), library books, and tricks received for holidays. I honed my craft and by the age of thirteen I was advertising. In the beginning, I put up flyers in the community, was performing at birthday parties, at community centers, and in retirement homes. Between my early teens and early twenties, these events were quite satisfying. Then, I saw a life-changing ad for an International Brotherhood of Magicians competition and entered. I won the stage category, competing against other magicians of western North America. Yes! This was pretty heady stuff, precisely the introduction needed, and I looked ahead to unlimited possibilities. Little did I know how instrumental magic would be for my future.

Highlights of my career have been performing for the band U2 and also for a Microsoft group when Bill Gates was in attendance. More excitement! Then, the day of my accident came.

One day, I was driving to an engagement. The drowsy driver of an oncoming car fell asleep, drove across the center line, and hit my Jeep head-on. Looking at the pictures of my destroyed vehicle, I find it hard to believe I am still alive. A new chapter of my life was born that significant day. For months and years, I recovered from traumatic brain injury (TBI) and other physical aches and pains. I recuperated with the help of innumerable doctors and medications, therapists, and therapies. One other element was essential to recovery—my determination to heal, physically, mentally, and emotionally. This was also the required order of healing. I was told by the neurologist I would forever require assistance to walk. Really? He apparently thought he knew me better than *I* knew me. I was certain I would recover, because unquestionably, I believe in healing.

The physical injuries to my body healed more quickly than the TBI. Some of the evident symptoms I displayed from the TBI were short- and long-term memory loss, confusion, repetition, and sleep disorder. Mentally and emotionally, I experienced lack of motivation, depression, anxiety, emotional control issues, and hopelessness. After the accident, my future seemed bleak and unworkable to me. Family always loved me, but the experts are necessary to take the load of therapy off the family. Because I could not remember or recognize certain things, my ex-wife would lovingly call me "brain boy." It was a welcome bit of humor at critical moments!

It was a while before I had my brilliant idea. I moved to a small community and purchased a house. Online, I came across a site with magic tricks. For me, the passion had been rekindled! I ordered about $1,000 in tricks. Having plenty of time to practice, I did so relentlessly each day, and the most amazing thing began to happen. The uninjured portions of my brain became less confused, I was remembering more, and making connections again. Other portions of my brain were creating new pathways. I learned this is called neuroplasticity, a remodeling, so to speak. In essence, my brain was an alchemy experiment; it had been lead which was turned into gold. I had a golden brain! I began to manage my own life again. What a great feeling!

Now I have a job which fulfills me. I work part time at Staples and lead a fairly normal, stable life. I also do inspirational speaking on an exclusive topic: TBI.

In my younger years I had become dependent on substance use. It was in my early twenties when I became clean and sober. Then, I started speaking to schools. My goal was to raise awareness and to have some meaning in what I was saying. To this end, I would release myself from a straitjacket to demonstrate the difficulty of freeing myself from addiction. When I speak now, I use a combination of magic, humor, and inspiration to encourage people. Those living with or without TBI can also discover their passion and build on it. My future goal is to create an online community, coaching clients. My background suggests success, and I look forward to it.

From painful and unpleasant to fabulous, overcoming addiction to healing through magic, experiences have been a vital part of the process of growing and learning. Perhaps others can find their own bliss, pursue it, target undamaged portions of their brains, and work toward constructing new lives. It is most rewarding!

Melissa

Four years ago, I lived near the ocean, and it seemed like a good idea to finally make the purchase. I bought my first boat; I was to be a proud skipper. You will notice I said "was."

Before setting out on the high seas, it seemed important to familiarize myself with all things boat-related. So working toward this end, I took a class. Isn't that what one does to gain knowledge of something new? We were learning how to flip a boat after it had capsized. The instructor made it look so easy! When it came my turn, I was standing on the dock, flipping the boat over. This was okay, but when it was half the way over, for some reason, I lost my balance and into the water I went. Simultaneously, the boat, still at its apex, suddenly came crashing down on my head and kept bouncing like a basketball on it! Immediately, I went under the water, unconscious. About the incident, I have only the memory of waking up in the hospital. I stayed for a couple of days and left with a diagnosis of acquired brain injury/traumatic brain injury (ABI/TBI). My boating adventure had come to a tragic end, but at least I had survived!

Having lived through this trauma, it seemed that I was well enough to go back to work. It was then I began noticing symptoms. I was sitting in a meeting when I began to have strange sensations. People would be talking, but the words spoken were unintelligible to me. I always heard ringing in my ears, and I could be sitting down but felt like I was trying to balance on a high wire. I would be at my desk and try to work, but I kept starting projects only to leave them unfinished. I kept telling my coworkers there was something wrong with me, which they knew already, but I had difficulty telling them what was hard for me to understand. How could I expect any of us to realize what was going on until I had a clearer picture? So, I went to a general practitioner (GP), thinking that perhaps he could shed some light. No help. I went to another, and it was a repeat of the first. I have found that this is generally true of GPs who are presented with ABI/TBI. They have little, if any, knowledge about it. This challenged me even more to try to get my life back! By God, I would once again survive! And so I have.

After the accident, I would see the chiropractor fairly regularly for this or that. He understood my situation pretty well. He was able to recognize ABI/TBI symptoms and referred me to the Brain Injury Society. I discovered a second home! I was so grateful there was recognition of my troubles that I cried many happy tears. At the Brain Injury Society, I found several programs from which I could benefit. There, I was finally understood that I was really okay! My symptoms were also the symptoms of others, so we are alike. I had found others with brain injury and I had true friends. My life is different now because of my new family. The people I have met since the accident are patient and loving.

My ex-husband and children have been less understanding. Following my accident, I was abused mentally, emotionally, and spiritually. I was constantly told the pain and confusion I had was laziness, so eventually I said, "Enough is enough!" My ex-family and I are distanced now in most ways. I currently have very little income and have been unable to find work, yet. My children help me pay bills, but even then, I have to be cautious, because the kids tend to use my checking account to pay their own bills! That could be a reflection of their father's denial that there is anything wrong with me, or it may be some of their own thinking. My parents try to understand, but have trouble. So, my true family is made up the individuals at the Brain Injury Society. They accept me for who I am. I sometimes miss the fair-weather friends and family of the past. At those times, I concentrate on the wonderful people of my present.

This family and I share similar experiences, like cognitive (thinking) issues, trouble sleeping, neck and back pain, migraines, difficulty with everyday living skills, and with work-related skills. I have been blessed by knowing and being helped by good people who understand what brain injury is all about. Two-and-one-half years of rehabilitation really worked wonders for me. Emotionally, a diagnosis of post-concussion syndrome has helped to lift a great weight from my shoulders. When I heard that my symptoms were common enough to have a name, I knew I was justified in following my instincts! Brain injury rehabilitation has also taught me a most valuable skill: recall. Repetition made a huge difference. Recalling what I need to do and when I need to do it, has helped me tremendously with daily activities. Currently, I can plan my days and what to do, like knowing what to have for breakfast, what clothes to wear, when to eat a meal, and when to have a snack. I know when I'm tired and need to rest, so I can wake up rejuvenated with a "fresh" brain.

Having structure is a most valuable tool, and it helps with recall, so I attend the BI Society workshops faithfully. I know that this is the right place for me. I believe my drive and willingness to succeed has also been a plus in overcoming the trials of ABI/TBI. In the past, I have worked in an administrative job and hope to work again in this position. That would provide some income. I could then move into a place of my own, start my life again with the revitalized me, and be my own person! There are some new things I know now.

Through the years and many experiences, I have learned when to be patient and when to kick it into gear. Through the rehab program, I have a much better understanding of what confidentiality means and when it's applied. I have learned that I can handle life without the drama, and I am proud of my ability to listen rather than rushing to speak. Fundamental knowledge and understanding of ABI/TBI is exceptionally lacking in the general population and in general practitioners. This basic knowledge could have helped me sooner, so the impact on my life would have been minimal. Unfortunately, things transpired in a different way, and though I grieve my losses, I rejoice in my successes. At a certain point, I had to decide if I would take care of others or if I would take care of me. I chose to take care of me for a change, and I have my achievements to display as a result!

Nora

Before the defining moment, I was an artist who drew, painted, and wrote stories as a hobby. I went to Georgian College for marketing business, and I was working in the retail aspect of marketing, looking for a marketing research or marketing advertising job. Then I was in the accident. It was a car crash, and we were hit almost directly head-on. I was riding in the backseat, on the passenger side, at the time of impact. I was unconscious for about ten to fifteen minutes, and when I came to, I had no feeling from the neck down. For that instant I thought I was in heaven. When I got to the hospital, they drew my blood and it was purple. I learned I had a head injury and a bruised heart. Both of those were reasons for being in the intensive care unit (ICU). Then I understood that I also had whiplash. It was only later I discovered there was another issue. The symptom indicating I had a brain injury was, first and foremost, memory.

To demonstrate, when I was just moved to the usual hospital room from the ICU, I was asked what medication I was taking at the time. I gave it a tremendous effort, but could not remember how to spell the name of the med. Why couldn't I remember? I always remembered how to spell words! After leaving the hospital, I would forget appointments, the names of people I did not and did know, stutter, show no emotion on my face, misunderstand directions, get lost, have anger issues, sleep a lot, and have horrible headaches during the day that could drop me to my knees. Also, I would run into the wall on my right side whenever I had those headaches, not recognize who I was anymore, slur my words when I was tired, need to have naps, feel no pain, get dizzy, and was unable to paint and draw like I used to. They're all symptoms indicating whiplash and brain injury. Though the accident has defined me in many ways, it has allowed me to flourish in countless others.

At that time, I couldn't understand why this was happening and what was going on. I was confused because one doctor would tell me I had a TBI, while others would tell me, "That isn't right." Their explanation was that I was mentally impaired. It made me very upset! Now I refuse to believe doctors who are paid by insurance companies to take tests and say there's nothing wrong at all. I know what I have; it's a TBI. I refuse to be treated badly, or as if I have no idea what is really happening. I can and will go on!

My experiences with brain injury vary from low to high. When I was first diagnosed, I became depressed. I thought, *Why me? Do I really have this, or am I really insane?* After I went back to work, I kept thinking, *How can I have a normal life?* In the brighter moments, I would think, *I can help people understand what a brain injury is, I can make a difference.* One of the lightest times was just hilarious. I was working at my job and asked a lady, "What is your phone number?" I needed it to put her clothes into the system for dry cleaning. She said, "Wait just a minute. You know, I really do have a wonderful, delightful, amazing mind. There is just one little problem." I said, "Oh, what is that?" She said, "It's just a little short!" That was incredibly funny to me, and I started laughing uncontrollably! When she told me she also had a brain injury, it was all the more comical! I smiled the rest of the day. As you may be able to tell, it still makes me smile.

Many things have inspired me since the diagnosis. My primary emotional support has come from my cat. She was there with me for the three months that I was sick, and did not know what was going on. She never left my side. The second source of emotional support was a place called the Opportunity Centre in Kitchener/Waterloo, Ontario. I really do miss that place! The people who go there all had brain injuries. They help each other out as much as possible. Even though we weren't friends to begin with, we became each other's support system, and came to feel like a family. Patients there also have dealt with horrible insurance companies, who fight them every step of the way. That in itself is an inspiration, because I refuse to let the insurance company win. They seem to miss the point of an insurance company: to help the people who need it! Another inspiration is my goddaughter. She is a darling, smart as a whip, and truly a gift from God. There are those even more deserving of praise.

The people who have helped me from Hamilton's ABI neurology department are terrific. They help people with brain injuries get better, and they also help teach strategies. Sometimes they have to work with anger or violent behavior that can come from a brain injury. With their job, it could get to be too much to handle every day, but they never lose their sympathy or caring for their patients, which is amazing! My greatest inspiration comes from my family, who were with me every step of the way. They have cared for me, supported me, helped me, and cried and laughed with me. They still may have some confusion about brain injuries, but their love is unwavering.

From the people at Hamilton's ABI neurology department, I learned new skills that can be used in place of my drawing and painting. I learned how to do pottery, mosaics, glass fusing, scrapbooking, woodburning, and carving. I also learned how to knit. Each ability helped to make me feel better about the new me that was coming out of the brain injury. With this irritating situation, I can get frustrated from all the challenges. Then I think about how far I have come, and I can't believe it. My life is so much better, and I got there with the help of my friends who also have brain injuries. We all believed in each other, and that makes us much stronger than before.

The most important thing I learned about this challenge is that if something is taken from you, you can make something even better come out of it. People with brain injuries are not lazy; their brains really do need that much sleep to help heal. If a person doesn't sleep, instead of getting better, his or her brain could get even worse. The brain doesn't bounce back 100 percent, but if we work hard, we can get some things back, maybe even better than before. Brain injuries are mostly invisible, while still being present. It means only that others may have to dig harder through the symptoms to find the information they're looking for.

Finding the strength to go to the Opportunity Centre to see what it was all about was tough for me, but I faced the challenge with courage and a plan. I could stay angry and depressed, or I could do something about it. If I had stayed away because I was confused about whether I had a brain injury or not, I believe I would be so much worse. I would have gotten more and more depressed. Without that support, I wouldn't be as well-rounded as I have become. Also, getting help from the ABI neurology department of Hamilton's Cedoke's Hospital led me to my new beginning. I never realized how strong I really am. There are two things that happen almost daily. One is waking up in the morning and being unable to move or talk, and I pass out or am too dizzy to get out of bed. The other is having pain in my hands that makes them feel like they are on fire. When that happens, I sleep all day and night. However, without a TBI, I would not have done or gone places and met the most amazing people I now consider my friends. They are really the most astonishing survivors I have ever known!

My brain injury has resulted in many achievements. An article I wrote about brain injuries was printed in the Kitchener/Waterloo *Record*. I was able to get a petition to the government about people having to live with disability and not receiving enough money to live. I climbed a thirty-foot rope ladder and went down a zip line. I rock climbed up a wall. I learned to do innumerable crafts and to open my heart to the world around me. I also sell my artwork on the side. It is not a lot, but a bit does sell. What a thrill! I can do almost anything!

Each day, I look forward to waking up and being alive. What else do I look forward to? Spending time with my friends, my family, my significant other, and my cat. Another thing that might happen is that I help my friend at her store, have a nap, then stay up a bit late. I may work on beading, woodburning, or scrapbooking. Sometimes, I go on the Internet and get on Facebook. I am so addicted to that site! Many subjects interest me, but experiencing life means always learning new things. New experiences help a TBI survivor to know we are alive and to see how strong and wonderful we really are!

TBI

— *Definition*

Psychosocial—pertaining to a person's psychological development within a social environment.

– Is/Cause

A) The National Institute of Neurological Disorders and Stroke states a TBI is the result from a sudden, violent blow, or when an object pierces the skull and enters brain tissue – http://www.ninds.nih.gov/disorders/tbi/tbi.htm.

B) The Brain Injury Association explains a BI may cause nerves or a nerve pathway to cease functioning or be impaired. This can change a person's actions, thought, or movement – http://www.biausa.org/living-with-brain-injury.htm.

– Symptoms

A) The NIH Medlineplus tells us that BI may be mild or moderate/severe. When BI is mild the person remains conscious or is briefly unconscious, with other possible signs. When moderate/severe there is a continual headache, vomiting, or other indicators – http://www.nlm.nih.gov/medlineplus/magazine/issues/fall08/articles/fall08pg4-5.html.

B) The Center for Disease Control (CDC) indicates there are four categories of symptoms, each with several identifiable items: thinking/remembering, physical, emotional/mood, and sleep – http://www.cdc.gov/Features/BrainInjury/.

– Tips

A) The American Occupational Therapy Association notes several steps that can be taken to help a person with BI. One is to help the person perform meaningful tasks important to them and another is to implement a weekly checklist of household chores – http://www.aota.org/Consumers/consumers/Health-and-Wellness/TBI/35146.aspx.

B) As shown on the television show *60 Minutes*, the medication Ambien ® may assist those who have brain injury, are not in a chronic vegetative state, and respond to sound – *60 Minutes*, CBS, *Awakenings: Return to life*, 8/31/08.

Step 1. Consult a professional.

WHAT IS CEREBRAL PALSY (CP)?

Michelle and Laura's Story, as Told by Their Mother

"Mom, why can't I read like my friends?" This question tore at my heart. One of my twins asked the question in second grade. She wanted me to support her and provide reassurance that some day she would be able to read. She felt like there was something really wrong with her. After I answered her question with, "Sweetie, we will work on your reading, and in no time, you will be a reading wonder." I cried like a baby.

Michelle is the twin who asked that question. She is absolutely terrific. Her dad and I couldn't ask for a more wonderful child. She is very caring and loving, but she does have some trouble. Michelle has been diagnosed with nine different disabilities. They include cerebral palsy, Asperger's, learning disability, audio processing disorder, visual processing disorder, etc. If you looked at Michelle, you would never know she has any difficulties at all.

Now let me tell you a little bit about our family. Our household consists of the two children, Mom, Dad, two dogs, one turtle, one parakeet, and a lot of fish. My pregnancy was truly horrible. I was in the hospital for the majority of the time and was never allowed to get out of bed. Was it ever boring!

At twenty-nine weeks, right after the nurse finished monitoring the girls' heartbeats, my water broke. Well, Michelle's water broke. We have a theory about why only Michelle's water broke. The theory goes that Michelle was the child receiving nutrients, medicine, and whatever else. Laura, Michelle's twin, got the leftovers. We imagine the girls heard the nurse tell me that my doctor had ordered another shot to help the twins' lungs get stronger. Laura asked Michelle, "How about sharing some of the medicine? I need it, too." "Go stick a pacifier in it," was the response. When Laura heard this, she kicked Michelle and made Michelle's water break. So even before leaving my womb, the girls had their first argument!

Michelle, the oldest by one minute, weighed in at two pounds, ten ounces. Laura weighed a whopping two pounds, thirteen ounces. Initially, the girls were separated to individual isolettes. When they were able to rejoin each other, I requested they be put in one isolette, so I could finally take a picture of them together. When the nurse actually put them together, it was so cool! They looked so happy to be together again, like they knew exactly who each other was. Michelle put her hand on Laura's cheek, as if to caress it, and Laura promptly responded by leaning over and sucking Michelle's nose!

When we were able to bring the girls home from the hospital, it was such a great feeling finally to have them at home so we could be a family together. To be able to watch the twins sleep, to hold them, feed them, and yes, change their diapers, was a joy.

Soon, we began to notice some differences in Michelle. For example, she would only lay her head on the left side. Then we noticed that she stayed in the shape of a "C" bent backward. Fortunately, a health department nurse was checking on the twins, as she did with all premature children. I spoke to her about the situation with Michelle, and she suggested I contact the area agency which deals with children aged zero to three to have both of them evaluated.

When the evaluators came, their results showed that Michelle did have difficulties. She showed signs of cerebral palsy, had trouble tracking objects, and didn't make a sound, not even crying. Laura's results showed that she was extremely "floppy," meaning she had low muscle tone. A therapist began to work immediately with both girls. They received physical therapy, occupational therapy, and speech therapy. This extensive regimen went on for a few years.

The girls began formal education at a charter school, where they received education similar to that in a private school, but it was public. This school had a smaller student/teacher ratio, which provided perfect assistance for Michelle. Laura was sailing along nicely, with few difficulties. However, she was still receiving speech therapy for pronunciation. Michelle still receives services through the exceptional child program.

Michelle struggles in school, but the loving and caring teachers make her feel very proud of herself and help her know she can accomplish anything she puts her mind to. Michelle has stick-to-it-tiveness, and will go not only from point A to B but from point A to Z. After the second grade, she told me she wants to be a teacher for kids like her. I asked her why, and her answer was, "Because I know them better than anyone."

Michelle and Laura are very close, and I believe Michelle's difficulties have made them even closer. One day on the playground, a little boy came up to Laura, asking her what was wrong with Michelle, probably because she is less advanced than other kids in her class. Laura told me, "Mommy, I put my hands on my hips and told him, 'Absolutely nothing!'" Such sisterly defense warms my heart, and I feel sorry for the first boy to hurt one of them, because the other twin will defend her somehow and goodness knows what will happen!

My husband and I are blessed with two beautiful daughters, and they are the highlight of our lives. The twins have demonstrated to us that life does throw some curves. Some of those curves are gradual, and some are 90°. We find the best way to deal with curves is to keep moving forward, walking tall, with purpose. Our children will become whatever they choose, and we all will be the benefactors of their choices!

Miles

The warm climate of the western U.S. is where I was born with cerebral palsy (CP). CP affects my legs, and I used crutches when I was younger, but I have used a wheelchair for some time. I love living life, having new and exciting experiences, and believe one's perception of oneself can have tremendous implications for the future.

From the time I was born, my parents raised me to know two things: I could do whatever I chose to do, and they emphasized getting an education. There were three siblings who followed the lead of my parents and treated me no differently than they treated other people. My dad was in the armed service, and my mom was a homemaker before going to school to earn teaching credentials. We lived in a community of middle-income families until my dad's retirement, which is when we went upscale. We bought a house on a golf course, as the first family of color to live in that community. One day when I was in high school, I came home to hear the words, "Your father is gone; he has left the family," and my life was instantly changed. Up until that time, I had direction, was in high school, and was involved in jazz and marching bands. Some pretty cool transportation was designed so I could march with everyone else. Things were different now.

Circumstances dictated the family move from our golf course home back to the same area we thought we had left behind. Because I was the oldest, I graduated, changed my plans, and worked to help pay the bills. That will strengthen a person's character! I have had many fascinating experiences since.

Working at different occupations, I was always searching for the highest-paying work. I was in many bands to earn some extra money, and while still in this frame of mind, I began working construction. At that time, construction was quite profitable, and funds were plentiful. I was introduced to a more unsavory way of life, and I began to sell methamphetamines when I was a fairly young person. The monetary profits were incredible, and the more I sold meth, the less unsavory it seemed. This was my life for four years until one day I thought, *I want to see what methamphetamine is all about,* so I began using. Unfortunately, meth use led to three different and relatively short, though any restriction of freedom seems an eternity, confinements. About that time, I was ready to settle down and recognized the futility of the revolving door my life had become. I decided to find a life partner and quit using meth. I had some very, very low times, because the women I met saw me as a handicapped person instead of a man. After much searching, Brenda and I met, and we connected. She is now my beloved bride.

I have been married fifteen years to a fully functioning, remarkable woman who deserves the highest pedestal possible on which to stand. Living with a person using meth, a detainee, and someone trying to leave the use behind, is almost always confusing and is undoubtedly a challenge. I am enormously proud of myself when I say I have recovered fully from substance use, going cold turkey. My early learning, which told me I could do anything, was quite useful! It also helped that I had my wife's love and support through it all. There was a time when Brenda tried to do everything for me, until I explained it was necessary for me to be as independent as possible. We now seem to be on the same page, and I am truly grateful to her.

It seems I have a talent for repairing computers, so now I have a computer repair business out of my home. My wife, Brenda, educates others, and my admiration and love for her knows no bounds.

I mentioned early on my willingness to try new experiences, and throughout my life, I have undeniably reached this goal. I play the guitar, which has led in many different directions, such as working for Columbia Records as an engineer's apprentice. I started a band once, while detained with Robert Downey Jr., who played the piano. I have tried water skiing—which I have declined to do since—I worked on cars, and I have drag raced. At this time my excitement is a bit more tame, I am writing a book, and I enjoy inspiring others. I mentor younger people, one of whom is learning to repair computers. The other is in high school, so I built a computer to help her learn. Think of it: I have become a solid citizen who gives back!

Faith has been a strong component throughout my years, though for much of that time, it lay bubbling below the surface. My faith has now burst forth, and it is very strong, so I am unashamed in praising the Lord. I believe in the goodness of others, and I realize everyone truly has a purpose for living. I look forward optimistically to waking up each morning, as today may be the day I inspire the next person!

Sam

My name is Sam and I was born in Cairo, Egypt, in 1963. To my parents' dismay I was born two months prematurely, with cerebral palsy, stillborn, and pronounced dead. At that time, when babies were stillborn in Cairo, customarily their bodies were disposed of in the trash. When tossed onto the pile, I screamed loudly in protest, to let the world know I had arrived, and wanted to stick around! Thank goodness I was immediately retrieved, which both my family and I greatly appreciate, and our journey began. My father investigated and found Shriner's Hospital in the U.S. These hospitals are international places of healing, they accept qualified children up to age eighteen, and provide assistance to improve lives.

With my beginning breaths, perhaps my protests were an indication of the toughness I would exhibit in the future. Much about my early years is a mystery to me, but I do know that I was in America when I had four surgeries before the age of four. After the surgeries, I went to physical therapy every day, so my dad had to attend with me. "Why," you ask?

"My father was my translator," I answer. Because I was unable to speak English, the nurse suggested to my father that he teach English to me. Apparently I was an unwilling participant in this project, because when my father said he would help me learn another language, my response was, "I came here to learn to walk, not to talk!" However, I did learn to walk with crutches, and to speak English. My father always saw me as a part of our family. To him I was more than a child with a disability; I was his child. What a great man he was and my first inspirational figure. He taught by example and devoted time to all of his family; there were others for whom to provide. My father would visit me twice a day in the hospital, riding the bus each way, and was always there for me.

My physical challenges have continued, but I have a strong and firm faith which has developed along with the knowledge how capable people with health issues can be. Starting a business can be a daunting task, though my attitude from the start has been; failure is not an option. So when I decided to begin this venture, in my mind at least, success was inevitable. Working hand-in-hand with the local community and others, I am now the proud owner of a totally accessible coffee shop. We function with sixteen people who also have health challenges. The many volunteers working at our coffee shop lend their talents to keep it running smoothly. We gladly train workers to move on to paid positions. The shop has an online store, so we are able to maximize our benefits to others. You might view our wares at morethancoffee.net.

A pay it forward project has been developed with the local community; I believe in paying it forward and encourage others to do the same. I am also developing a nationwide marketing campaign, so it will be interesting to check us out. Part of the coffee shop profits go to charities for those needing a helping hand, as I once did, and I delight in empowering people. To me, the rewards of helping are immeasurable.

I have been married many years to Lois; she is a remarkable woman. We have two exuberant sons, Tyler and Steven, who help me at the business. Through much of my life, my dear family has been my second inspiration, just as my father was my first. With the support provided by them, their patience, their belief in me, and their unconditional love, I have been able to be a successful person and proprietor. Through the years, I have had many operations, and when I was told I needed a neck operation, the 30th of my life, it was the hardest of blows! Dying, or being completely dependent were very real possibilities, and I was concerned for my wife and children. I didn't want to be a future burden. I had things yet to do; I had promised my wife we would grow old together. I still needed to be a father to my youngest son, and I had to live so that my older son could be a teenager, and be a pain in my butt!

The years have always been a challenge for me. I have survived life-and-death surgeries, employment disputes, and the difficulties involved in starting a business. Prior to becoming a husband and father, the tremendous joy of those experiences was unknown to me. I have God to thank for my abilities, my family, for being able to give back for the goodness in my life, and knowing how to love and serve Him.

The coffee shop, my family, and my deep faith are my most splendid successes, for which I give thanks every day. Paying it forward and doing good things for others is also a focus of mine. I believe when one receives, one must demonstrate gratitude by giving back with all of one's being; which I happily do. What more fitting way is there to glorify God?!

CP

– Is/Cause

A) The National Institute of Neurological Disorders and Stroke tells us that CP appears in infancy or early childhood. It may effect muscle movement and coordination, but stays stable over time – http://www.ninds.nih.gov/disorders/cerebral_palsy/cerebral_palsy.htm.

B) Medicinenet explains mental function is unaffected by CP – http://www.medicinenet.com/cerebral_palsy/article.htm.

– Symptoms

A) For babies, a symptom of CP is when the infant lacks muscle control and intentional movement, according to the Cerebral Palsy Info website – http://www.cerebralpalsyinfo.org.

B) The 4MyChild site of the Cerebral Palsy Organization lists specific symptoms such as difficulty buttoning buttons, or trouble walking – http://www.cerebralpalsy.org/what-is-cerebral-palsy/symptoms/.

– Tips

A) The University of Michigan states that programs should focus on throwing, walking, and rhythmical movements – http://www.fitnessforyouth.umich.edu/cerebral_palsy.htm.

B) The Mayo Clinic lists some treatments such as medication for spasticity and physical therapy – http://www.mayoclinic.com/health/cerebral-palsy/DS00302/DSECTION=treatments-and-drugs.

Author's Note—A device called a "DeltaTalker," or other types of voice synthesizers, might be appropriate and may assist a person with communication by speaking for the individual. Also, a picture book might be helpful, so a person with CP who has communication difficulties could point to a picture.

Step 1. Consult a professional.

WHAT IS STROKE?

Desiree

There came a time in life when I had to let go of all the pointless drama, and the people who created it, so I surrounded myself with people who made me laugh so hard that I forgot all the bad. Then I could focus solely on the good. After all, life's too short to be anything but happy!

Both English and German were spoken in our home. As a German-American I have also traveled several times between Germany and the U.S. I was raised by my grossmutter and grossvater (grandmother and grandfather), my mother's parents. Grossmutter died when I was ten and my mother was far too busy partying, finding "The man," and working to pay much attention to a child. I was mostly on my own. By choice, when I was nineteen, I stopped having contact with my mother. I didn't want to listen to her constantly demoralizing talk about my younger days. Whenever we did speak, I almost had a nervous breakdown. Who needs it?

Though I easily could I don't feel any grudge against my mother. She was eighteen and quite young when I was born. What was life like when I was living with her? I once had a savings account, but we had to use that money, because my mother needed it to buy food. When I objected, she said, "Well, you're the one who's eating it!" When I was grounded for two weeks, it was more like two days, because my mother wasn't checking on my whereabouts. I learned early how to be responsible for my own actions, and I was my own guide.

It seems the unstable living situation was reported, and the people from child care in Germany came. They wanted to take me, but the neighbors were great. They said I was alright, and they would keep me for the time my mother was at work. Terrific people! I had to take baths and showers at the neighbor's house, because the water heater at our place had to be fired up for the water to get warm. Well, my mother wasn't there to help me do it. When I was twelve, I moved in with my cousins because Grossvater died. When I was thirteen, I moved to a really small town with my mother and her present husband. I guess she wanted to get back the time we lost, but I finally told her, "If you want to start raising me now, it's just too late." I didn't have headaches until later.

The first symptoms I had were when I was fourteen. I had horrible, migraine-like headaches, but the doctor just gave me an injection and that was it. I went there five times for relief, but the doctor rationalized them away and no MRI was ordered. I just never went back. After that, I continued to have headaches, but took over-the-counter medicines. Those got me by for the next few years.

When I was sixteen, I was offered an apprenticeship and there was only the contract to sign to make it happen. Well, my mother had to sign the contract, because I wasn't eighteen yet. Instead of signing, she called them up and told them, "My daughter's going to the States with us." When I was eighteen, I moved back to Germany, all by myself. I was told, "If you go to Germany, you will get nothing; if you stay in the States, you get everything." Oh really? I moved to Germany, worked three jobs, and went back to school. I also got a dual citizenship because my dad is American. I was a person with two languages and two countries.

Actually, I was in the States when I got headaches with migraine symptoms. I was throwing up and could hardly move my right side, so I went to the doctor. At first they thought it was tense musculature in my neck. That is, until they ordered an MRI. They noticed that I had an arteriovenous malformation (AVM), which is an abnormal connection between veins and arteries, and is usually congenital. Arteries (arterio) carry blood away from the heart; veins (venous) carry blood to the heart. Congenital means damage occurs when a fetus is developing.

The symptoms I had were typical for an AVM. Overall, I was admitted three times to the hospital for what were always the same symptoms. Those three times include once in Scotland, where I had gone on vacation; I was cleared by the doctors to fly. Luckily, I was in a U.S. hospital when my stroke happened. The doctors went up with a catheter to check my brain and noticed I had an aneurysm as well as the AVM. But they actually caused my stroke, because they glued the weakened area, which fixed the aneurysm, but glue also went into some of the wrong vessels. A stroke was the result.

For about two days, I was unconscious. I can remember only bits of the week in the hospital and the time after. My parents just told me that the doctors said I had a mild stroke, because I could still use my arm and leg, just not as well. That got better when I went to rehab for three weeks, but at first, it seemed to me that the stroke was quite severe.

Rehab was tough, but I think I would have had more to give if I had been pushed! After a couple of months, the decision was to radiate my head as if I were a cancer patient, just not as aggressively. I thought, *I'm gonna die!* when they put that "helmet" on me. They administered injections in my head, because they had to numb it for the helmet. After that, I was exhausted.

Since then, I have Googled "AVM," and I think I'm really lucky, because mine was located in my temporal lobe. I could have been more impaired. Thankfully, my impairments are only physical. Every day now is a blessing for me, and I just enjoy every minute of it. The stroke has made me even stronger, because these have been my accomplishments: I have been in a wheelchair, I got up and walked with cane and AFO (ankle-foot orthotic), walked without a cane (with just the AFO), and now only need a bandage to support my foot drop. Yea! I can wear little heels again! I am bilingual, very independent, a citizen of two countries, have traveled transcontinentally alone, worked, gone to school, and I am successful in spite of limitations.

Now, cleaning can be a challenge, because I live by myself and do everything with one hand and arm. I can hold things in my right hand, but can't let it go again, so that's an issue. One day, and hopefully soon, I would like a job, a husband, and a child. That's actually the scariest thing, because there are so many obstacles in having a family, but I'm ready. I'm only twenty-seven, and I already have a lot; I have seen a lot and have done a lot. I've learned that life's a roller coaster: just sit back and enjoy the ride! My life is filled with humor; I laugh my butt off every day. It's like I said: I had a stroke, recovered, and have moved on. Things are looking up!

As it happens, I have coped pretty well. Sometimes I think I just want to be lazy and let people take care of me. But what doesn't kill me makes me stronger, so I do for myself. A lot of people can't deal with that. It's frustrating sometimes, but I always cheer myself up somehow. I'm confused right now and don't know what to think. The laws in Germany for the disabled seem foolish. I want to go back to the States, because it is easier to get a job there, but then the health-care system isn't the best and neither is public transportation. I'm also confused about my love life. Most men can't deal with me, because I come up as a strong and independent person, and nobody's willing to see what's behind it. As I have always done, I will forge ahead.

Just two months after my stroke, I went back to my job. I was cutting pizza with one hand! That's all I will say about that job. The stroke happened in June 2007, and in April 2008, I went back to Germany. In the U.S., I had the choice between job, college, or getting my health better. The fact is, I would have been broke if I had stayed in the States. So I came back to Germany with nothing. I had already traveled here in 2001, but I had to figure out everything again. Well, I got the offer to go back to school and to do an apprenticeship. Now that I'm done with both, I am trained to be a management assistant for freight forwarding and logistic services. I am unemployed at the moment, but I am sending out applications. I'm hopeful they will soon be productive.

The stroke is actually the best thing that could have happened. I know it's hard to believe, because I was enjoying my life before, but I enjoy it more intensely now. Before I was just living, but not really thinking about it. Today, I do think about it, and I am loving it. I feel very lucky! I'm not a real church person; I was as a child, but not anymore. I do believe in God, and the only thing that kept me going after the stroke was this—everything happens for a reason. God probably has a bigger plan for me; otherwise, He would have taken me! Of course, God has inspired me. Other inspiration comes from all the people that were there for me after the stroke and who believed in me! My parents and my boyfriend at the time, who traveled from Scotland, are among them. Also, my aunt and uncle traveled from Germany after rehab. My aunt is so inspiring! Even strangers came up to me and told me I could do it. If I set my mind to do it, I will get it done!

There are no siblings for me, but I do have an aunt and uncle here in Germany. I'm really grateful and blessed with my family. People come and go. I count everybody that is in my life as family. I met my dad when I was twenty years old. I have gained a whole new family and lost an old one; I'm actually glad about it. When I was twenty, I called up my U.S. grandma. I hadn't had contact with her since I was fourteen. I called her up around Christmastime in 2002, and I'm very glad I took that step. She gave my e-mail address to my dad, and we started talking. In 2003, when I first visited them, I didn't know that I could be so loved by people who were almost strangers. Since then, I have a whole new/old family. It's not the days we remember but the moments! My motto is, "I'm a stroke survivor and pretty proud of myself; even if you think there isn't a way, I will find one!"

Tom

It may become evident that I am a determined competitor, while my story is real, touching, and ends with a smile. First, the real. Trying is the only way to know what is possible, and anything is possible if you just keep trying! "I can't" is an excuse that never worked for me; "I can" is the way to make things happen. Each day builds on the next. The more I heard, "You'll never," it gave me the drive and inspiration to prove that I could. Get ready to re-write the stroke textbooks, for I am here to prove I am different. I am the exception to the rule. I believe winners never quit and quitters never win! There is an I in my team! I am team Tom, and I will do it!

Belief in myself was instilled early. I was adopted at nine months and my sister at three and one half years. My parents were great, and my grandparents lived next door. It was really an ideal living arrangement. I graduated from college with a psychology degree and started with a computer company shortly after. Sadly, my sister and I haven't spoken for some time and live in different parts of the country. I'm fifty-four now and though I miss working very much, I am happy.

I was a field systems engineer, specializing in diagnostics and disaster recovery and data backup planning. I did a lot of traveling. I loved my job, the complexity of unraveling and fixing the problems I worked on, and the people I worked with. Then one day, Sunday, October 16, 2006, I was sitting and talking to a friend on the phone at one in the afternoon.

That day everything was going as usual, until it wasn't. Suddenly, I had left side numbness, trouble talking, and inability to control my left side. I didn't understand what was happening! Thinking the feeling would go away, I waited to go to the ER until standing became impossible. After I got to the hospital, I was told I'd had a stroke affecting motor function. A stroke. Me? This was only the first of many dark moments. The doctor and the neurologist told me, at different times, that I would never walk again, wouldn't have the use of my left arm, that I would have balance issues, and that I would forever be disabled. I did not want to believe it! I had always had my body to rely on! I was always active, had played sports, run, and more. Now, the body that had done so many enjoyable things for me, had let me down. At the time I thought, *I eat right, exercise, watch my weight, and quit smoking seventeen years ago. Why me?*

Other thoughts I had were, *Why bother caring what happens to me? Who else will?"* I thought I was useless, and everything was a waste of time. I felt broken and that I was no longer me. I wanted my body back. I wanted it very badly and right away! I was single. I had no family, no money, and no car. Why should I even try? I was depressed and thought, *Just put me in a care facility, feed me with meds, and throw away the key.* I was done! Enter my friend Kathy.

Kathy has been an extremely good friend to me. She gave me a place to live and the verbal, mental, and emotional support I needed. Kathy said, "You still have that amazing mind of yours, it's fast, and you are so smart. You are miles ahead of many, so don't waste that gift." She told me that my left side might be different, but said I was still there mentally. I could still speak. I still had the ability to try to walk. Kathy also told me that I had to work on my issues. She said she knew I was depressed, but that I didn't have time to be. I recognized at some point that I was still me. Additionally, Kathy gave me extra incentive when she said, "If you think you are going to grow roots and die here, you can get out now!"

That was the day I started to fight back. Life has thrown me many curveballs since then. It can be and was harsh, though I always believed in me. The effects of the stroke have become the competition; my body is the reward. I would win; I am a winner! The only thing that would stop me was me, and that wasn't and isn't happening! I still have a lot to do, and even a series of strokes will not stop me!

Back to before I left the hospital and "the incident." The differences between my sister and me stem from her actions when I was about ready to be discharged. She and her boyfriend came to see me. My sister handed me a document, drawn up by a lawyer, which said that I would turn over all my financial decisions to her, and she would have the say in all transactions. I was floored! What made her think I would sign such a document? Had she even bothered to note my mental faculties? My mind was clear and had been completely checked out; I was 100 percent mentally clear. This wasn't going to happen! When I said, "No" to signing the piece of paper, my sister tried to physically assault me and had to be restrained by her boyfriend. My sister wouldn't let me stay with her, she didn't care if I lived or died, and her boyfriend drove me the one hundred miles home to my upstairs apartment. I had no food at home and was not allowed to stop to get any. I had no meds—we weren't stopping for them, either—and I had no feeling on my left side. All the way home, the boyfriend was as unpleasant as my sister had been. Greed was apparently uppermost in their minds, and denial of any profits was a rejection to them. Their behavior was unbelievable! Compassion in my family was non-existent.

After the stroke, my left side was totally numb, though there was pain through the numbness. I had spasticity, tremors, imbalance, and dizziness; I was left handed, so I had to learn to use my right hand. I had to re-learn to walk with a cane, then without a cane. Though I wasn't fine, I was creating the illusion that all was well. Through it all, I kept trying and have greatly improved! Even so, retirement was necessary, so now I look forward to furthering my college career. There's always another goal to look toward!

Recommendations for help after discharge from the hospital were limited. I was told that my previous habits would help me in the future, and that formal therapy might be of assistance. I did some research, and the National Stroke Association says that of stroke survivors, 10 percent recover almost completely, 25 percent have minor impairments, 40 percent have moderate to severe issues, 10 percent require care, and 15 percent die shortly after the stroke. I vowed to be one of the 10 percent recovering almost completely! The therapy, after I decided to go, was helpful but limited in length. Through the excruciating pain when I did exercises, I always had hope for a better tomorrow.

Now came the tough part of recovery. I do more daily therapy than any therapist ever recommended. I do stretching, pool therapy (pool therapy takes many hours, because stroke survivors cannot store energy), and I go to the fitness center to walk the track. I have worked hard and am now on my own. I love life and continue to learn and understand my situation.

Many medications help me throughout the day. I take Lipitor®, Plavix, benazepril, Lyrica®, baclofen, Niaspan®, tramadol, and hydrocodone. The joint pain just has to be worked through. I am at a point where I'm able to laugh at my foibles. I'm not disabled, the rest of the world is! One day, I walked up to a counter, and I was asked, at ten in the morning, "Are you drunk?" I said, "No! I had a stroke and was never supposed to walk again!" Patience and understanding are valuable tools and are often useful.

Since the stroke, there have been some emotional and trying days but even more great days. I have still more to do; I'm far from done! I enjoy it when people say, "I would never have known you had a stroke. You look great!" It makes all the hard work worthwhile. My doctors all said, "With all you have been through, you are amazing to have survived and done so well!"

The touching and inspiring part of my story came when my friend said, "Tom, you always face your challenges head-on. You're not a quitter; you're a winner. You love competition, so fight back." I did just that, and I'm now able to live on my own, do for myself, and be a capable human being. I *am* a winner. After the stroke, I have moved five times in four years. Right away, I was unprepared to be disabled and to live in a care facility in Connecticut. I needed help and have no wife or children. When the stroke happened, I had the choice of living in an institution or being homeless. It was wintertime, and I still chose homelessness because I know that institutions breed helplessness. That is not for me! Kathy stepped in at the last minute, so I was relieved of that worry. I am so grateful for all of the help I've been given. Kathy has been an incredible friend who didn't enable, pushed me when it was needed, and helped me on my path to recovery. I now live in Florida, and I am beating the odds. So many cry and say, "I can't." But, I can, and so can others! I am proud of me, because I feel I have done amazingly well. I am ready to inspire!

Some things I have learned through this process are that stroke is something only the survivor can work on. Firstly, we have to be able to say, "I had a stroke." Secondly, we need to work at getting back whatever abilities we can. At the same time, we must have hope and believe there is always more to do. Our recovery is up to us! We must never give up! Also, we need to beware of those who take advantage of the disabled. They are legion! I am truly disgusted with those people. We are the ones who are the most vulnerable and can afford it the least. How often do we hear of raises in pay for those with health challenges?

In spite of my trials, I am completely independent. I have beaten so many odds, I am so proud of me. I am doing it! What makes me even more proud is that I never get complacent. I feel I can beat this. I will show the world, through my actions, I can and will do everything in my power to succeed. I believe that I can do anything! School, school, and more school has been a theme for me, and meeting all challenges is another theme. Learning new things is crucial. Having fun with activities is important, so that's how I meet my challenges. I have always felt that if I set my mind to it, I can do it. Stroke survival was just another challenge for me. My next chapter will be just for fun, and a challenge can be fun.

The ending with a smile follows. My future looks bright. I look forward to waking up in the morning and getting ready for the day, to building myself up, and knowing the future is now. I'm ready to go back to college so I can work again. The Florida sunshine helps my attitude, so I'm in the right place. It's time for a new beginning: a new chapter in my life. Now is the time. It's my turn to give back and to show people the great possibilities that lie ahead. Nothing life can throw at me will beat me. Just like a cat, I always land on my feet, and it may take time, but I have always figured out a way to survive. There is no real ending to my story. I am happy as I am, and I still build for tomorrow. What's the difference between a stroke survivor and a stroke victim? It's simple— many, many, many decades of happy life! After the stroke, Kathy's mother asked why I continued to walk each day, even though it hurt. I told her, "If it's easy, it ain't no fun." I just think of the walk as fun, and it feels better. When I'm walking through the pain, I am a winner!

What follows is a poem I wrote after the stroke that shows how I feel.

It's not about the money; it will always be about people.
Never concern yourself with what they look like.
Those whom prejudge, are just so wrong, and foolish!
A person should be viewed by their: character, words, actions, and
strength of spirit. Decency is the key!
Instead of setting someone into a mold, see them!
When you come to the fork in the road
You are supposed to choose which path to take.
Be daring!
Walk up the middle, create a new path ...
So you can see both sides!

Then the person behind you,
Might choose not the given two paths,
But the path less traveled!
"That's my path"

Kolleen

What was your life like when you were thirteen? Did you read, listen to or play music, sleep in, or play sports? What I remember is pain and confusion. I began having petit mal seizures in 1973. I have since learned that I was about the age this usually begins, but at the time, I knew only that they were brief: sixty seconds or less. I would go blank or stare off into space, and the seizures were combined with terrible headaches, which persisted into adulthood. The seizures continued until I was twenty-seven, when I stopped drinking excessively. Heaven knows I tried many ways to deal with the constant, excruciating headache pain. I saw numerous doctors, always with the complaint of terrible headaches, but I was also having tunnel vision as I got older. Medications did not help, but I would take them for a while, hoping that this was the time I would find relief. I wanted to believe I could control something in my life. The doctors seemed to think my input was useless, that I was a hypochondriac. Where could I go for assistance?

All the while I was seeing doctors I had the loving support of my family. Original family, and my husband and son have continued that trend. What wonderful people they have been to sustain me! My father has had to deal with his own difficulties, and my husband has been my rock and my friend. You will notice that none of the doctors are mentioned as I speak of support. That's because they weren't supportive, ever! "Contempt" might be a word I would use to describe my considerable ill will.

When I was thirteen there was a CAT scan done of my brain. At that time a spot was discovered, but little consideration was given to it. The answer was always medication, and the headaches continued. I saw a neurosurgeon when, years later, my left pupil dilated to twice the size of the right. At the hospital, my doctor and the neurosurgeon together looked at the results of my EEG and CAT scan. They decided nothing was wrong because they were looking for an aneurism, and found none.

I wanted to shout, "Something must be wrong. I'm no doctor and even I know it!" As before the answer was medication, and the headaches continued. My mom worked at a lab doing imaging, so we asked to redo tests; the answer was no. My mom knew about a new test to do: an MRI. When I asked the doctors, their response was, again, no. I saw many other doctors, and most often the diagnosis was migraine. When I would point out that I had no other symptoms that usually accompany migraines, they couldn't believe I knew there *were* other symptoms! Again, medication was the answer, and the headaches continued.

One doctor found my septum was deviated, so he repaired it with surgery, and still the headaches continued. At least his answer was different, "Well, we tried." Unsatisfactory! The vision in my left eye started getting cloudy, and the optometrist could find no eye-related reason. He suggested going to see my regular doctor for a CAT scan. I thought, *Oh boy, here we go again.* When I did see the doctor and told him what the optometrist had said, he still saw no reason to order a CAT scan. That was it! No more! I would be heard this time! The doctor *did* order the CAT scan, and when results came back he said he would order an MRI. Finally! I had asked for one only five years before! When these results came back, the doctor called me at work. I was apprehensive and hopeful at the same time. The doctor said, "You have a benign brain tumor." Hearing these words sent me into frenzy. I felt like I had been a spider trapped in an upside-down champagne glass, ramming into the edges time after time. I felt as low as I ever had.

The years of suffering, and my feelings of anger at the medical profession all came tumbling out at that moment. The dam burst, the water flowed, and I cried uncontrollably. I was incoherent. It became so out of control that my boss called my husband to come get me. I was thirty-one, and I had a growth in my head. My crying was rage at every doctor I had seen in eighteen years. Murder and suicide were two disjointed thoughts entering my mind, but murdering doctors would have been quite an effort, and suicide was an undesirable option. I had to live for my family. There was nothing I could do! I cried all the while, until my husband, the one person I could depend on, arrived.

When I was twenty I had married; however, that marriage failed. Although the marriage didn't survive, I did have the most wonderful experience of my life: my son was born! When I was twenty-eight, I married Mace, the most patient, loving, caring person I could hope to meet. We are together still. I had brain surgery on 3-11-92. Several hours after the surgery, my middle cerebral artery collapsed, and I had a stroke. Even though I was in a coma for several days, I eventually woke up to hear my husband's voice. He explained that everyone had been talking to me; however, I thought his voice was the sweetest. I was fortunate to survive, and with lots of rehabilitation, things are better than they were at first.

A couple of months after the stroke, we were temporarily living with my mother-in-law, when I went to my home and saw many gardens. I thought they were beautiful and wished creating such a gorgeous setting was something I could do. I didn't remember that it *was* something I had done! My life was changed forever. Once I recognized it, I was overcome by despair, and sat on the porch to cry. My husband came out and cried with me. When I re-analyzed how things were, I understood I'd have to look at things differently. I chose to be grateful for what I have: the perfect trifecta—my husband, my son, and my father. Others have also been there for me.

Since that time, I have looked to them all as my inspiration. My husband and son support me, and then there's my dad. He is a remarkable man, who has had many challenges from an impressionable age. He was paralyzed from the waist down when he was shot while in college. He has gone on to live a productive life. Dad uses a wheelchair and lives his life as he desires. So when I began therapy, I could always use Dad as an example of success.

When I began going to speech therapy, because the stroke had caused me to lose my ability to speak, my grandmother was sometimes with me. She was there the day that the therapist was using flash cards. I was to say what was pictured on the card. Things were going well when a card she flashed was a picture of a gun. I started to cry and the session ended; I was impacted too deeply by the picture. My grandmother explained to the therapist why it was so very moving for me, and we left. Other times at rehabilitation, I used to make up words and combine sayings. Oh, how I wish I had kept a journal of those words! I would often combine two words into one or substitute words in an unusual way. For example, I'd say, "I have a beef to pick with you," when I meant to say bone instead of beef. I might say, "The horse is on the other foot," when I meant to say shoe instead of horse. Once when I was at rehab, I was trying to say my stepmother's name. I tried and tried. No luck.

Frustrated, I finally said loud and clear, "Why don't you go home?" That sent us into fits of laughter and broke the tension.

Survival since the stroke has been an adventure for me. My right arm and hand are useless, I have no sight in my left eye, I have a pronounced limp in the right leg, and I have had three surgeries on my back because it's so painful. But, I always live my life the way I choose. I wanted to have some accomplishments under my belt, so I went back to community college and received an associate's degree in applied science (Grounds and Turf Management) with honors, cum laude. It was an effort, but with books on tape, a note taker, and unlimited time to take tests, I excelled!

I am proud to have been a volunteer for Johnson County Extension for eleven years as a trained master gardener. I have been a proud volunteer for the American Stroke Foundation for thirteen years. When I facilitate stroke support groups, I tell a story to the class as a way for people to learn to laugh at their own challenges. One day I went to speech therapy, and the speech therapist asked, "What day is this?" I said, "Thursday." She said, "You're right. What day is tomorrow?" I said, "Thursday." She said, "What day was yesterday?" I said, "Thursday." "Thursday" was the only word I could say for the whole session! I had the choice of crying or laughing, so I chose to laugh at myself. I can be a victim or a survivor; I choose to be a survivor.

Other things I would like people to know about strokes are, firstly, spouses/significant others can be unintentional enablers. For no discernable reason that person feels guilty the stroke happened, and wants to help, while the person who had the stroke feels entitled to the help. For example, once, after the stroke, my husband called me into the kitchen. He pointed to the cabinet with glasses, and to the phone. He told me that from now on, it was my responsibility to get my own water and to hang up the phone when I was finished. Secondly, many times doctors give no hope, because they don't want to give false hope. Doctors need to factor in the *inner you,* because the meaning of prognosis is *educated guess.* Thirdly, it would help if people were educated about different health challenges. When I was still doing rehab, I couldn't talk very well, so people would talk to me loudly as if that would help me understand better. At that time, I was hearing at a heightened level, so it just was annoying! Some people would turn and talk to my husband as if I didn't understand at all. He would tell them simply to talk to me. Salesmen would sometimes ignore me altogether. I like to think things have improved a little. To demonstrate where I was to where I have come, I wrote this:

My starting reality

I was paralyzed on my right side.
I could not talk in a coherent way.
I could not read, not even the alphabet.
I could not walk, skip, or run.
...
I was an infant all over again.
I did not even know how to feed myself.
I drank perfume ... it smelled good!
I had to learn to talk, read, and walk.

My current reality

I learned to compensate.
I learned to talk.
I learned to read.
I limp but I learned to get around.
...
I grew.
I can eat.
I learned not to drink perfume, even though it smelled good.
I did learn.

Required elements

Determination
The will to succeed
Persistence
Love and support

What might a typical week be for me? I clean house, within limits. I have a one-step stool to use. It's safest, because I have a balance issue. I can do laundry and spend time gardening, which is a passion of mine. I Facebook and find games on the PC, I volunteer, and am able to inspire other stroke survivors. I pay bills for home and my husband's work, and do data entry for my husband's work. In other words, I'm living my life as I desire.

Like I said, my family has been terrific throughout everything. My husband has been my anchor to sanity and my friend. He took care of me and loved me and has been incredible. When I had the stroke, my son was eleven years old. He inspired me to set a good example for him. Mom had trouble at first, because seeing me with so much difficulty caused her pain. She has become an ardent cheerleader. I've already talked about how inspirational Dad has been. Their inspiration for me has left me striving to be an inspiration for others. I have no religion, but I follow the Golden Rule. Looking forward, I have about three books I'd like to write and have published. I deduced that there are Stroke Survivors, Stroke Existers, and Stroke Victims. I chose to be a survivor, so I wrote this.

To be a Stroke Survivor rather than a Victim

- Believe in yourself *(the inner you)*.
- You have had a stroke, you are not dead; get on with your life!
- If you want to get better, *YOU* have to work hard.
- Look to the future, not the past.
- Seek support from *family, friends, church,* and *other stroke survivors.*
- Have a sense of humor.
- You must be able to laugh at yourself.
- Your whole body doesn't have to work to be a whole person.
- If what you do doesn't work try again, again, and again.
- Push your brain.
- You must re-learn basic skills in order to regain higher skills.
- Be adaptable, find a new niche in life, and be happy.

Stroke

– *Definitions*

Embolism— a traveling blood clot.
Thrombosis— a stationary blood clot.

– *Is/Cause*

A) The National Stroke Association says there are two types of stroke. One is when a vessel is blocked by an embolism or thrombosis, and one because a vessel burst. An aneurism is a weakened vessel. http://www.stroke.org/site/PageServer?pagename=explainingstroke.

B) The American Stroke Association tells us stroke is the third leading cause of death in the United States and is the leading cause of disability - http://www.strokeassociation.org/STROKEORG/AboutStroke/About-Stroke_UCM_308529_SubHomePage.jsp.

– *Symptoms*

A) The National Stroke Association says acting within the first three hours of a stroke is crucial. They have tips to spell the word FAST:
   Face—Ask the person to smile; does the face droop?
   Arms—Ask the person to raise both arms; does one drift downward?
   Speech—Ask the person to repeat a simple phrase; is the speech slurred or strange?
   Time—If you observe any of these signs, call 911 immediately.

B) WebMD also says trouble understanding simple statements and vision changes could be indications of stroke - http://www.webmd.com/stroke/guide/stroke-symptoms.

– Tips

A) The Family Doctor.org tells us some risk factors for stroke can be uncontrolled diabetes, smoking, and high cholesterol level – http://familydoctor.org/online/famdocen/home/common/heartdisease/basics/290.html.

B) Medicinenet details the rehabilitation process and says this can include: speech therapy to relearn talking and swallowing, occupational therapy to regain as much function in the arms and hands as possible, physical therapy to improve strength and walking. Also, family education will orient them in the care of their loved one at home and the challenges they will face – http://www.medicinenet.com/stroke/page6.htm.

Step 1. Consult a professional.

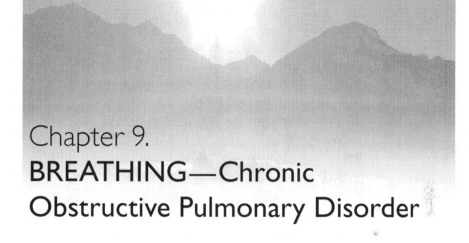

Chapter 9.
BREATHING—Chronic Obstructive Pulmonary Disorder

What Is Chronic Obstructive Pulmonary Disorder (COPD)?

Mark

Living in a rural area of the Midwest was influential for the type of life I was to lead. My parents, five siblings, and I were a happy family. We spent our time working around, caring for, and learning from farm animals. We also developed close relationships with family, the animals, and others. I say others because there were few social options available, so we focused on 4H. Our neighbors were also in 4H, which did lead to social opportunities and to relationship building. This organization provided excellent training ground for my future endeavors, and when I was a teenager and state 4H officer, we went to a national 4H competition in Washington DC. We camped on the Mall and even met with the vice president. Exciting! It seems I was already establishing foundations for the future.

Health issues began when I was a baby, which have plagued me throughout my life. You will see this as the story goes on, however, I will mention I was seriously ill as a one-month-old, then came down with the flu when I was seven and was extremely sick. That flu is comparable to the current H1N1 pandemic, where pneumonia can be involved. The family doctor finally gave up and told my parents, "I can do no more." Thank goodness my parents found another physician more familiar with effective treatment. One parent also became very seriously ill, and my grandfather lost his life due to the illness.

Following my trip to Washington, WWII started, and I decided to enter the armed service. I qualified for officer status and instructed military personnel on aircraft maintenance, so I would be stationed closer to home. "Closer to home" means still in this country, but I was less, or more, fortunate the next transfer. At this new location, I taught foreign cadets, in their language, on aircraft maintenance. Having been culturally isolated most of my life and unfamiliar with different ways, it was an eye-opening experience! This alone would have been informative for a young adult, and taking a crash course in another language was even more educational. Because of the understandable suspicion caused by the war, and the general fearfulness WWII had produced, my next learning experience was the result.

My friend and I were riding a bus, speaking in English, when I felt something brush the hair on the back of my head. I turned my head to see what this irritating thing was and froze immediately. My military training was insufficient for what I had glimpsed. A man had come to stand behind me with a gun pointed at my head! Believe me, my attention was riveted! The man said low and guttural, "Speak our language." Military training had drilled us in following directions: Yes, sir! The rest of the bus ride I had no problem speaking appropriately with my friend, and I understood instantly how important it is to speak the language of residence.

After returning home, I attended veterinary school in my home state. I graduated and moved to start a clinic for large and small animals in yet a different city. Certainly, my upbringing and experiences provided the impetus and courage to make these decisions. My first wife and I had two children, one of whom has become an environmental engineer in another state. My first wife passed away, and I have been happily remarried for numerous years. I would be hard-pressed to find a more dear and devoted partner. After practicing at the clinic for many years, I moved again because I was appointed state veterinarian. It was a challenging and interesting job, and I worked in that position for many tiring, but enjoyable, years. I have received other honors as well. During my tenure as state vet, I judged many animal competitions at the state fair and was then named state veterinarian of the year. The year following that service, I was elected president of the state veterinary association. After living many years in my adopted locale, I am now headed back to live where I first practiced. No doubt, many changes will have occurred while I have been gone, and I look forward to exploring.

As I think back, it seems throughout my years of ministering to animals, and being around them, I have had periodic bouts with pneumonia. Usually, I worked through the difficulty breathing, coughing, congestion, and nose discharge. The symptoms were generally a serious issue only when the "cold" settled in my lungs. Then it was a tenuous situation, but with antibiotics and sulpha, the signs always retreated. That is, until several years ago. I was in the hospital with pneumonia, that old adversary, and developed congestive heart failure. The heart was then the focus of attention, so now I have a defibrillator implanted in my chest to keep my heart muscles working. Focusing on my breathing again, it was at this time I was told I have COPD. The doctors also discovered an infection in the lining of my lung. This may have been caused by bacteria from being around animals so much of my life, but we are uncertain. Once the infection was eliminated, I felt great for a couple of years, but then other issues developed. I eventually took up temporary occupancy in a nursing home. Occupational therapy and exercises were extremely helpful, so now I am at home and require only some assistance. I am truly disappointed I need any assistance at all, but I am grateful for the help.

It is unfortunate that I require oxygen twenty-four hours per day and all its accompanying accoutrement. Any type of exertion is agonizing, because it requires more breath than I have. My trials may be traced back to the illness when I was young. I remember, before COPD was diagnosed, a time when we visited family in the mountains. When we arrived, I stepped out of the motor home, and instantly, I was besieged by shortness of breath—like a fish out of water—because of the high altitude. It was quite a memorable event! Another issue I have is breathing difficulty when it is humid. Midwest summers can prove to be a problem, which necessitates always remaining in air-conditioning. So, my day's activities are governed by circumstances, location, and energy level. When I feel illness coming on, I immediately take steps to prevent it, such as using cough syrup or an analgesic. When there are flu or other shots available, I take advantage early.

What do I think about my life as a whole? Service to others, whether animal or human, has been my focus. I feel rewarded to have had such interesting and life-changing experiences. Certainly, those experiences have developed thoughtfulness on my part and have provided me with purpose. Having purpose has been my goal; wonderful experiences have been my reward.

Julie

Family is a huge part of my life and always has been. I have two brothers, a mother and father, aunts and uncles, and cousins. We lived in Kansas and had lots of family get-togethers, and we shared both tears and laughter. I now live in the western U.S. and we are a happy group, with different strengths and talents. Mine lie in the artistic area.

Breathing issues are a fairly new experience for me, personally. I started having trouble this year, when I felt faint and dizzy with numbness in my face and hand. This was somewhat alarming, as I had a mini-stroke several years ago, and I thought I was having another. Driving home from the grocery store was unnerving, to say the least, and took tremendous concentration. At home, I took my blood pressure, and it was fine; so what was going on? I sat and rested a while, until I felt better. I knew I had a doctor appointment soon, so I decided to wait until then to talk to him about this scare. Things would be better, I was sure. All was determined to be well, and I relaxed.

It was about a month later when I started coughing terribly. My job was driving school bus for three-to-five-year-olds in Head Start. The bus overheated three times in one day, and as a result, I was breathing in massive amounts of fumes. Two days later, I was in the ER, because I was very sick and having trouble breathing in *and* out. I could only speak a few words at a time and was, again, dizzy and light-headed. A nebulizer treatment helped me, and I was diagnosed with acute bronchitis and COPD. COPD is emphysema and chronic bronchitis. Since then, the ER has become a very familiar place. I have really gotten to know everybody there! Having trouble breathing, and learning about it, has truly been a roller-coaster ride.

Now I need oxygen twenty-four hours a day, so I wear a cannula and carry a tank with me wherever I go. I have been declared totally disabled by a doctor. I do smoke, but I have cut way down, and plan to quit. I use patches, and they seem to be working well for me! I am finding this disease involves so many different things. The biggest issue is that I feel totally in the dark on the subject of COPD. I would like to know more instead of just following directions. I am computerless, so maybe I could use the computer at the library, maybe even find a book!

I have learned that I have asthma, along with emphysema and COPD, and I have diabetes on top of everything else. My pulmonologist described my condition as severe combined obstructed and restrictive ventilatory defect. My lungs were described to me by a different doctor when he put his two fists tightly together. He said my lungs are so compressed, that's what it's like when I try to breathe! I have COPD, with frequent flair-ups of acute bronchitis and asthma with bronchialspasms. Quite a mouthful isn't it? I have difficulty sleeping. I'm tired, exhausted really, even though I use a continuous positive airway pressure (CPAP) machine at night. They are used primarily for sleep apnea, which is waking up periodically because breathing stops, but I do need it to breathe at all. I remember that Mom died of pulmonary fibrosis (PF), and she had a sister who also died of lung disease. It may have included PF. There is a sister still living with various lung diseases, including COPD. So, breathing difficulties are quite possibly a hereditary condition. Positive thoughts are my antidote.

My struggling aunt is my inspiration. She helps me know about the condition and gives me pointers. My aunt has gone through hell, and thinking about what could happen to me is stressful, mostly for others. I wish not to be a burden; after all, I've spent my life trying to help others see the bright side of things. In addition, my deep faith helps sustain me. I know many people are praying for me, so maybe that's why I'm at peace. Income is my main concern, and I'm working toward relieving that worry. I have made some lifestyle changes. Also, I am enrolled to learn more about what to do to breathe, and I do have the treatments regularly. As far as I know, there is nothing more that can be done at this time. Talking to others helps me, so I use Facebook a lot and use the phone for the Internet connection. For my own sake, I am unafraid of dying; I'm just unsure when it will be and care only for my family's sake. They light up my life.

My emotions vary from depression to happiness. I know the ending to my story; I just think about what my mother went through, and my quality of life toward the end is a concern. Right now, I'm just starting to take medication. Some prescriptions are left unfilled because of the funding issue, but I look forward to an improved situation in the future. COPD and other problems are just new to me, because they involve my health this time. I'm trying to grasp the immensity of everything that's happened in a few short months. It's a lot to accept!

It's also clear that the difficulties I'm having developed over many years. I think back to the time I spent as an over-the-road truck driver and driving school bus. The diesel fumes I inhaled were ever-present, and combined with the smoking, have been unhelpful. I've been around diesel fumes my whole career. After giving up the over-the-road trucking, it was my brother who started me on the path of driving school bus. Then he began driving over the road. We are honoring our father, who drove trucks and was killed in a car accident. I thought it was pretty great that I, being the only girl in the family, was doing a job that my dad had done all his life, to support his family. I drove in memory of him, as I traveled the miles on some of the same roads he drove. I felt fearless and strong. I was privileged to deliver loads, several times, to help the survivors of Hurricane Katrina. I thought that was pretty cool, and it sure felt good!

My faith has to come first when talking about any success I've had. My kids run a close second. I have four fantastic children: two boys and two girls. They are amazing, and two of them have master's degrees. My daughter-in-law also has a master's. She and I are very close, and my son has chosen phenomenally well. He is a captain and chaplain in the army, and is an exceptional person. I am extremely grateful to my son for paying my rent during this trying time. One daughter has a secure job, which I decline to discuss, and the other daughter went back to school to become a phlebotomist. Now she runs a lab. My grandchildren are wonderful, and some also have health issues. So what? All my grandchildren are marvelous and beautiful.

Currently, I am writing a children's book with a religious theme, and I'm also illustrating the book. I am an artist who does pencil drawings and paintings. It is my dearest wish to be able to finish my book, and I will work toward that end. When it is time, I will go as a happy person. I've had a good life. I will be sad to be leaving my loved ones, but they will know how much I've loved them!

I was very mature when I married at sixteen. I stayed home and raised our kids with a spiritually oriented home life. I helped the children grow with a strong moral theme, and my ex-husband stressed education for our children. It seems that each of us had a powerful influence on our kids. Because I was sixteen when I married, I never graduated from high school. I did go back to get my GED, and I am quite proud of my accomplishments!

For a long time my guiding principle has been, "We are only here for a short time, and we are somewhere else for eternity. We choose where that will be." I have always lived with a focus on my family and will lovingly continue to do so. I made my choices long ago!

COPD

— *Definition*

Acute—rapid onset and severe.

Chronic—ongoing.

Nebulizer treatment—administering medicine through an inhaled mist.

Pulmonary—involving the lungs.

— *Is/Cause*

A) The NIH-Pub Med explains Chronic Obstructive Pulmonary Disease (COPD) is trouble with breathing. The two forms are chronic bronchitis or emphysema. A combination of these is the difficulty for most people - http://www.ncbi.nlm.nih.gov/pubmedhealth/PMH0001153/.

B) The Mayo Clinic states COPD is the leading cause of death and illness, worldwide. Much of this lung damage is caused by long-term smoking and cannot be reversed – http://www.mayoclinic.com/health/copd/DS00916.

– Symptoms

A) Two of the symptoms explained by the National Heart Lung and Blood Institute are constant coughing, "smokers cough," and shortness of breath – http://www.nhlbi.nih.gov/health/dci/Diseases/Copd/Copd_SignsAndSymptoms.html.

B) Medicinenet provides additional indications of COPD: frequent lung infections and with advanced COPD, bluish tint to lips/nail beds, headaches, and weight loss – http://www.medicinenet.com/chronic_obstructive_pulmonary_disease_copd/page4.htm.

– Tips

A) The Heart Lung and Blood Institute states that two of the goals of treatment are to relieve the symptoms and improve exercise tolerance – http://www.nhlbi.nih.gov/health/dci/Diseases/Copd/Copd_Treatments.html.

B) National Jewish Health suggests oxygen therapy and medications as possible treatments – http://www.nationaljewish.org/healthinfo/conditions/copd/treatment/index.aspx.

Step 1. Consult a professional.

Chapter 10.
DEVELOPMENTAL DISORDERS—
Asperger's Syndrome, Learning Disorder

This section deals with disorders occurring in a child's development.

WHAT IS ASPERGER SYNDROME (AS)?

Catherine

I am in love with other people's bookshelves and my aunt's in particular. One day when I was visiting, I wasn't looking for anything specific when I came across a book in her shelf called *The Curious Incident of the Dog in the Night-time*. Reading over the dust cover and through the first few pages intrigued me, so I borrowed it. When I arrived home, I had some time, so I started reading right away, and I couldn't put the book down! The main character had been diagnosed with Asperger's syndrome (AS). I thought it odd that people found his behaviour strange; to me, it seemed perfectly normal. Coincidentally, when discussing the book with a friend, she told me about her brother having been diagnosed with

AS, and everything changed for me. She referred me to a website, which helped me to make a preliminary self-diagnosis.

Then, I went to a psychiatrist and got a formal diagnosis of Asperger's syndrome. The main emotion I remember at the time was absolute relief to have a name for what made me different from so many other people. It was such a boost for my self-esteem to know that there is actually nothing wrong with me! I wasn't at fault! It wasn't something I'd done to myself. Then, I adjusted my life to avoid as many hot spots as I possibly could.

My list of AS symptoms is extensive. It starts with social awkwardness, inability to understand hidden meanings, work politics, etc. There is also my issue with not being able to block out sounds, my dislike for people in my "personal space," and anger meltdowns resulting from me not being able to understand what people mean when they say something. More symptoms include taking many phrases literally, being too straightforward, hurting people's feelings even when I had no intention of doing so, and having an obsession with patterns and numbers.

Sometimes when I do something "wrong" or inappropriate or rude, I struggle a bit to remind myself that I needn't beat myself up about it. If I can, I must just try to avoid doing it again. However, my main experiences have all been focused around people getting very angry with me.

Undoubtedly, there are incidents that my friends and family can now laugh about, but at the time, they just wanted to kill me. Since the formal diagnosis, I realized I have fantastic positive qualities on which I can focus. I make people laugh, and they always know where they stand with me. There are the days I'll make mistakes, but heck, even neurotypical people make mistakes. So what? Shit happens! When I make errors, I just try to learn from them.

In coping with my challenge, I got divorced and removed myself from difficult situations that traditionally led to meltdowns. Now, when I don't understand people's behaviour, I try to sit back and relax. It doesn't matter anymore, because when I don't understand, it isn't an indication of my failure as a human being. It's just that I won't always understand, but people who really care for me will try to help me out. What else matters?

Through my experiences, I have learned to not sweat the small stuff. Also, I don't allow other people to make me feel worthless or inadequate. Doing these things can help others with AS; I promise. Just relax and try for the best possible outcome. It works for me, because when I don't feel like trying, I give it a rest for a day or two. Then the answer comes to me: voilà! There are a few things I choose to not do. Being in a roomful of first-year university students who struggle with chemistry, just freaks me out. So, too, does many people talking at once. I'm terrible with time management, and I'm very easily distracted. I will sometimes think, *What will I do next?* Then I read news websites or play Sudoku. After that, I have to focus on the fact that I get paid to do a job!

My days are full, but might seem lazy to others. I get up, have a cup of tea, and a cigarette. Then I wake up my sixteen-month-old daughter, dress her, and make her tea. After I drop her off at the nursery, I get to the office at around eight. I work until the afternoon, when I pick up my girl from school and take her home. At home in the evenings, I fix dinner for her at five o'clock, play piano, to keep her happy until about six thirty, when it's bath time. At seven she goes to bed and by then, I feel like I need the bed. I have a glass of wine, work a bit if I have to, watch some TV, shower, and go to bed at nine. I read a book or play Sudoku until I fall asleep at around ten thirty.

I have a mum, dad, stepmum, stepdad, two brothers, one stepbrother, and two stepsisters. When I'm in any of their company, I feel relaxed and under no pressure to be "normal." My family loves me unconditionally, and they make me laugh.

I have an undergraduate degree in chemical engineering, as well as a master's degree. I was a consulting editor for a chemical magazine and the vice-president of the South African Institute of Chemical Engineers. I am a lecturer at a South African university, teaching third-year students how to set up mathematical models of chemical processes.

I look forward to the day I complete my PhD thesis, but I know myself well. Following that, I'll just set another goal. I feel that my accomplishments far outweigh any challenges placed in my path and I will continue to love my daughter, my family, my job, and my life!

AS

– Is/Cause

A) The NIH tells us AS is a developmental disorder and explains its characteristics – http://www.ninds.nih.gov/disorders/asperger/detail_ asperger.htm.

B) The Asperger Syndrome Education Network (ASPEN) comments it is a neurological disorder on the higher end of autism spectrum disorders (ASD) – http://www.aspennj.org/aspergers-syndrome.asp.

– Symptoms

A) The Mayo Clinic states that children with AS tend to be socially awkward and might become totally absorbed in a specific topic – http://www.mayoclinic.com/health/aspergers-syndrome/DS00551.

B) According to the Asberger's Society, there are other symptoms of the syndrome, such as sensitivity to noise or touch, craving for routine, and communication or motor skills problems – http:// www.aspergerssociety.org/indexsymptoms.htm?gclid=CI3_z_OV_ qgCFULsKgod5E-AUg.

– Tips

A) WebMD tells us that many with AS do better with verbal rather than non-verbal instructions – http://www.webmd.com/brain/autism/ tc/aspergers-syndrome-home-treatment.

B) The Mayo Clinic says that among treatment options are communication, social skills training, and cognitive behavioral therapy (CBT) – http://www.mayoclinic.com/health/aspergers-syndrome/ DS00551/DSECTION=treatments-and-drugs.

Author's Note—Anecdotal evidence suggests that talking to many people, like at the mall, might help the person with AS to become more comfortable and less socially awkward.

Step 1. Consult a professional.

WHAT IS LEARNING DISORDER (LD)?

Sarah

When I was younger, I remember growing up in smaller-sized communities of the Midwest. There are four in my family: two parents, a sibling, and me. Our parents are wonderful people, hardworking, and intelligent. Suburban areas with colleges were located nearby, so I traveled there for testing when I began having trouble. Actually, I was the troublemaker—in the classroom especially. I didn't understand a lot of what we were learning in class, and eventually I was told that I have a reading and writing learning disability. Upon entering elementary school, it was soon clear I was experiencing difficulty with lessons. Why oh why couldn't I stay focused?

It made little difference how hard I tried; I was unsuccessful with any subject to be learned if written words were involved. Verbally I did well! This was quite frustrating, so I began to feel very foolish and angry. Acting out followed. A caring instructor noticed this change in my attitude, combined it with her other observations, and chose to notify my parents. My very caring parents immediately had me tested for learning disability.

Until the time I was the only child to leave the classroom, to see the nurse about my medication, I thought all the kids were having the same difficulty as I. Imagine my surprise at being the only child to stand up and walk out! As the only one to parade in front of the others, it was quite humiliating for me. About second grade, it was necessary to change schools. I was being teased mercilessly, which made me feel even worse, if that was possible. As we know, kids can be cruel. At my new school, there was acceptance, because each day when I would leave, it was taken as a matter of course. No teasing, no drama. My reason for moving to another classroom was to learn how to best compensate for my inability to comprehend as others do. Finally, what a relief it was to be able to focus, understand, and learn.

What I came to realize is that I can read on my own, sometimes help is needed with responses, and hearing questions verbally poses little difficulty. I also learned that, given enough time and effort, I can work through any reading or writing task required. When taking a test,

I would be allowed extra time and would be given necessary help so I had a "level playing field" with other students. I learned that though it may take me a little longer, I function almost the same, but just a little differently than others.

Since graduation from high school, I have volunteered helping children with special needs while they are doing their lessons. There have been times I could show them devices I have used myself. It's priceless to see the gratification on children's faces when something helps them understand. This, then, is my goal: to assist children with special needs to learn and develop as I have.

In one of the classes necessary for my employment, which helps others, I mentioned my learning disability. Following class, the instructor called me to the front and complimented me on what a good job I had done during the class. The instructor also mentioned how quickly I could respond to questions and, when asked to read, how well I accomplished the task. To my delight, it would seem I have overcome my difficulties!

Since I have grown up with a learning disability, it is normal to me. I know now I am equal to any undertaking, in spite of difficulties. I have learned I can accomplish whatever I am determined to achieve. I have only to be patient, so I can carefully work through the item before me. Also, because I have a limitation, I am creative and able to figure out ways to work around usual methods of solving a problem. Maybe I will go on to be an inventor. Who knows? At any rate, if there is a way for me to help others, I will find it!

Brandy

Learning disabilities may be congenital or acquired, according to the Merck manual. Mine is congenital. Non-verbal learning disorder (NLD) means a person may be lacking other skills, but is highly verbal. That's me! Personally, I don't remember the first signs that people noticed because I was so young, but likely others might have noticed my delay in learning to walk. Walking was not so delayed as to be troubling, but I also learned to talk early and had a good vocabulary. Taken together, they are possible indications of NLD. Looking back, it's easier to recognize now that I know.

What my teachers must have noticed was that I was not learning to read, do math, and do some physical things—like climbing a jungle gym—at the same pace as other children. It took me a month of trying before I could climb; the rest of the students in my class seemed to have little difficulty with any of these types of activities. While those things were discovered at school, my parents also noticed other things at home. They often refer to the "milkweed pod" story when I was a preschooler.

We lived in a rural area, and my parents encouraged my sister and me to play outside with them. I loved nature and found milkweed pods to be fascinating. Monarch butterfly caterpillars fed on them; sometimes they were filled with a liquid like milk, and sometimes they were filled with seeds. They were awesome to my three-or-four-year-old brain, and I wanted to share this with my parents. I would tell them what I thought, but they couldn't make sense of what I was trying to convey. Although I had a good vocabulary, sometimes I wouldn't be able to choose the right words to describe something visual so that others could comprehend. It was extremely distressing! It came to the point that I almost had a meltdown every time I saw a pod. This is often the case with children with NLD, as it is extremely hard to live in a world where we are almost there, our IQ is high, and we understand things, but can't *do* things. I was lucky to have a great mom, who talked me through life as a child, and now I have the skills to handle these challenges.

"Brandy, have you ever heard of dyslexia," my mom asked? She had taken me aside to explain to me that I was recently diagnosed with a learning disability. My diagnoses were dyscalculia, which is difficulty in mathematics, and dysgraphia, which is difficulty in spelling, grammar, and handwriting. My other LD symptoms were described as specific learning disabilities. I wasn't diagnosed with NLD until I was twenty-eight. During my school years, I was okay with having a learning disability. It isn't like something had happened to me. I was the same me I always had been; we just knew why I was "different" now.

My mother and I both misunderstood when I was diagnosed. She thought she just had to get me through college and then it would all be fine. I thought if I was willing to work harder than any other LD child at school, I would be learning disability–free by eighteen. I thought everything would eventually turn around. Together, we both learned that I had learning disabilities for life. I have to hand it to my mother, though. She helped me believe in myself, she did whatever she could to make my life easier and more successful, and kept the whole household running smoothly.

My childhood was lovely, and I didn't really get down about my struggles until high school. Elementary school was hard for me, but that was just the way it was. Some people with NLD are great with spelling and learn to read early. I couldn't read until I was eleven, and spelling has always been tough for me, but I had many other things going for me. Home was great, vacations were great, and I felt accepted socially. The other little girls in my class always came to my birthday parties and played with me on the playground, even though I didn't have a best friend. I didn't mind, because I liked playing with my classmates, and I also liked my family time. NLD-ers often have trouble socially, so I was doing well. I was close to my younger sister and two cousins, who were near to my age and lived in another state. That worked well for me at the time. The world was so much fun, and there was so much to do and learn. Inquisitiveness and perseverance have been traits of mine since birth. I've always laughed in the face of adversity; I admire others who have taken adversity and used it as an advantage. It's also what I choose to do!

NLD, like other learning disabilities, affects every day of my life. I can't seem to learn a foreign language, though I completed French written assignments in school just fine, and I actually got an A in sixth-grade French! I can't play team sports, because my sense of space is faulty, and all the teammates around me are too much. Also, my mind tells my body to do things at a slower pace. I do love alpine skiing! It took me six years to learn—from first grade to seventh grade—but I am glad I stayed with it. I love the feeling of freedom when I am skiing. I teach first-and-second graders how to ski every winter, and just love it!

NLD has affected most choices I've made, like where to go to college. I learned colleges and jobs do not have to follow learning disability guidelines the way earlier public schools do. Two colleges weren't willing to acknowledge waivers I had for math and foreign language. Three colleges did acknowledge them though, and even told me they liked the rest of my application a lot!

When I choose jobs, the NLD is uppermost in my mind. Physical jobs, jobs with money, or jobs that require sequenced tasks are unwise choices. I know I will always avoid drawing, singing, and dancing. I've succeeded in writing and speaking in front of groups. Knowing my weaknesses and strengths has definitely helped me when seeking employment. Dreams of things I wanted to accomplish in my future have been my inspiration since I was young; I've wanted to reach out to as many people as possible through my writing. I've been told that as I grew up, I kept my childlike love of exploration. I'm motivated to learn about nature, people, the arts, and politics, though I wouldn't be comfortable holding any public office. I would, however, love to campaign for the laws, rights, social awareness, and research funding for NLD and other learning disabilities.

Every day, I'm motivated to be a part of everything the world has to offer. I want to put my own little dent into it whenever I can. I've been a newspaper reporter and an educator at a science museum. I want to freelance write and be a public speaker about learning disability awareness. I want to be the best darn NLD-er out there and help to present learning disability to the world as a positive. It just needs to be viewed differently. Then other people might be encouraged to display their creativity, in spite of their difficulties. Because I understand my LD, I now care about helping others to understand about it.

Sometimes people say things like, "Your learning disability shouldn't define you," or, "Don't blame your learning disability for the difficulties in your life." Those statements just don't feel right to me. NLD and the essence of Brandy are intertwined and one in the same. Because I'm Brandy, I am not exactly like others with NLD or who have dyscalculia or dysgraphia. Also, because of my learning disabilities, my life is a little different than a neurotypical person. I feel it is okay to explain that I have a learning disability. It is part of my definition of self, and I think it is fine to acknowledge that my learning disability is the reason that certain tasks are a challenge. I feel that pretending otherwise implies that having any LD challenges are bad things, and not to be mentioned. I am proud of my accomplishments in spite of, and because of, an NLD diagnosis! I drive, while some people with NLD never learn. I had tons of friends in college, and I'm a published writer. These are things about which any person can be very proud. I am extremely grateful, because NLD encourages me to be a thinker. I know my political opinions. I know why a movie could have been better; I feel a world of new thoughts open up when I hear a favorite Beatles song. I have great self-esteem and feel my self-worth does not have to be the result of performance perfection. It comes from knowing who I am. I just naturally think outside the box, because I am unable to live *within* the box. Mostly, I realize that I can find a different way, that any point in life may be imperfect, and if there are flaws, things will get better. I still feel I will find a more settled life in the near future when I find a way to support myself that is just right for me.

Every day I feel a passion for life. There will always be angst, but a sense of humor goes a long way. In college I even used my verbal skills to joke around with friends. Instead of saying things simply, I would make up new words or string sentences together in a new way to say something. This wordplay often brought laughter from friends, because I am an imaginative person.

NLD is either very rare or it is underdiagnosed. I have one friend from college who has NLD, but most people I know with NLD have been discovered on NLD message boards. Many of these message board posters have become great friends! NLD is part of the definition of Brandy. It is why I've had trouble finding the right romantic partner as of yet, but I hope to work on this soon. NLD is why I don't play soccer, and it is why I never apply to work as a waitress or a cashier. That is fine with me. It is also why I am a great interviewer and reporter, why people feel comfortable talking to me, and why I get so excited by what I'm doing. I'm like a square peg in a round hole when I look for jobs. I believe that I can find employment to provide needed talent in a way that works for me. Right now, I'm exploring the possibility of self-employment. It is my way to keep moving forward; I will keep striving to find the right fit!

Paige

Growing up in the Canadian foster-care system was a struggle, until I knew there were people who really understood and cared about me. Foster care was filled with uncertainty and fear, as I never knew what to expect. I learned social workers were to be feared; they usually only showed up when I was in trouble or being moved to another foster home. I was always treated as if I didn't belong to any family and was often referred to as the "foster kid." I felt unneeded and unloved. Love and caring was, for me, defined by how many names I was called, how often I was hurt emotionally, physically, sexually, mentally, and spiritually. I began to believe that *I* was the reason for being in foster care, and that I was a bad kid. It seemed that I was unwanted by everyone! This would probably be traumatic for those who had some sense of family, love, belonging, and safety. I knew nothing different. When I mentioned this to social workers or therapists, they seemed incredibly clueless. They would say, "Oh, just go love yourself," or, "Go be nice to yourself." It's clear to me now that I easily could have said, "Please tell me, what does that look like?!"

Because of my situation, I was busy trying to survive. I just tried to get through each day without upsetting someone. This was the case so much so that I couldn't focus in school. When I would wake, I was relieved to be going to school. At least it wasn't home: well, wherever I was living. When I got to school, I struggled with learning, reading, and with other kids constantly making fun of me. At school, it was also unfavorable but was better than any other option. Because I was unaware I had a learning disability, I would do everything I could to try to focus my attention. I tried as hard as I could. I studied and paid attention, to the best of my ability, and I would still fail exams. A long time later, I learned why: I was diagnosed with dyslexia.

At school, on-the-spot situations like going to the board to do math problems and reading out loud from a textbook were shameful experiences. Teachers often sent reports home that reading was a problem and I wasn't making an effort. Most teachers thought I wasn't even trying, so I also thought there was something wrong with me. All of us compared me to other students.

Living in foster care with this going on, I was adopted at the age of seven. By this time, I didn't know what it meant to be part of a family. I continued to live in fear, and didn't know how to adjust to having a family. The adoptive family didn't know about my history. I was bullied and made to feel like an outsider by my adoptive sister. My adoptive parents always took her side, and once again, I was the bad kid. When the adoptive parents were angry, they frequently used the threat of giving me back to the government, and I quickly learned *they* couldn't be trusted. Then, my adoptive parents were frustrated when I withdrew from them! I lived in fear of the social worker, and came to believe that even adoption didn't mean forever. The problems at school continued. I had the same struggles with reading, writing, and learning, and that got me into trouble at school and at home. I continued to feel like a failure. Eventually, the adoption broke down. Undoubtedly, my adoptive parents thought they cared, but I couldn't adjust to their life nor they to mine. It seems that compromising was not considered. I have had lifelong experiences showing me that lasting relationships are vital and precious. It was a few social workers that have really demonstrated their depth of commitment to me.

As a child, what adults first recognized was my inability to fit puzzle pieces together. I couldn't comprehend how the shapes fit to make a whole. By grade five, I couldn't tell time on an analog clock; I didn't understand how long five minutes was. When people would say quarter after the hour or half past whatever time, it made little difference to me; time was time. After telling my friend I didn't understand about clocks, she explained it using money. In Canada, we have a one dollar piece we affectionately call the "loony"; the coin has loons pictured on it. My friend then told me to think of the loony as a clock, and of the four quarters equaling the dollar as fifteen minutes each, which adds up to an hour. After she made it concrete for me, abstract thinking was unnecessary; I was incredibly excited to understand!

What I came to realize is that I have to break things down into smaller sections. When I read, I need to read and re-read paragraphs in order to understand them before I move on to another paragraph. Sometimes even that doesn't work; sometimes I do understand. As you might infer, I also have memory problems. Here's a link to the video I once used in a presentation: http://www.youtube.com/watch?v=gwZLFTW4OGY; it truly shows what dyslexia can be like.

For me, words do move off the page, or words can jump around on the page. When I read, I often read words that aren't there, skip words, switch with and which or then and than. I sometimes see big spaces between letters and words. I have problems reading some fonts, like italic. If I read too long, I see different colours of the pages or letters. When I read, I can't have any noise or distractions. I need to read with earplugs in, so I can focus. Sometimes when I read, I don't know the word I'm reading; I don't recognize it. Then, I need to look at each letter to try to sound out the word. It's common for my eyes to jump to different sentences on the page. Reading something can take me three times longer than others. When I'm in class, it's very hard for me to listen and write notes, because I write a lot slower, but I really need to write to remember at all.

Several situations in high school led me to the conclusion that I was differently abled. Tests were always tough for me. If they had been given verbally, I could have demonstrated my knowledge, but written exams were a nightmare. One time, a particular teacher was handing back exams and giving encouragement to students, until he came to me. Then he said, "Do you work hard at being retarded, or does it come naturally?" Did he know how that affects a young person? Clearly he knew and didn't care, or he was devoid of knowledge. If his comment was meant to be funny, I sure didn't get it! I stood up, marched out of the room, and went to report this inexcusable, horrendous behavior to the principal. I was told, "He'll be retiring in a couple of years." I wanted to scream, "What do I care about that? How many more times will he insult me and other students in those few years?" I had to go back to the classroom, be brave, and tough it out until school was finished for the year. After that, I'd be on my way and show him! I guess he was influential—in his own way.

Other teachers, upon hearing I was thinking about university, told me that it would be impossible for me. It seemed to them as if I was not trying, even though it looked like I was paying attention. These were my darkest days, because school, home, and now even teachers were all discouraging me from trying to be someone who wanted to succeed! I had a desire to learn. Shouldn't that be encouraged? Something inside me urged me on. It seems my guidance counselor recognized that "something" and nurtured the flame. Apparently, he heard about my thinking, and I'm grateful he followed up with action. He had a different viewpoint from the others; he saw potential all the teachers had missed. That has changed my life!

When he broached the subject of university with me, I was ambivalent. The counsellor finally asked, "Would you meet me for coffee?" I was mystified and intrigued, so I did. But we didn't go to the coffee shop; to my surprise, we drove to the university. Oh boy, I was excited and a little bit fearful at the same time! Having the counselor there sure helped, but was I really going to do this?

It seems I would, because that day I signed up for a course introducing me to computer usage and many other helpful items I would need for university life. With accommodations I learned about, I passed this first course! I had learned what was needed to go forward! Then, with this encouragement, I continued to attend school part time, and I became much more comfortable. In my third year of university, a professor of one of the classes I was attending had a speaker come and talk about learning disorders. One of these was dyslexia, and when it was explained, I thought, *That sure sounds like me!* So, when I spoke with the professor, he suggested I be tested, and the result was a dyslexia diagnosis. Finally! After so many years of difficulty and struggle, I now understood. I knew what caused my difficulty, and I could do something about it. I had always been making the effort! I was relieved that I wasn't just a failure, and I felt sick because the teachers, social workers, and foster parents were all incorrect. I wasn't lazy; there was an explanation for my troubles. What I have learned is that the way things work for others is almost always different for me, so I must rearrange things in a way that *will* work. I've gotten proficient at adjusting my thinking, at searching out accommodations, and planning. It's so much better! After years of "failure" in the homes, at school, to myself—and constantly being told what a failure I was by all—I felt victorious!!!

Further demonstrations of how things are for me can be shown in a couple of off-campus instances. Once, a friend and I were enjoying our free time, and we were also getting some exercise. In explaining to my friend how to play the game, I was saying the words "speed boost," and it sounded right to me. But my friend laughed hysterically every time I said it. What was this? Why was it so funny? When I finally asked about her behavior, she explained to me that the words coming out of my mouth were actually "spood beest." Well, that was even funny to me! Other instances of me saying mixed-up words have been pointed out to me. One time I was talking about the Craig Ferguson television show. It seems that I was saying Freg Curgeson. This was why school was so hard for me: the way I see and sometimes say words, is different than other people. That's why some words don't make sense to me. Now I understand!

At university, I learned that lights flicking, any flicking lights, make it harder for me to read. Clocks ticking seem to sound really loud for me; I can't focus when clocks tick in class. When I'm writing exams, I write in an office by myself, and I put earplugs in. Otherwise, I can hear pen or pencil writing on paper. I really struggle with sequences of directions, math, and sentence structure.

I graduated university with two degrees. I am now working on my master's degree in social work. It's hard for me to believe, and I am amazed I have come so far! It makes me feel exceptionally proud to have achieved so much, and I am appreciative for the help I have received at key points in my life. From six months to nineteen years old, supportive people were few and far between. There was the adoption that didn't work out, twenty-six foster homes, that many or more social workers, continually protecting myself because some homes did have abusers, verbally abusive teachers, and through it all, I had little support. Hopelessness is often taught to those with unsupportive situations, so one learns to depend on oneself. I can truly say, "I am still here, and I *have* been successful!"

Specific social workers and teachers were some of my most important allies. I can remember only a handful that seemed to really care about me, but they entered my life at crucial moments. One social worker stands out, and that was Carrie. Because of my experiences, I can size people up within minutes of meeting them; it's a useful tool to have. Carrie actually spent some of her valuable time with me, and I enjoyed every minute. She was genuinely caring. Carrie always wanted to know about the good moments, and she was there for me during some of the darker times. She offered supportive advice, someone to talk to, greeted me with a hug, and was there to just be with me when there weren't words for what I was going through. Despite challenges at home and school, Carrie was there to help me learn strategies to work through them. Living in many abusive homes, it was impossible to ignore emotional pain, but I learned to ignore the physical pain. Bruises heal more easily than a heart.

With other very tough situations, I was lucky enough to have Don stick with me through some of the more difficult. It meant a lot to me, because Don was one of the people that understood. He had a connection to me and my history. When I was in care, I moved often, and many social workers might not have understood how moving affected me emotionally. They also seemed to not know how that's connected to one's ability to learn and focus. I couldn't focus on school when I was always trying to adjust to change and coping with a new way of life.

What made a difference in my life was having social workers, teachers, and a counselor who went out of their way to try to make life more bearable. They brought stability and safety for me. All I ever wanted was someone to stick around and be involved because they wanted to be there. When I felt someone cared and wanted to be a part of my life, not only because they were paid, that meant the world to me.

In order to be able to learn, I needed support. For foster children, social workers tend to become one's family, because they're the only constant in young lives. The teachers in high school and university, as well as staff, are also more likely to be understanding. When I had to have a university class in statistics, which I knew would be trouble, I was able to substitute three other classes instead. Planning ahead pays off! Even though some accommodations are difficult to access, most are easily attained. The university wants to graduate good people, and that's me!

What makes a difference in my life is when people believe in me, especially when I don't believe in myself. As a result of a difficult life, when I was going through some of the darkest days, it helped when others would hang onto hope for me. It's the little things in life—such as a text, e-mail, or calls from people—that helps me cope with tough times and stay focused on overcoming challenges. My favorite quote is by Martin Luther King Jr., "Our lives begin to end the day we become silent about things that matter." Thankfully, I was quite vocal.

School and working have been my focus for a long time. I have been volunteering at a long-term care facility for seven years, and I also work at a student-run medical clinic on campus. Between these activities, I have found time to rappel down a twenty-two story building in record time, twice. Once I rappelled for prize money, once for a donation to a good cause. I can succeed at many things! My goal is to become a social worker at a hospital, in a pediatric oncology unit. It is just another step toward becoming who I want to be. Challenges have become strengths for me!

LD

— Is/Cause

A) According to Kids Health.org, learning disorders are, problems with the brain's ability to receive, process, analyze, or store information ~ http://kidshealth.org/teen/diseases_conditions/learning/learning_disabilities.html.

B) Help Guide.org tells us that trying harder, paying closer attention, and improving motivation are impossible for the child to do alone. Help is needed to learn how to do it ~ http://www.helpguide.org/mental/learning_disabilities.htm.

— Symptoms

A) The Learning Disabilities Association states some symptoms are poor coordination, difficulty following directions, and poor memory ~ http://www.ldanatl.org/aboutld/parents/ld_basics/symptoms.asp.

B) Medicinenet explains that he/she may have difficulty with spelling, expressing ideas in writing, or have very messy writing ~ http://www.medicinenet.com/learning_disability/page2.htm.

— Tips

A) Help Guide has information for those aiding students with LD. The first suggestion is to help them help themselves, to give them tools to work through challenges ~ http://www.helpguide.org/mental/learning_disabilities_treatment_help_coping.htm.

B) The University of Michigan lists helpful tips for those with NLD: keep the environment predictable and familiar, prepare the child for changes with logical explanations, and state expectations clearly ~ http://www.med.umich.edu/yourchild/topics/nld.htm.

Step 1. Consult a professional.

Chapter 11.
MOVEMENT—Amyotrophic Lateral Sclerosis (Lou Gehrig's Disease), Fibromyalgia, Paralysis

WHAT IS AMYOTROPHIC LATERAL SCLEROSIS (ALS)?

Lana

We were a happy family of six, living in the Midwest, when I was young. You might say we were two families in one. My parents, one sibling and I were one of the families; and ten years later, when two more siblings came along, they were another. My father changed jobs when I was just a child, so we moved to another state. My parents then remained in the same house, while I have since lived in different locations. I was taking the scenic route, you might say.

Upon moving to a new area, usually the first thing to occupy one's attention is finding a job. When I moved away from home, it was also mine. I worked in a non-traditional environment, which provided great salary and benefits to raise children; however, it was unable to give me a sense of achievement. After being abused, I divorced the abuser and met my true life partner at a new job. How? With one of my later moves to a new locale, I discovered a new occupation much different than the previous one. This new job suited my personality much better. It seemed, at least for me, I had to try different jobs before finding my calling. Where we worked, my husband and I were both extremely good at our jobs. We are "people persons," which was necessary in our positions, and my husband tells me others still ask after me. They are very kind.

We are inordinately proud of our family. Between my husband and me, we raised six children. They produced thirteen grandchildren, who now have provided us with seven great-grandchildren. They all, especially the young ones, light up our lives! We had lots of family get-togethers, and it was at a family holiday celebration that I first noticed symptoms. On one of my many trips to the kitchen, I was going up the steps and noticed that my legs felt extraordinarily heavy. What was this? I usually took off like a greyhound, and others had to keep up with *me*. I didn't understand. Here I had to sit and rest while others did the work, which was very unlike me! After this first instance, I found myself resting and waiting frequently in other situations. This stuff, whatever it turned out to be, was sure teaching me uncharacteristic patience! I was learning to live with the unknown when the pain started. Okay, now my style was really being cramped and a visit to the doctor was in order. Many, many tests were required; however, when all was said and done, ALS was diagnosed. It was clear this was the worst possible diagnosis! I knew what it meant, but maybe the researchers would find a cure before the disease came to its inevitable end. I was determined to make the best of things!

Because my body was slowly becoming paralyzed, by the time of the diagnosis I was using a wheelchair. Our house was designed for people who could walk. Some magnificent friends decided to do something about that, banded together, and raised the money to make the house wheelchair accessible. These remarkable friends not only adapted the house for access, but donated their time and talents to design other modifications as well. What can one say about such wonderful people? I was unaware others were so caring and giving and I have a hard time finding words to express my gratitude. I get choked up just speaking of the sacrifices of these friends, and "thank you" seems so insufficient. Still, it is what I have to offer so I say, "Thank you."

With help, I was able to stay at home for four years before going to a nursing home. My husband eventually became unable to provide the total care I needed, even with family assistance supplying days off. My husband retired to stay with me. Hubby, along with friends and family, is totally incredible to give so much. Friends continue to demonstrate their support; a walk promoted by the same group of fabulous folks raised $5,000 for the ALS organization. What more can I say?

What I have found is that every day with ALS is a new adventure. Some days I do not have pain; some days I do; some days the pain meds do not help; some days they do. I have had to quit working, have been in hospice, and moved to a nursing home. Each experience has been a new undertaking. Having me move to a nursing home was a particularly traumatic decision for my husband. We agonized over this solution for many months; however, after residing here, I realize we are both now more appreciative of each other.

Now I live at the nursing home, and my husband visits when he's not working part time. We do enjoy each other's company. My days begin with getting ready for activity, and all preparations require the assistance of others. My husband arrives mid-morning, and at lunchtime, we have the choice of eating in the room or visiting the cafeteria. I wonder sometimes about the wisdom of eating with others for two reasons. I use a power wheelchair, and my steering control is sometimes questionable. I can just see myself pulling up to a table and accidentally pushing it away from others already seated! My other concern is self-consciousness. Because I am not able to eat as others would, I do not want residents to lose their appetites seeing me eat, or to feel as if I need help.

If I need to, I go back to the room after lunch. There I have various things to do. Sometimes we watch movies rented by my spouse, or caregivers will bring movies from home for us to watch. Sometimes I listen to books on tape. Chronic fatigue can be associated with ALS, and I often fall asleep during the movie or books on tape. Oops! I also play bingo with other residents, and we have gotten to know each other well. The caregivers here are all good friends, as were the hospice caregivers, and we enjoy each other's company.

I am well aware of the eventual outcome of ALS; it is now a waiting game. While I still have some function, and my voice still works okay, I wish to enjoy my time. What has and will sustain me through numerous trials are family and friends, of whom I have spoken, and a very deep faith. I attend services here each week, sometimes twice a week, I watch a person speak about God on television daily, and I am always silently giving thanks. I feel truly blessed, and I am the same person I have always been, even though I function differently. I choose to utilize my time constructively, be happy, and be positive!

ALS

— *Definitions*

Degeneration—refers to damage or death of cells.

— *Is/Cause*

A) The ALS Therapy Development Institute describes ALS as a gradual degeneration of nerve cells which control muscle movement - http://www.als.net/AboutALS/Glossary.aspx.

B) The Focus on ALS website explains two to five years after diagnosis is the usual life expectancy. About twenty percent live ten years or more and up to ten percent live even longer - http://www.focusonals.com/alsfacts.htm.

— *Symptoms*

A) The ALS Association suggests that the initial symptoms may be so slight as to be overlooked, such as muscle weakness, twitching, or "thick speech" - http://www.alsa.org/about-als/symptoms.html.

B) The Amyotrophic Lateral Sclerosis Organization states muscle cramping and swallowing difficulty may be initial signs - http://www.amyotrophiclateralsclerosis.org/ .

— *Tips*

A) The ALS Association lists books in order to find information about living with ALS - http://www.alsa.org/als-care/resources/publications-videos/manuals/.

B) The Mayo Clinic has suggestions for several therapies, including physical therapy, occupational therapy, and speech therapy - http://www.mayoclinic.com/health/amyotrophic-lateral-sclerosis/DS00359/DSECTION=treatments-and-drugs.

Step 1. Consult a professional.

What Is Fibromyalgia? (FM)

Lori

It was February 2002, a morning like any other. I put the coffee in the coffeemaker, added water, and pushed start. I stretched hard, reaching toward the ceiling. It felt so-o-o good, until—I felt it. Heard it, too: a "pop" in the back of my neck, followed by extreme pain through my entire back. I couldn't move my head at all. It was later diagnosed as a herniated disk at C5/C6. But what no medical tests could indicate was that this damaged disk was just the beginning of a cavalcade of events.

It was the trauma that triggered my fibromyalgia. Fibromyalgia is a collection of symptoms and is not considered a disease, but a syndrome that is often triggered by a physical trauma or incredibly stressful event. It is characterized by long-term, body-wide pain and tender points in joints, muscles, tendons, and other soft tissue. That's the medical description. What it feels like is a gnawing, burning pain that goes bone deep. Some days, it feels like my skin is on fire. I can't stand to be touched on those days and, sometimes, can't even bear to have clothes touching my skin. If I slap my thigh (you know, like you do when you hear a funny joke?), the pain is excruciating. But it's tricky. I don't feel the pain sometimes, until I slap my thigh or someone grabs my arm. Then I practically go through the roof.

The pain worsens with weather changes, lack of sleep, and stress. While many people have fibro "flares," meaning they feel good most of the time and experience only temporary flare-ups of pain, my fibro is a daily companion that I have learned to live with. But then, I've had a lot of practice at being sick. As a child, I had severe asthma and allergies from the age of two. In the 1960s, there weren't any very effective asthma medications or treatments for children. I was placed on an experimental medication—a green liquid with so much sugar in it to counteract the taste that all of my baby teeth rotted by the time I was in first grade. I was also extremely thin, partly because of the many food allergies I had. As it turns out, people with fibromyalgia often suffer from allergies, too.

Other conditions that are common among the fibromyalgia-afflicted include irritable bowel syndrome (IBS), chronic dry eyes, migraine headaches, sleep disorders, mitral valve prolapse, irritable bladder, depression, and anxiety disorders. None of these disorders have been found to cause fibromyalgia, nor does fibromyalgia cause them. They just seem to co-exist in a large number of fibro sufferers. I live with most of these co-existing conditions, but the one that has affected me the most on a daily basis is the fatigue. It is unlike any feeling of tiredness one can imagine. The only way I can describe it is to say that it feels like something is sucking the life right out of my body. It is the worst feeling of physical exhaustion I can imagine. I used to be fatigued, to some degree, every day. But my physician prescribed an anti-viral medication that has been a Godsend in terms of restoring my energy levels. As with many things related to fibromyalgia and its treatment, no one really knows why anti-virals work for some people; they just do.

This brings up one of the many lessons I've learned about fibromyalgia in the eight years I've had it. What works for one person doesn't necessarily work for the next. Just as the symptoms of fibro manifest themselves differently from person to person; the treatment needs to be individualized as well. It takes a lot of patience on the part of the physician and the patient to get the right mix of medication and physical therapy, an important part of living with fibro. I've also learned that avoiding activities that cause me pain is actually the worst thing I can do. People with fibro need to maintain some level of physical activity. Otherwise, muscles stiffen and eventually atrophy. In the beginning, I had to work through a lot of pain to get to the point where I felt relief. It took two years from the morning when I stretched in front of the coffeepot until I received a diagnosis of fibromyalgia. I was diagnosed with everything from stress-related muscle spasms to torticollis (wry neck).

I think my primary-care doctor thought a lot of it was in my head, which brings up another lesson I learned: don't just go to one doctor and accept a diagnosis that doesn't seem right to you. See other doctors. See different types of doctors. It was a rheumatologist that finally diagnosed me as having fibro. Until I had the right diagnosis, nothing I was doing was helping me. My primary-care physician just kept prescribing larger and larger doses of narcotics along with massage therapy. Before my diagnosis, I was a very busy advertising copywriter. Today, I cannot hold a full-time job. I can't even hold a part-time job, because I don't know which days I will feel good and which days I won't be able to get out of bed. Fortunately, I've been able to find freelance work and perform it from my home.

My biggest concern was what I was going to do when my COBRA insurance ran out. Because of fibromyalgia, I couldn't buy health-care insurance from anyone, except as part of a group policy. I was hoping and praying that universal health care through the government would become a reality at some point in my life! Well, it was differently successful!

I call my fibro, "the gift that keeps on giving." Part of me says it in a tongue-in-cheek way that borders on sarcasm. But the other part of me knows that good things have actually resulted from having this syndrome. I've had to learn to accept my physical limitations. But because of them, I've drawn closer to my family for support. I've lost my job, but because of that, I am now living in a smaller place, closer to my daughter, parents, and grandchildren. I'm in pain a lot of the time, but it has helped me to understand the pain of others and offer support based on experience. In fact, for almost every thing that fibro has taken from me, it has given me something back. They are gifts I would never have asked for, but those gifts have made my life more complete.

Jen

I am one of two children. My older brother will be mentioned only here, because I could have had a more positive role model. An understatement! My mother was my hero, and I recognize her sacrifices and love for me. It was after her death that I realized what a great friend she was. Each day, her example inspires me to keep moving and do what I must, without complaint and with a smile on my face. When I went to college, I graduated with a mathematics degree. Afterward I married, so when I became pregnant I chose to wait until after my two children had started school before I began teaching. I taught for a few years and tried different grade levels, first elementary then high school. I found teaching could be stressful, but there were times I really enjoyed it.

The marriage was unsustainable and I had to swallow, or you might say gulp, very hard to get past residual angry feelings after the divorce.

Since then, and for that reason, it might seem likely my ex-husband and I would have a tense relationship. However, in actuality we have become friends. Our thinking is that whatever differences he and I had, it would be better to unburden ourselves for the sake of our children. We find, rather than being marriage partners, we get along much better as only partners.

When I was in my mid-twenties, I started waking up from a sound sleep with a severe leg cramp, or "charlie horse" in my right leg. It went on for several years and drove me to distraction! Then, when I was in my mid-thirties, I was in a horrible car accident. It happened six years ago, as I was waiting for a red light. I was thinking family thoughts when out of the blue, wham!!! My head snapped back violently, and the seat was almost ripped from its foundation! So what exactly had happened? It took me a few minutes to take it all in. A car had plowed into mine from behind. My spine was fractured in the neck area and nicked lower. Pain? It fails to accurately describe what I felt then and for the next year and a half. I needed a couple of shoulder surgeries, innumerable procedures, and injections. I was losing all hope and was ready to throw in the towel when an amazing thing happened: a neurosurgeon told me that walking would be out of the question. Oh really?! Determined to prove him wrong, I began to walk, and the pain began to subside. Morphine helped me a great deal, and it took a long time, with intensive rehabilitation for me to walk again without agony. I succeeded and came away with a fibromyalgia diagnosis in addition to a sense of satisfaction.

You will notice that rather than say pain was "eliminated," I mentioned it "subsided." Pain is a constant companion. Over the years, I have tried different fibromyalgia pain meds, which have varied in their usefulness from non-effective to temporarily helpful. People sometimes fail to understand my reality. They think I am healthy. Possibly this is because I work full time to support my family; I am our only source of income. I love my job working for a store which offers home improvement items. Mobility has become an issue for me and it can be hard to understand my pain until it is visible. Now, I walk with a limp. The type of work I do can seriously impact how much pain I feel. Sometimes the pain is worse, sometimes better; sometimes I cry myself to sleep at night, and sometimes I feel blessed relief. While there are too few of nights of relief, they are wonderful!

Lighthearted moments come all too infrequently and usually happen when I am cooking. My arms or legs jerk periodically with a spasm. This alone causes little pain; it is when my hand hits the skillet or my leg hits the stove that the most severe pain results. I think, *There I go again,* or my kids say, "Oh yeah, Mom did it again!" Even my boyfriend gets into the act, laughing with us and helping to keep me upbeat.

With all of this pain you might wonder, "What does Jen do to cope?" Well, spirituality has entered my life in a big way, and my faith in God is strong. It teaches me to live positively. Prayer is my solace, and I also follow my mother's example. She was diagnosed with cancer, and two weeks later she was gone. It all happened so quickly; I was left breathless. My mother was the strongest person I have known and I try to emulate her every day. I try to find ways to cope with my pain. I talk to it, challenging it, and I am confident in knowing I will be the victor.

When I'm away from work, I am learning to use a wheelchair. I need to give my spine and body a break, so I use the chair about thirty-five percent of the time. In the future, I will have surgeries on my legs to help me to walk better. I am cautiously anticipating positive results.

My suggestions to others are firstly, educate yourself about medications. Meds can relieve pain, so read about them extensively to know what exactly is going into your body. Currently, complications have caused me to stop all meds, and without them the pain is excruciating! Sometimes we must do unpleasant things to achieve a desired result. Well like I said, I will succeed! Secondly, talk to your doctor and ask questions about your care. If you write questions down you will be sure to remember them all. Third, avoid narcotic medications whenever possible. Fibromyalgia is often caused by a trigger: learn your triggers. It could be illness, injury, or something else, but it will help you know your body better. For example, I eat healthy foods and take the proper meds, so I avoid obesity and stave off depression. Fourth, anxiety also tends to rear its head, so I think positive thoughts. I am constantly learning about fibromyalgia, and now there is research supporting underperforming glands around the brain, such as the thalamus, pituitary, and thyroid. After being tested, the doctors and I have recognized another diagnosis: hypothyroidism, or a low-performing thyroid. This situation can also be rectified with medication.

My illness has greatly impacted me, considering both my pain and mobility limitations. I must work, so my days are long and hard. I rise early, get my daughter off to school, get myself to work, and come home to fix my daughter's lunch. I go back to work and come home totally drained after four more hours of labor. Then I cook and clean, make sure my daughter does her homework, spend time on the PC if possible, get ready for the next day, take my nightly meds (because my heart also needs medication), and hope the night will be restful. If I have any time at all, I enjoy many and varied interests, like travelling, swimming, reading, riding horses, gardening, writing short stories or poems, listening to good music, and watching a good movie.

I live with my children and my boyfriend. I look forward to our upcoming vacation during the week of the 4th of July. We plan to visit New Orleans, the zoo, and an aquarium. My family has always been my rock and stabilizing force. My intelligent, handsome son is seventeen and is on the A/B honor roll at school. My daughter is nine, smart, and beautiful. My dad is terrific, and my boyfriend is the love of my life. They mean the world to me and because we are together, I have everything. This provides an incredibly strong, unshakable foundation for me. The structure built on this foundation is my own design, and even though it is bruised and damaged, I choose to stay with it and stay active. Each day, I find the strength to push on in the dark until the sunlight hits my face once again. Like the saying goes, I am getting busy living!

Tara

Being an Australian stay-at-home mum was my profession until about five years ago. After that, going to college and graduating top of my nursing class helped me have confidence, hope, and a direction. Nursing has been my profession since then; my family has always been my life. Living would be impossible without Darron, my wonderful husband; my teenaged sons, Brendon and his older brother, Simon; and Paige, my daughter. Their love and support are so very important to me.

A while back, I realized lower back and knee pain had been plaguing me for several years. As nursing was my job, it made sense to me to see a doctor. My first step on this long journey was tentative, but I was sure I was on the right road. The doctor referred me to an orthopedic surgeon for my knees. After X-rays were taken, I was told I have a deformity in my shins. He said, "The knee does not join the femur bone in your lower leg correctly, so both legs need to be broken, or cut through, to correct it." Without expressing my thoughts, I quickly walked out on that person, his recommendations, and felt I was back to square one.

I began to notice the pain was worse on days off, when I was sitting and relaxing, than on the days I was working and active. I also started having severe headaches and pain in my shoulders. I had never been one to suffer headaches, so it was very curious to me. I also found that the excruciating pain in my neck, shoulders, and back was causing my strength to diminish. Even with this pain, I continued to do my job. To do otherwise might seem to the other nurses as if I was whining or slacking off. That was certainly unlike me! Then one afternoon at work, a persistent headache that I could not shift, nagged at me. Removing my long, heavy hair from a ponytail was ineffective. I was observing a procedure when my vision began to blur. I returned to the nurse's station and was told I was very pale. My colleagues sat me down, checked me out, and found my temp was high, and my blood pressure was through the roof! They sent me to accident and emergency (A&E) at a nearby hospital. I left there, unseen by anyone, even though I waited many hours. I then took a fork in my road and saw my general practitioner to treat these headaches, etc.

My pain was unresponsive to the usual types of analgesia. I thought perhaps I could have viral meningitis (VM), as I had nursed a patient who died with suspected VM. The doctor also thought it was possible, but at that moment, my headaches and neck pain were so severe she rang for an ambulance to take me to A&E again. With a doctor's referral, I was seen. The tests didn't reveal a pain cause, even with a blood test and doing C.A.T. scans. Fortunately, they did rule out a tumor, which was a relief. I continued on Endone and Panadiene Forte for a few more weeks, ineffective as they were, and even had a morphine injection at one point to treat the continual pain. By this time, I had also been through gallbladder removal and had pneumonia. My system had gotten so run down, it's little wonder I was suffering fatigue! It was an added detour. The pain was getting worse, so I asked my doctor to refer me on to a specialist I knew from work. I described my symptoms and pain to him.

The doctor made his determination using pressure points. He found I had sensitivity at all of the fibromyalgia "tender points," and he also diagnosed chronic fatigue (FM/CFS). He knew how hard I usually worked at the hospital and could also see that I was now exhausted after only a small exertion of energy. Another indicator to the doctor was when I told him about my relaxing weekend getaway. My husband took me away for a weekend, and I described to the doctor how physically drained I was. I was hit by fatigue so badly, I needed to return to our accommodations for a nap. I came home feeling even more tired than when we left. He said, "Everything you've told me about how you feel and all the symptoms, lead me to diagnose chronic fatigue syndrome (CFS) and chronic fibromyalgia (FM)." At the time, I was not particularly worried. There was no tumor, and I was relieved of that worry. I was incredibly distraught when the hospital contacted me, said I had used all my paid leave, and they were going to advertise for another nurse to take my spot. I felt like they were kicking me whilst I was down! After years of hard work, I had reached the position where I wanted to be; then it was snatched away from me. So, I kept pushing forward on my road.

More information would be helpful, so I started doing research about FM/CFS. I read some articles on the Internet about the XMRV retrovirus. My doctor knows nothing about the virus, and testing for it is non-existent in Australia. I worry that we are lagging behind in this country; we have trouble getting Lyrica® for treatment of FM. I was first diagnosed with no tumor, then when my pain worsened, I Googled FM and CFS and started to learn what to expect. My symptoms were mostly different than the descriptions provided, and doctors seemed unsure how to help. I began to think there was something very wrong with me. Then one day, I started searching on Facebook to find some chat and information sites.

These sites helped me find friends! I read the stories of other sufferers and realized that I had lots of company. What I was experiencing were normal FM symptoms. I learned about different medications and specialists who might help. I am now referred to see a professor that specializes in CFS and have been given information on other sites about other specialists in different areas. I have also done a lot of research into the XMRV virus suspected in CFS. It seems CFS and FM have very similar symptoms, so a test might show XMRV presence. I wait anxiously for Australia to test for this; in the meantime, I continue to watch reports from the USA and continue to try any treatment that I hear has had some success. I've learned this condition can vary day to day, depending on whether there is stress, how much of it there is, and how much sleep I've had. Planning ahead can be tricky, because every day is different. Day by day, I'm learning more about my condition and its effect on daily life. For example, I am sensitive to noise, to many stimulants at one time, I am nervous and jumpy, my vision is affected, and so are my eating habits.

During my research, I discovered FM used to be known as fibrocytis. My mother was told she had this when she was in her thirties, but didn't realize it was a condition that would stay with her. Back then, an explanation for her pain eluded everyone. For many years, she complained of pain and now she's fifty years older, and has arthritis. While I can tell Mum it's all explainable, the symptoms are always with us!

It amazes me how quickly the condition spread to all my joints! I also have face and bladder contractions and bowel disturbance. I call FM the disease that just keeps on giving. Drug treatment seems to be the only way to control my yearlong situation. My husband procrastinated before finally reading about FM. I'm grateful he eventually did. My teenage sons don't understand how debilitating the pain can be. To them, you just take some Panadol and get on with it. My daughter is very understanding. She learns from her friend's mum, Kelly. Kelly has had FM for fifteen years, and I've learned a lot from her. I have always been very strong and capable; that's how my family has known me to be. My father was a builder, and he taught me to be able to tackle any D.I.Y. (do-it-yourself) project that needs doing. Before, I would paint a room while everyone was at school/work. Now, I either can't tackle it at all, or it takes me a l-o-n-g time.

My family and I will continue to face new and difficult situations. Together, we will learn to understand about FM/CFS, and because we love each other, we will support each other and become stronger because of it. It demonstrates how important family is to me.

One time, we were visiting my mum and dad for my dad's eightieth birthday. This was a day I was having terrible trouble with my bowels.

I knew the birthday cake I'd eaten wasn't going down well at all. There were seven of us there, with four chairs to sit on, so some of us had to stand. I was happy to do so. My tummy was gurgling and popping loudly enough for the others to hear! Finally, I decided to excuse myself, so I could relieve some of the gas. I could hear the family talking away and timed things carefully with their loud moments. Coming out of the side room, I told my hubby, "We should go home soon." We said our good-byes, and on the way home, I began talking to my husband and daughter about how painful the cramps had been. They broke into fits of laughter and went on to explain that the whole family was listening and pulling faces! Embarrassed doesn't describe my mortification! I couldn't face any of them for a few days, at least.

Just one day at a time is how I am getting on. Darron does what he can and often turns to Fiona and Tennille for assistance. My friend Fiona visits weekly, is there for me to talk to, and does spiritual healing for me. She has provided much help with the headaches. My nursing friend Tennille and her husband often cook dinner for us. I have been retrieved from the depths of despair with their help and Darron's. Some days I want to give up, and others I feel I can fight on, so I do. My family is the how and why I keep forging ahead. Seeing me in pain is hard for them, I know. I have been strong in the past, and they give me courage to be strong in the future. I know my husband, who I have been with since I was fifteen, sometimes feels helpless. Other days, he can give me the help and hope I need.

Darron describes me as the hub, meaning of the wheel or of the family, and the spokes going from hub to wheel are him and the kids. He always tells me, "If the hub isn't strong then the whole wheel falls apart," and that's my reason to live. Looking forward, I see a day when I wake up without pain and to when I can alertly drive my daughter to school. That day, my journey will have reached its destination. There will also be a day when it is finally recognized that while FM/CFS may be less prominent than cancer, it affects more and more people every day. For now, we are treading water. However, I am confident there will be a day when a treatment is available that enables FM/CFS sufferers to return to functioning lives. Even so, there may be crises to deal with along the way.

A while back, my middle child Brendon, then ten years old, had a freak bicycle collision with another boy. His top jaw was smashed, and he lost some teeth. I received a frantic call from my then twelve-year-old son, Simon. I flew out of the house to arrive at the scene shortly afterward. What a horrific site! I went into control mode, organized all available help, and did what I could for Brendon before the ambulance came. I could see immediately that the injuries were quite severe. Poor Simon suffered delayed shock from seeing so much of his brother's blood, passed out, and fell to cut his own lip open. Suddenly, I had two children as casualties! It was three days in the hospital for Brendon. On returning home and caring for Brendon, whilst continuing my studies, I noticed he could no longer interact well with his siblings, or cope with normal family noise. After many meetings with neurosurgeons and specialists, they finally believed me that something was wrong and agreed to test my son further. They discovered he had a moderate acquired brain injury (ABI) from the impact; his injuries totaled those expected from being hit by a car! Fortunately, he would heal with time and effort.

Brendon went through months of treatment, and the children's hospital was an hour and thirty minutes' journey, each way. I made over two hundred trips, often having to spend all day at the hospital, whilst trying to study for my exams in between appointments, driving, and attending school. Talk about multi-tasking! My husband struggled to cope with the fact Brendon had an ABI, as it made my son aggressive toward siblings and others. He couldn't get along at school and couldn't be left alone at all. Brendon did not function in my absence. This meant that when I wasn't at college, I had to constantly care for Brendon. My husband began to seek comfort from our friends and found his greatest comfort from a female "friend," which was totally unknown to me. When I finished my studies, I fell in a heap. I could no longer cope with the pressure, and the hub of the family collapsed. I was at wits' end and called a friend I could trust. She took me to the hospital, and I spent the night in the psychiatric department, talking to a specialist. When I got home, my husband had packed his stuff and was leaving. He then told me he was having an affair. My road had led to a mountain!

Soon, I gathered my strength and managed to convince welfare I was a safe parent for my children. I was picking up the pieces of our broken lives, and my children were well cared for. We were on a new road, marching forward. I spoke to friends about Darron's mental state and begged them to get him help. A week later, I suddenly had an urge to text him and tell him we all loved him. I pleaded with him to get help. He received that text just as he was laying his wallet and other items on the bonnet of his car. He was ready to commit suicide by jumping off a bridge. My text message stopped him short and, thankfully, brought him home to his family. The path had leveled off!

Next followed months of counselling, talking, and forgiveness. I found a friend to talk to while Darron and I were in counselling. He helped me to put my family and my life back together. "Why me?" is a question I ask every day. I have been to hell and back, and I have survived. So, what is the reason I must fight on? Then comes my answer: I have three happy, healthy children. Simon has completed school and is in his first year as a motor mechanic. He is soon to turn eighteen years old and get his driving licence. Brendon is sixteen years old and is leading a normal life now. He has one year of school before he does a school-based apprenticeship as a chef. He has three jobs, a girlfriend, and is best friends with his older brother.

Brendon can be changeable; I believe it was described as emotionally labile. This can be stressful, so I concentrate on how successful he has been with our efforts to reintegrate him into the family. He is generally a happy, normal teenager. My twelve-year-old daughter, Paige, is off to high school next year. She is confident, happy, strong, and a great person to help care for me. She knows a lot about FM/CFS and does all she can to help me. Darron and I just celebrated twenty-six years together and twenty years of marriage. He has a stressful, busy job as a branch manager and works long hours. He is a great provider who tries hard to understand my condition. That is wonderful because Darron regularly takes us both for trips away to recharge and have a break. I sometimes feel I have used all the strength I have over the last five years, and have none left to cope with FM/CFS. Then I look at where I have come from and what I have had the courage to achieve. Maybe this is just nature's way of saying to me, "Rest and take some time out before moving forward!"

FM

— Is/Cause

A) The NIH-Pub Med states fibromyalgia has no clear consensus or a cause, but may be from a combination of events ~ http://www.ncbi.nlm.nih.gov/pubmedhealth/PMH0001463/.

B) WebMD describes fibromyalgia as constantly being looked at for explanations to its occurrence For example, some investigators are exploring hormonal disturbances and chemical imbalances that affect nerve signaling ~ http://www.webmd.com/fibromyalgia/guide/fibromyalgia-causes.

— Symptoms

A) The Fibromyalgia Coalition International explains FM is painful and chronic, primarily involving widespread muscle pain. It might be described as throbbing, shooting, or stabbing ~ http://www.fibrocoalition.org/pages/fmssymptoms.html.

B) The National Fibromyalgia Association lists many other symptoms that could overlap the previous listed. They can include irritable bowel and bladder, headaches and migraines, skin sensitivities and rashes, and dry eyes and mouth ~ http://www.fmaware.org/PageServerb3b4.html?pagename=fibromyalgia_symptoms.

— Tips

A) Fibromyalgia Symptoms says treatment usually involves several health care providers and may include physicians, chiropractors, occupational therapists, physiotherapists and psychiatrists ~ http://www.fibromyalgia-symptoms.org/fibromyalgia_causes.html.

B) The Mayo Clinic tells us medications for symptoms and exercise, relaxation, and stress reduction may help ~ http://www.mayoclinic.com/health/fibromyalgia/DS00079.

Step 1. Consult a professional.

WHAT IS PARALYSIS?

Ray

Growing up as I did on the fringes of a large Midwestern city, life was in fact, quite rural. As a child, I spent most of the year focused on school and various sports. I spent the other portion focused on yet a different sport. School, playing sports, attending sporting events, camping, and hiking allowed me to spend a great deal of time with my two sisters. Over the years, that has helped me realize a tremendous appreciation for them as people. Another group of individuals for whom I have great appreciation includes the educators of my early years. It is possible that my eventual chosen helping profession stemmed from that early teaching. Little did I know there would come a time when I would be the one needing assistance.

Looking back on earlier days, living near a large city allowed for plentiful opportunities. I took advantage of the readily available employment to work my way through college and to visit the city. I was an observer of the turmoil caused by the war in Vietnam and the hostility of the Democratic National Convention in Chicago. They were very unsettling experiences!

I eventually married and we had two daughters. Please know as I go on, I freely admit to bias when speaking of my amazing family. Many wonderful years and two fabulous children resulted from our marriage, before my wife succumbed to the ravages of ALS (Lou Gehrig's disease). Throughout the battle with the deadly illness, my spouse maintained her dignity and a positive attitude. She also constantly helped others and continued to work part time. Fortunately, our sweet, lovely, exceptional daughters exhibit numerous parental influences, which displays our pride in each other and love of family.

Throughout my life, many experiences influenced my choice of employment. I have worked as a physical therapist for thirty years. After much time experiencing an on-again off-again malady, I underwent surgery to correct a spinal condition; it was the first of several. More recently, an unfortunate mishap has caused me to have related paraparesis, or weakness, in my extremities. The morning after my accident, I tried to get out of bed and fell "splat" on the floor. I have since progressed from walking slowly with a cane for three or four blocks, to walking with difficulty and two canes for one block, to traveling more quickly and efficiently with a wheelchair. I am still able to master other daily activities, with much practice, and have greatly benefitted from the assistance of my fabulous children and the two magnificent sisters previously mentioned, as well as incredible friends.

Because my experiences are mostly recent, the most amusing story I can think of is one I am sure other professionals might find less humorous than I. Once, when I was at the local rehab clinic, I needed to be moved. I say this because my legs are not functional, so I could not do the moving. A Hoyer lift is commonly used in this situation. With a lift, a piece of canvas is placed under the person, the canvas is attached to a machine, whether manual or electric, and the person is lifted into the air. The Hoyer is then maneuvered to the specified location, and the person is placed gently in the desired spot. Again, this is what generally happens. From my experience, things do not *always* happen as desired. When I was being raised, I tipped and went "plop" on the floor. I thought, *Oh man, they're going to be worried!* The consternation on faces of the professionals was really something to behold. Apologizing profusely, their first question was, "Are you okay?" Right away the next morning, I was off to the main rehab clinic to be checked over and was pronounced none the worse for wear, thank goodness.

Following my last surgery, I needed to learn a different way of living, and it seems I am now the student. Before my daughter was married, I used a manual chair, which worked well for me. However, it was important to me to be able to use an electric chair to "walk" my daughter down the aisle. One had been ordered, but the wedding was almost upon us, and status of the chair remained elusive. Anxious times! Three days before the wedding, the chair appeared, so I was able to escort my daughter instead of using all my effort to wheel or have an assistant help me. Wouldn't that have been interesting?

Work has been my most glorious achievement. I was fortunate to enter on the ground floor of a physical therapy clinic, which has become quite successful. I am now a partner of that firm. Even though I am unable to perform physical therapy, I am looking forward to consulting in that field.

I am quite proud of having been one of seven tenors in the church choir for twenty-two years. It continues to baffle me how I was considered good enough to be a part of something so wonderful. As time has gone by, different functions at church and our daughters' school have needed volunteers, so my wife and I were happy to comply. We believed children learn in many ways, and leading by example is an excellent way to teach. So we taught and have been pleased with the fruits of our efforts.

Looking back over my life, I am able to say it has been pretty terrific. I am grateful for the time with my lovely wife, I am exceptionally proud of our daughters, and I am most proud of my achievements. All in all, I can say I have never had a bad day; some are just better than others.

Brenda

Five years ago, on a Saturday night, a colleague and her husband, my husband and I spent a pleasant evening together; we went out to eat. When we were driving home, we were stopped at an intersection to turn. We were waiting, discussing many things and nothing in particular. That's when our world exploded! We were violently thrown back in our seats, and our car was thrust across the highway into oncoming traffic, where it was immediately smashed in the front by another car. It happened so quickly that the oncoming driver was unable to avoid a collision. Twisted metal and blood was everywhere. Emergency vehicles came swiftly and whisked all of us away to the hospital to be checked out. I was the most affected and stayed in the hospital the longest.

Seven people would definitely remember this night forever! I was in the hospital two weeks and in rehab for six. Right about now you're probably saying to yourself, "What in the world happened?" We were in just the right place at just the wrong time. A drunk driver plowed into our car from behind, while he was driving about sixty miles per hour. Naturally, we wanted to be compensated for our injuries, time away from work, our cars, our hospital time, and our pain and suffering. Fifty thousand dollars, split between the seven of us, was all that was covered. That's just a drop in the bucket! This fact would be revealed to us later, but it was the day after the accident that was most memorable for me. It's when I learned that my spine was injured, so I would be *using a wheelchair for the rest of my life.*

Because of the accident, I had been instantly changed to non-ambulatory status. My only consolation was that the offending driver just barely survived *his* injuries. What was my response, otherwise? Fury! Agitation! Bitterness and thoughts of vengeful actions all coursed through me. I think one of the hardest things for me was to go to court. When I saw the man who did this to us, I could only think, *You decided my fate in life, and you had no right to do that!* I sincerely believed he would be in prison for many, many years. Wait for it—five years in prison was his sentence. Surely that couldn't be right; it wasn't enough! Mine is a lifetime sentence of using the wheelchair and this guy had done it! Thank goodness for my family, friends, and supporters. They all played a major part in my recovery. These wonderful people made it possible for me to succeed, and my fury abated over time.

My husband was also badly injured in the wreck, so he couldn't come to rehab with me and had to spend his time healing. My parents were with me almost all of the time. My sisters and brothers were a major support. The people in our farming community came to our place and brought in trucks and combines. They harvested all of our crops in one day! They cut wood for us and sent us meals, doing everything to keep our family life going. We didn't have to worry about any of those things. These fabulous friends and neighbors just wanted us to concentrate on getting our lives back together.

My son lived in Lawrence, and my daughter lived in Manhattan at the time of the wreck. My son stayed with his dad during the week and commuted to work every day. That was so he could help with all of the chores and be with his father. My daughter was in college and came back every weekend so that she could help out with everything. They did this for about a year. Everything that needed to be done seemed to have friends and family involved. It was pretty unbelievable, and it still brings me to tears when I think of all that was done for my family! How could I not be strong and move forward with all of the care that was surrounding me? I have undying love for these fantastic people. They were there to encourage me when I got the news about my injuries, and they have sustained me throughout. Their affection and dedication will always be remembered.

Those thoughts were a godsend the first time I encountered a barrier to my mobility. The life I had known was radically changed, and that fact became a crushing reality when I needed something from the second floor of our house. My eyes were suddenly opened wide, because I was very willing, but someone was going to have to go for me! I was aggravated beyond words, disbelieving that something I had done so easily—going up the steps—now was impossible. I silently screamed, shed a few tears, and depended strongly on the love that I knew was there from my family and friends. The wheelchair would make me a stronger person in many ways!

Teaching has been my career for about twenty years now. Educating ten-year-olds has been therapeutic. They are so open and honest! When students first see me, they are unsure how to act. Many students have lived their young lives without encountering someone who functions differently than they do. I address my wheelchair first thing and invite questions for us to discuss. That way everyone can learn. The most frequent question asked is, "How do you put on clothes?" It always makes me smile. There are tricks to dressing, but it's possible. It takes about two months before students feel totally comfortable.

My students are now more aware of different situations for people, are extremely helpful, and are very caring. When I returned to work, my school family treated me as I wanted to be treated: helpful while allowing my independence. Also, the school made sure that my room was set up so that I would be able to move around easily and have all the technology I needed to be successful in teaching my students. They have worked with me every step of the way, and my coworkers have been the best. They always make sure that I have what I need. What wonderful people they are! Work and home are places of emotional healing, so I am well covered.

We live in a small Midwest community, and the people here are incredibly supportive! They have had fund-raiser after fund-raiser to help with the cost of renovating our house. It's at the point where it is almost completely wheelchair accessible. There are few words to express my immense gratitude. We have ramps, counters are open underneath, faucets stretch out over sinks so I can reach the water, the bathroom facilities have been altered, and my life is facilitated. I drive the car with hand controls and can push my wheelchair wherever else I need to go.

The events of that night, and the result, have made me a stronger person. I am ready to move forward and continue with this wonderful life. I have a fabulous husband; our children are both working and live independently; they are lovely people. Our daughter is a social worker and our son is a project manager for a utility company. We see them often, as they live in this area. I was recently asked what living in a small town is like for young people growing up. I think it gives them solid footing. It's what I recognize as true, having always lived here. I found that strength in family is great inspiration. I just did things for my family, because they had to be done. That was it. Our kids went away to go to college and now appreciate living in a close community, which is why they have returned. To say they have been supportive and helpful to me is insufficient recognition and praise.

I look forward to marriages and grandchildren, as parents are given to do, and teaching, because I enjoy my students every day. Education has always been my bedrock; I've always wanted to teach others. Becoming an educator has been a fulfillment rather than a goal. After teaching for twenty years, I take things as they come and see where to go from there. I also know now that things can be well planned, but it takes only a moment to irrevocably change those plans.

My family has been, and still is, amazingly supportive. I love them all dearly. I believe there is a reason for all things, and I try to use my experience in a positive way. I do get frustrated and feel sorry for myself, but then, what is, is. I have learned to deal with it. Above all, I have learned patience. That's quite different from the way I used to be! I have also learned to involve much more thought in working things out. Using the wheelchair provides unlimited problem-solving opportunities. It's even become routine to think through things critically. What an interesting and enjoyable activity. What about the man who hit us? Though I used to be angry, unknowingly he gave me the chance to grow and flourish. There are positives to every situation!

Ed

Farming has always been my life, whether here at the farm or studying agriculture at Purdue University. We have raised grain, livestock, and truck crops on our seventy-two-acre family farm. We currently grow asparagus and several acres of strawberries. You might want to visit our website at www.EatMoreStrawberries.com. There are a lot of photos and even more information there.

Some additional background items would be helpful about now. I was in college and visiting my girlfriend when we lived through a terrifying experience. We were attacked by her jealous ex-boyfriend. When I say attacked, I mean threateningly and viciously attacked! I defended us to the best of my ability so that my girlfriend, who is now my wife, was unhurt. Thank goodness! My fate and the fate of our assailant were quite different. I was shot in the leg and neck and have used a wheelchair since that day. I am paralyzed from the collarbone down. My disability happened as a result of an intentional act of evil. When the police arrived on the scene, it took several officers to wrestle the man to the ground. He was convicted of two felonies and incarcerated for over fifteen years. He is free now, but has never bothered or tried to contact us. We have purposely and happily closed the book on that part of our lives.

At the time I was shot, I thought I had received a mortal wound and was sure I was dying. God had other plans. I was conscious and knew I was bleeding to death when, miraculously, the blood stopped flowing. I felt God saying to me, "I'm not done with you yet." Since that fateful day, I have strived to persevere, and I feel good about my accomplishments.

Sometimes problems do come my way. There was a time when I didn't want to be disabled anymore. My thoughts were always gloomy. The idea of permanence weighed on me like an anchor pulling me underwater. My disability was forever and inescapable. I wanted to be someone else. I grieved the loss of who I was and hated the limitations I now had. This disability anchor was pulling me down, down, down, and I was drowning! I felt powerless to change my situation. I just wanted things to be different. I became depressed to the point that I wanted to run away, but with the disability, even that wasn't possible! I felt so bad I gave up, got into my manual wheelchair, rolled down our long country driveway, stopped, got out, and just lay on the ground in despair.

My problems had become bigger than me; I had reached my breaking point. I could only ask God to handle them. I cried to God and told Him how unhappy I was. I begged for His help and told Him I couldn't do it on my own. As I lay there crying and praying, my dad came slowly walking down the drive. He quietly picked me up to set me carefully back in the wheelchair. Dad pushed me back to the house and helped me into bed. He comforted me and his only words were, "Come on, Son." My father had physically picked me up and emotionally encouraged me to move forward when I couldn't do it for myself. He gave me what I needed, when I needed it. I realized then that God had provided.

God blessed me with Dad, family, and friends. They were there to pick me up whenever I crashed, especially in the early days after the injury. I have mediocre days, and then there are the good days. It's been a long time since I've tasted true despair. When burdens get me down, I find great comfort in knowing that God is bigger than all of my problems. He, like my dad, loves me and is there to pick me up, take me home, and comfort me. That makes all the burdens seem smaller. Surviving a murder attempt tends to put life's troubles into perspective. My outlook now? Life is very do-able.

There is no feeling on my ring fingers, little fingers, and the bottom sides of both arms, yet I have nearly full function of my arms. Unfortunately, I am unable to move anything below my armpits. I can do all my own personal care in the morning. However, I am unable to regulate my body temperature in harsh weather. This is comparable to a person with quadriplegia, and therefore, I must be careful in extreme weather conditions, heat, and cold. After the attack, I still wanted to live and work on a farm, so I redefined success to fit my circumstances. We made lots of modifications, and despite my disability, I have continued to farm. There are times, once or twice a year, I accidentally tip over in my wheelchair. When that happens, the people around me generally freak out, though I am hardly ever hurt. The usual reaction is people running to my aid and yelling. The first question is always, "Are you okay?" My usual response is, "Well, I can't feel my legs." My wife thinks this is never funny; I prefer to think of it as dealing with my issues in a humorous way.

It's possible, even likely, that many people die not knowing their full potential. A long time ago, I made a choice and decided to be not a victim but a survivor. I have faith in a loving God, who is bigger than all of my problems. So, the way I look at it, instead of saying, "I can't do that," I ask, "What can I do about it?" Some of the modifications we have made at the farm began with changing direction. I was a pig farmer, and that was not at all feasible. So we got rid of the pigs and started raising strawberries. That kind of production worked much better for me and fit well in this area.

Next, we adapted the tractors with hand controls and a homemade lift. I have a van with hand controls and a lift, and I carry a cell phone with me everywhere I go. I use larger hand tools that provide me with extra needed leverage. I have a canopy on my tractor that keeps me shaded from the hot sun. I use a standing wheelchair. I recently purchased a new loader tractor; it has a commercially made tractor lift. I do consulting work for the Standing Wheelchair Company and Purdue University's AgrAbility Breaking New Ground, which serves farmers and ranchers with disabilities across the country. As a side note, I also do lots of motivational speaking. Other changes have taken place over the years. In 1995, our house burned down, so we built a new accessible home. Just like many other things, out of a negative comes a positive. I firmly believe that people in my situation are worthwhile; we can contribute to society. I value life, liberty, independence, relationships, and the management of time much more than before. I take little for granted.

In doing what I can, I was awarded the Governor's Trophy for surmounting a disability and for employing people with disabilities. Also, I received the U.S. Department of Labor 2005 New Freedom Initiative Award as part of the Breaking New Ground team, and the 2006 Indiana Farm Family of the Year Award. Speaking of my family, mine is amazing, which is an understatement. I am blessed to be surrounded by wonderful people.

Without them—family and friends—survival would have been much harder. My wife is an exceptional woman. Most women would walk, or run, away from men like me. Debbie, who is a part-time RN, has faithfully stood by my side for well over a quarter of a century, and I have been very blessed. My parents were always there to pick me up whenever I was down; they have been my biggest cheerleaders. At the time I was hurt, the doctors told me that I would never walk or have children. They were only half right, so far. My eighteen-year-old natural daughter will be a freshman at a state university in 2011. She is presently a state officer for the Future Farmers of America (FFA) organization. My daughter is a gift from God. She, my wife, and friends are quick to fill in the gaps when I am unable to do something and are helpful when it is needed.

I look forward to getting older with my wife and to seeing my daughter get married and start her independent life. I look forward to holding my grandkids someday, Lord willing. I look forward to Heaven. My life has been about several things: faith, family, friends, and perseverance. Life has also thrown many curveballs my way, but I believe God is closest when you live on the edge.

Paralysis

— Is/Cause

A) Medlineplus states that paralysis is loss of muscle function when something goes wrong with the way messages are sent from the brain to the muscles ~ http://www.nlm.nih.gov/medlineplus/paralysis.html.

B) The NIH explains that most paralysis is caused by stroke or spinal cord injury ~ http://www.nlm.nih.gov/medlineplus/paralysis.html.

— Symptoms

A) Step Ahead Australia defines two types of paralysis resulting from a spinal cord injury. Paraplegia is when hands and arms are still useful and quadriplegia is when all four limbs fail to function ~ http://www.stepahead.org.au/pages/spinal-cord-injury-facts/types-of-paralysis.php.

B) The Brain and Spinal Cord Organization explains that the effects of paralysis have an impact on other systems of the body. It can cause changes to circulation and respiration, the kidneys and gastrointestinal system, joints, bones, muscles, etc. ~ http://www.brainandspinalcord.org/spinal-cord-injuries/signs-and-symptoms-paralysis.html.

— Tips

A) An article about sleep disorders talks about sleep paralysis happening frequently. Tips to cope include making an attempt to observe sleep patterns, sleep positions, and emotional or the psychological condition before an episode. This will help identify factors that can stimulate sleep paralysis and help to avoid it in the future ~ http://sleepdisordersinfo.tk/symptoms-of-sleep-paralysis-tips-on-how-to-cope-507

B) Arch-online.org mentions bathing accessories which may help those with paralysis, such as bath seats, handheld shower heads, or grab bars - http://arch-online.org/disability-safety-bathroom-safety-tips-for-disabled-people.htm.

Author's Note—Through personal experience the author has learned the following tips:

- Asking for help sometimes is okay, most people are glad to assist.

- A "grabber" to reach what is not reachable can be quite useful for those with arm movement.

- Physically moving to maintain or gain range of motion can also be beneficial; assistance may be needed.

Step 1. See "Autoimmune, Multiple Sclerosis," this book.

Step 2. Consult a professional.

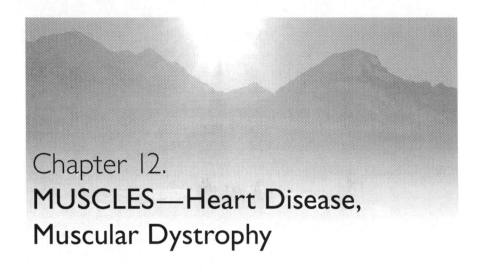

Chapter 12.
MUSCLES—Heart Disease, Muscular Dystrophy

WHAT IS HEART DISEASE?

Nate

It's been at least a hundred years since my great-grandparents homesteaded this parcel of land. These one hundred sixty acres have sustained our family, past and present, which gives me immense pride, a sense of history, and a legacy. I have always lived in this house, on this land, and continue agricultural and livestock activities today. I care deeply about my family and helping crops and animals to grow. What a rewarding way of life it is.

I grew up with kind, firm, and fair parents and an older sister. Located just outside of a growing rural community, our family was small, but happy. My early years were enjoyable, though we did experience some financial hardship when I was young. I remember rationing during WWII, when many people had a common goal. Because my sister was older, really a surrogate parent, it was somewhat traumatic when she graduated high school and began working in town. I was still in elementary school at the time, so I began working at home, which helped to fill the void of her absence. It seems worthwhile effort is a family tradition.

After graduating high school, I went to town myself and attended junior college. Though I enjoyed high school immensely, a year of further education proved to be less to my liking. Then, armed service was my choice for a four-year enlistment. Leaving home was an interesting experience, as I traveled to the southwest and graduated first in my class from a highly technical maintenance school. Now I understood how college had been inappropriate, because my talents lie in the mechanical arena. The service had given me a direction.

My next post was to be in Hawaii. Before I left for another distant part of our country, my wife, JoAn, and I married. We had just spent a year apart and now we weighed our options. We could move together to an expensive island paradise, or spend another three years apart. We decided to tough it out and be separated. My period of service seemed endless, but we appreciated each other more and have been married fifty-six years. It seems we decided well; perhaps being away from each other helped us strengthen our union. Following an honorable discharge from the service, I worked agriculturally. I eventually decided to supplement agricultural income with alternative funds, sold some equipment, and began working in a mechanical position at a nearby manufacturing plant. I remained there twenty-two years, until my retirement.

It was following my retirement that I began to have heart difficulties. Firstly, I could work only mornings, and the remainder of the day was devoted to resting from morning exertion. Was I that much older that it was causing my weariness? Secondly, I woke up one day with uncomfortable chest pressure. Was it indigestion? It felt like it might be. Then my chest tightened and it felt like I had a load of books stacked on it. I was more concerned now. Was I truly having a heart attack? This awful feeling worsened and I knew I really needed help. After we called the doctor, I was at the hospital in short order. He knew where I needed to be.

Open heart surgery with a triple bypass was performed. It was an unpleasant experience, and though I spoke in rehab with a person who had surgery twice, once was enough for me. In addition to physical pain, there was post-surgical depression. I have been told this is common, though for me, depression coupled with excruciating and overwhelming pain was a new experience. I was at my lowest ebb. Just starting rehab, my foremost thought was, *That morphine sure gave me weird dreams!* Other things I thought about were pain, always the pain, and what would my abilities be like in the future? It seems rehab was valuable, because the pain is gone, and my abilities are okay.

Going to rehabilitation, two different times—once after surgery and once after several stents were inserted—has been an effort. Even so, I was and have been very faithful about going to rehab and to see the doctor. I had drive and determination before, but since surgery, it's at a new level. A heart attack isn't going to keep me down. It was thirteen weeks after I got home before I could actually feel comfortable doing my usual activities. It took time, but with family love and assistance, things are back to normal. With adjustments, of course.

So a repeat performance would avoided, I vowed to keep myself healthy. Since the surgery, I have had nine stents inserted. I have a checkup every four months, and the doctor determines the need for a stent. The reason for a coronary stent is to keep the arteries from plugging up. It is a mesh sleeve designed to fit inside an artery to hold it open. What might cause arteries around the heart to plug? When asking this question, I was told that scar tissue and plaque could cause the plugging. Plaque is a buildup of fat. The stent procedure requires a day devoted to time at the hospital and resting. So to avoid frequent visits, we began eating less red meat and have foregone using added salt or sugar to our food. Also, I don't drink coffee, or the one item I miss the most—an ice cold beer after evening chores. I really want to live to enjoy my family.

JoAn and I have four children: Steve, Brian, Brent, and Scott. My wife remained in the home with our sons while they were growing up. All of the boys are now married and have children of their own. Each child is unique, with individual talents in construction, manufacturing, or agriculture, and we are quite proud of each of them. These days, I have cut back on the number of livestock for which to care and the amount of time devoted to the land. My children help me with the workload.

All in all, I feel I have lived a good, honorable, and fruitful life. JoAn and I have always concentrated on family, so why would we change now? Have I mentioned yet how proud we are of our children and grandchildren? We attend many functions of the grandkids; as many as possible. Our presence at events is a grandparent's privilege, and it is a great a joy to focus on the young ones. After all, it will be through succeeding generations that our family legacy continues.

Susan

We lived in the Midwest many years ago, when we chose to relocate to a warmer climate. Our new home proved to be not only a different, more suitable setting, but a nurturing environment for my husband, me, and our two children.

In May of 2008, my husband and I were back in the Midwest to attend our granddaughter's high school graduation, but for me, it was not to be. What could have caused me to miss such an important event? Two days before the graduation was to take place, I felt tightness in my chest. It was uncomfortable, but bearable at first, and I thought the tightness must be caused by the humidity. As time went by, this heaviness became an extremely uncomfortable feeling. I knew there was a cause other than humidity.

This tightness and heaviness was obviously going to stick around, so going to the hospital seemed the best and most prudent thing to do. Because we were unfamiliar with the area, we called our son, who knew where to go. We drove to a different city where we met him and he guided us to the nearest hospital. The tests there revealed the need for heart surgery. Who, me? Why now? It seemed I'd never had problems before. Well, it so happened that I needed a type of surgery that would have to be done at a different hospital. So off I went by ambulance to a hospital that did do my type of surgery.

The next day, I was scheduled to have the major surgery, but that night, to keep me alive, two stents were put in. Well, it seems to have worked, along with the other things that had to be done. My aorta had to be replaced and the mitral valve repaired, along with two bypasses. You might say I was in bad shape, but wait, there's more! Soon after the heart surgery, my kidneys and lungs began to fail, and dialysis was needed. I had tubes coming out of me everywhere! This was not fun! I felt like I had been wrung out and hung up to dry. These were dark days, because I had one additional tube in and I couldn't talk. Because I couldn't communicate verbally, my family and I learned to "talk" with our hands. We got creative and developed our very own sign language. Also, staying infection-free was crucial to me, so everyone quickly learned to wash their hands before approaching. We made light of the hand washing, but it was certainly vital to my health.

My family was told they could bring the grandchildren in to see me, as it was expected that I would not survive. Hah! It just showed how little the doctors knew me. I am a survivor and was determined to get well! I had many things yet to accomplish in my life. There were people to see and things to do. I had just been elected corporate secretary of a large homeowner's association. I wasn't about to let them, or my wonderful family, down! So I recited the Lord's Prayer, over and over. I learned my friends and family were also praying for me. I knew the hospital was state-of-the-art, and that it had especially qualified doctors and nurses, which were all comforting thoughts. The sooner I got well, the sooner I could go home. It would still be a while before I could leave.

As I was healing, there was also much time to reflect about how I had gotten to this point; then I remembered October 2007. At that time, I did have a warning that I took lightly. I was visiting my daughter in Oregon and carried two large, heavy bags of groceries into the house. Upon completing this task, my chest seared with pain. I sat down for a little bit, and the pain soon went away. I had priorities other than going to a doctor, so a visit was neglected. I was scheduled to attend my older sister's ninetieth birthday in a few days: it was a V.I.E. (very important event) and wasn't to be missed! Another time, I felt some tightening in my chest again, but foolishly thought my bra was too tight. Other times, I would be exhausted by just walking around the block. These were all significant signs, but they all happened at different times, in different situations, so a connection between them was, understandably, not made.

The day I was told I could fly home, my surgeon came to my room and said, "Susan, you were quite a challenge." After he left, I thought about his curious statement. Hmmm … he'd done many heart transplants and I hadn't received a new heart. Aha! I remembered that back in the fifties, I had both legs operated on because my veins were bad then. My existing veins must have been too weak to effectively supply blood to the heart. They couldn't be used, so mammary veins were. Challenge or not, I was very ready to leave.

After I left the hospital, we flew home. Our grandson drove our car back, cross-country, in one day. When he arrived, I said to him, "You may be a pilot, but our car doesn't have wings!" He is a healthy young man; however, it is important for youth to maintain their health by eating healthy food and keeping stress to a minimum.

To help me reduce stress and to stay healthy, therapy at a heart clinic was helpful. Also, regular visits to a cardiologist are now part of my routine. I am trying to eat more fruits and vegetables and have been going to a gym to exercise. This quote by Maya Angelou, "When we know better, we do better," is certainly true in my case! Fortunately, I have avoided post-surgical depression. Unquestionably, I believe life is what you make it. We can stay in bed and dream or get out of bed and fulfill those dreams!

Heart Disease

– Is/Cause

A) The Mayo Clinic tells us the term heart disease is a broad description of a range of diseases: coronary artery disease, heart rhythm problems, heart infections, and heart problems a person is born with are some ~ http://www.mayoclinic.com/health/heart-disease/DS01120.

B) The National Heart Lung and Blood Institute says
- High blood pressure
- Diabetes and pre-diabetes
- Overweight and obesity
- Smoking
- Lack of physical activity
- Unhealthy diet
- Stress

are all risk factors to having heart disease ~ http://www.nhlbi.nih.gov/health/dci/Diseases/hd/hd_whatare.html.

– Symptoms

A) The Cleveland Clinic states that the most common symptom of coronary artery disease is angina, or chest pain. It could also be described as heaviness, tightness, pressure, burning, etc. ~ http://my.clevelandclinic.org/heart/disorders/cad/cadsymptoms.aspx.

B) The American Heart Association (AHA) lists the warning signs of a heart attack

- *Chest discomfort.* Most heart attacks involve discomfort in the center of the chest that lasts for more than a few minutes, or goes away and comes back. The discomfort can feel like uncomfortable pressure, squeezing, fullness, or pain.

- *Discomfort in other areas of the upper body.* This can include pain or discomfort in one or both arms, the back, neck, jaw, or stomach.

- *Shortness of breath.* It often comes along with chest discomfort, but it also can occur before the chest discomfort - http://www.heart.org/HEARTORG/Conditions/Conditions_UCM_305346_SubHomePage.jsp.

- *Other symptoms.* May include breaking out in a cold sweat, nausea, or light-headedness - http://www.nhlbi.nih.gov.

– *Tips*

A) The University of Maryland Medical Center states studies show that following a just few steps will assist a person to become more heart healthy. The steps are to eat a healthy diet, quit smoking, exercise, and maintain a healthy body weight - http://www.umm.edu/features/tips_prev.htm.

B) The Family Doctor Organization tells us to talk to the doctor about specific risk factors and how to reduce the risk. The following are suggestions the doctor could possibly make: quit smoking, eat a healthy diet, control blood sugar if diabetes is an issue, exercise, lose weight, and control high blood pressure - http://familydoctor.org/online/famdocen/home/common/heartdisease/basics/291.html.

Author's Note—Perhaps rather than trying to accomplish all the previous suggestions at once, one might take a step at a time and work up to include all items.

Author's Note—When buying food, LDLs, or hydrogenated contents, can be harmful. LDLs tend to promote plaque buildup in blood vessels. Another suggestion is that high fructose corn syrup can promote fat increase.

Step 1. See "Blood, Diabetes," and "Mental Health, Eating Disorders," this book.

Step 2. Consult a professional.

WHAT IS MUSCULAR DYSTROPHY (MD)?

Kathy

Omaha, Nebraska is where I grew up; then I moved to Texas in 1985. Then it was on to Kent, Washington in 1989. When I had the opportunity in 2007 to live again in Texas, I jumped at the chance! My husband chose to remain in Washington, because Texas is too hot. Not for me. The heat and humidity sure make my feet and ankles swell if I sit in my power chair all day, but it's okay. Being near to my children takes priority over weather and discomfort. I have added incentive, I love Texas! Two of my three children live nearby, and so do my lovely grandchildren. My children's ages are thirty-six, thirty-five, and thirty-four. Back in the day, I was certainly a busy mama! Fortunately, I am still able to get around as needed. You see, I use a wheelchair when I am out of the apartment and stationary assistance at home. I have a form of muscular dystrophy called facioscapulohumeral muscular dystrophy (FSHMD). It certainly is debilitating, but I found out that FSHMD is, thankfully, non-fatal.

When I was in fifth grade, I noticed that when I wanted to raise my hand in class, it was impossible to extend my arm to its full height. Though this worried me, I said nothing, even to my mom. After two years passed, I remember once walking across our backyard in my bathing suit. Mom told me, "Stand up straight!" Apparently, shoulder blades sticking out are one of the first visual symptoms of FSHMD, as those muscles die. My older sister finally told Mom that I could not raise my arms up all the way. By then, both arms were affected.

Mom took me to our family doctor, who had no idea what was going on. Into the hospital I went. Because it was a teaching hospital, doctors and interns would come in every day and have me hang my little pajama top around my neck to protect my privacy. Then they would have me push against the wall, push against their hands, and just have me raise my arms. They let me go home, not knowing what was going on. When I was in about tenth grade, my doctor sent me to a neurosurgeon, who did yet more tests on my body. He diagnosed muscular dystrophy. A short time after receiving the results, my older sister said she heard my mom talking to someone on the phone, and they were discussing what a short time I had to live. Did this upset me? Yes! I was extremely upset, but never talked to my mom about this either. I just waited to die for many years. Back then if you looked up MD in an encyclopedia, Duchenne MD was usually the type mentioned, which we know now is mostly found in males. Females can be carriers. Individuals with Duchenne MD rarely survive beyond thirty years. Like I said, I have FSHMD, and so does my youngest son.

The idea that I have passed this disease on to my child devastates me. I know my children worry about *me* and wish things were different. I worry that my grandchildren may some day be diagnosed with FSHMD. My three children were all born within two years and four months. It was, at best, strenuous to carry a child for long. My arms would become painful and exhausted, so I would rest the child on the arm of a chair, with the baby's head resting against my arms. The pain continued when I was only holding the baby in place! Thinking back, I remembered the doctor would write notes to excuse me from physical education classes when I was in school. I was unable to participate in activities like the others. I wanted to, but as hard as I tried, the reality always was with me. As I aged, I would still try to participate in activities with the inevitable result. Always, the desire was there, but the ability was lacking. People would try to compensate for my physical faults without understanding how hurtful that was. The goal for them was winning, while being part of a team was mine. I once was told I ran like an "old lady." Do people realize how hurtful their actions and words can be?

Even walking could be an issue. Inclines were really tough for me to climb, and one time there was a man who saw how difficult it was for me. He offered to help me walk up the hill. What a surprise: a gentleman! It seems odd now, but I was embarrassed to have his help, so I declined. But what a nice gesture! I now realize that people really want to help and will almost always be glad to do so when asked.

For many years I used a cane, then two canes. Then, about six years ago, I started using a power chair. It seemed at the time I was "giving in," but I can get around and go places now. I sometimes get the "pity" look or "the stare of amazement," because I'm using a power chair to "walk," and I'm zipping right along! I'm so happy to have this chair. I live alone, work, have a carrier on the back of my car, and can get around by myself. In the apartment, I have everything placed so that I can hold onto things as I move around when I'm on my feet. My legs and hips are affected, but I can still get into and out of the car. I use cruise control a lot and am still able to drive at this point. I use a grabber often, and the grandchildren help me with things I cannot do. If I fall, I am dead weight, so it's difficult for others to get me up. I can manage to stand upright on my own, using a stool and chair if they are available, but it's becoming more difficult. Fortunately, I have found a way to get my wheelchair on and off the car carrier by myself. The weather is a concern, because the chair must stay dry and covered. But as a whole, I have my independence. I get tired sometimes, but I take care of myself and I am very proud and happy I am still able to be on my own.

My grandchildren like to imitate my walk and swinging hips, which is cute. I used to take my granddaughters, nine-year-old twins, to the park near my house by putting them on my lap. We would also take "walks" around the block. We thought my then five-year-old grandson would never walk on his own, because when he was with me, he automatically would climb on my lap, and we would go exploring. He is now almost six and still likes to climb on my lap and go through the store or up to my pool. When my granddaughter was a little over a year old, so she would be comfortable and come to me easily, I would set her on my lap in the wheelchair, and we would ride around the apartment complex. We were both thrilled to be having fun together, and she was excited to go for rides with Gaga! We still have fun now that she is older.

For work, I am a substitute teachers' aide at many different elementary schools. If they let me, when children are sick, I like to take them for rides up to the office. The school doesn't like them walking the halls alone. I do love my work. The children are wonderful and are unafraid to ask questions, which I am happy to answer. They all ask why I am using a chair, and some are very worried about me living alone. One little boy even said he was going to buy me a cat! I find children are much less judgmental than adults.

I would like for people to really hear what I am saying. There are things I am just unable to do, and I do what I can. Those people tell me to exercise more so I can do better. Horse manure! I wonder how they would respond in my situation. They are welcome to trade places with me anytime! My muscles are dwindling in size and ability, so how can I exercise or take walks? Sometimes I resent it when people tell me about their walks, hikes, or working out. Those things are forever lost to me. There are many things I would like to do that are impossible.

My grandchildren wish upon stars that I would be able to walk and play with them. I want to be able to run and play, as well. I wish I could go to the beach with them and be able to go into the water. I wish I could get into a swimming pool, but I cannot get in and out. I would like to take care of my apartment better. It is almost impossible to do much of the cleaning that is necessary. I would like to plan a fishing trip or a vacation and be able to walk, hike, fish, or whatever. I wish I could take a drive and not worry about ramps or where the bathroom is and if it will be handicapped accessible. Going to restaurants, if I must walk, is avoided at all costs.

People have told me, "We are very proud of you; you work and get around on your own very well!" Some have also said, "I don't know what I would do in your circumstances!" My thoughts are, *We cope with what we are.* I am very happy that I can work and go shopping by myself. I am able to take the grandkids to parks to work off some energy and play. After that, it's on to the fast-food restaurant! I am also able to do my own laundry. My grandchildren are my inspiration to keep going and I hope to be around when they have children. They are always happy to help and will do whatever I ask. My children and grandchildren are my life. I've mentioned my children: Daniel, Tammy, and Dennis. The grandchildren are Tammy's nine-year-old fraternal twins, Taylor and Alyssa, and six-year-old boy, Tyler. Dennis has a daughter, Kaitlyn, who is two. And even though Daniel has no children yet, if he so chooses, he will make a great parent, just like his siblings! My terrific children have raised terrific children of their own, and I love them all!

Larry

When I was a twenty-eight-year-old young man, I had just begun working as a mechanic in plant maintenance at the main post office. I was also in the Air National Guard and had been for ten years; I enjoyed my time serving in the Guard very much, and things were going well.

My wife and I had been married for several years and I was the father of three. Then, I began feeling the strangest tingling in the fingers of my right hand; I didn't know what to think. So I took this information to my doctor. The doctor sent me to another doctor, a neurologist, and that doctor diagnosed Charcot-Marie-Tooth Disease (CMT). It's a disease of the peripheral nerves and causes muscles to atrophy, as is the case with other muscular dystrophy situations. Maybe you can imagine how stunned I was at the news. An actual diagnosis of an illness; not me! I was in shape, felt great, and all seemed okay, except for this annoying tingling. I was told that by the age of about fifty or fifty-five I would have a lot of trouble walking. That's something that would stay in the back of my mind, but I couldn't change anything, so why worry about it? I felt I had to report the diagnosis to the Air National Guard, and CMT was the reason I was honorably discharged. Other than that, my life stayed pretty much the same. I have remained as upbeat as ever.

We live in what is for the Midwest a fairly large metropolitan area. Our lives have been uneventful for the most part. Our three children are all wonderful, upstanding people. As they were growing, there were a few incidents, but everything always seemed to work itself out. My wife and I have been married fifty-one terrific years next month. Good for us! We believe in family, and it has always been a dependable constant.

One of my brothers has CMT and one brother has no sign of it. My daughter has CMT and has passed it on to her twenty-year-old son. My grandson knows it came from me, so I told him, "I wanted to give you something that would last you a lifetime," tongue in cheek. My children and grandchildren have accepted my CMT admirably. If I'd known that I had this disease, I would not have had children of my own, but would have adopted instead. I'm very happy now, however, that we did have children. My brother who has the disease never had children of his own, and as a result, he has stopped the progression of CMT from himself, forever. Good move! After discussing it, my brother and I think CMT was passed on to us by our mother. Thinking back, we can remember times when she showed symptoms.

CMT symptoms have caused my share of falls, as my hands and legs are now seriously affected. Fortunately, I have never broken any bones, but I have suffered other serious injuries. Both knees have twice-torn tendons that can give me aches now and then. Thankfully, there is no need to replace the knees, though.

A few years after I was diagnosed, I started using a cane to help me walk. After several years, I began wearing braces on both legs, and that helped a lot. After a while, I started using a cane with the braces. The deterioration kept on. After another few years, my lower back began to hurt, so I set up an appointment with MDA to visit one of their clinics. They suggested that I consider using forearm crutches. What a difference they made! I get around pretty well and can get up off the floor with them in a heartbeat.

Though I do not have a problem with hammer toes, many people with CMT have a big problem with it. They may have to have their toes fused to keep them straight. Walking on the tips of one's toes would be very unpleasant, and hurt, to say the least! My brother has had all ten toes fused twice, as the first try didn't hold for very many years. Another symptom with certain types of CMT is quite a hearing loss, and my brother and I share that problem. We both wear hearing aids, as did our mother. We must look different to others.

People sometimes do not know what to think when they watch me walk. I try to put them at ease by making light of my situation. They are mostly curious, especially kids, so I explain to them simply what all the equipment does and why it's there. I find that people have really good hearts and they're always willing to assist. Women, especially, are quick to accommodate my needs and will often go out of their way to open a door or pick up something from the floor. I find most people are very good about things like that.

On the humorous side, I tend to move more slowly than others and perhaps walk like I may have had a smidgeon too much to drink. One year, I was appointed to serve a year as the Grand Tyler; it is a state-level assignment for the Masonic Grand Lodge of Iowa. The Grand Master who had asked me to serve gave me the title, unofficial of course, of "Corvair Tyler." The reason for the title was that Ralph Nader wrote a book many years ago, and being the consumer advocate that he is, advised consumers not to buy the then-popular Chevrolet Corvair, because it was, "unsafe at any speed." Do I need to say more?

Of the forty-odd diseases included in the muscular dystrophy spectrum, I like to say I have the best of them. No complaints here. When I was diagnosed, I knew that physically, things would get worse. There have been no surprises. But feeling sorry for myself will do little good, for those around me or for me. I decided early on that I would make the best of it for as long as I could and that I would continue to do what I can. My kids have caringly suggested a ramp so I don't have to step up the two steps to get into the house. That's very kind and loving, but I'm not ready yet! They can build the ramp, but I won't use it until *I* have decided that I have to have it.

Traveling with my wife is something I enjoy and we go on vacation once or twice a year. I drive the car with hand controls and have a scooter to help me get around better. I had a lift installed in the back of my Dodge Caravan and that makes it easy to get my handicapped scooter in and out.

My crowning achievements have been my family, my Masonic membership, and my job. My wife is a wonderful woman and she is so helpful. I believe that perhaps I have helped with a positive outlook and my determination. Our children are outstanding people. We have a close-knit family with three kids, seven grandchildren, and two great-grandchildren. They are fabulous people in their own right and we enjoy spending time with all of them. My Masonic friends are great guys to be around and are good, moral men. We have terrific camaraderie, a good time together, and do some traveling around the state to other Masonic lodges. I retired from the US Postal Service after an accrued thirty-six years. I had worked my way up from clerk to superintendent of maintenance, with sixty to seventy people under me and more branching out from there.

It's a great life, and while I wish I were disease-free, I believe pity and sympathy should be reserved for others. My outlook has always been, is now, and forever will be productive, positive, and optimistic!

MD

— Is/Cause

A) NIH-PubMed Health states MD is inherited, is a group of disorders, and involves muscle weakness/muscle loss - http://www.ncbi.nlm.nih.gov/pubmedhealth/PMH0002172/.

B) The Cleveland Clinic explains that some forms of MD appear in infancy/childhood, while some appear in middle age - http://my.clevelandclinic.org/disorders/muscular_dystrophy/hic_muscular_dystrophy.aspx.

— Symptoms

A) Web MD states the symptoms of Duchenne MD and Becker MD can be clumsiness, a waddling gait, and curvature of the spine - http://www.webmd.com/parenting/understanding-muscular-dystrophy-symptoms.

B) The University of Maryland Medical Center tells us that adult onset myotonic MD can appear as baldness in men and women, intellectual impairment, or respiratory problems - http://www.umm.edu/altmed/articles/muscular-dystrophy-000113.htm.

― *Tips*

A) The National Institute of Neurological Diseases and Stroke explains that no specific treatment for any form of MD will stop or reverse the progression of the disease. Physical and speech therapy are some options for treatment, corticosteroids to slow progression, anticonvulsants, or immunosuppressants might be drug therapies, and occupational therapy also may help ‒ http://www.ninds.nih.gov/disorders/md/md.htm#Is_there_any_treatment.

B) The Mayo Clinic states assistive devices or surgery could be solutions ‒ http://www.mayoclinic.com/health/muscular-dystrophy/DS00200/DSECTION=treatments-and-drugs.

Step 1. Consult a professional.

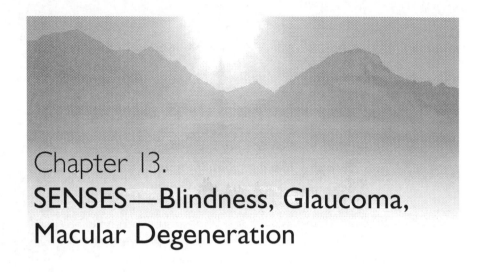

Chapter 13.
SENSES—Blindness, Glaucoma, Macular Degeneration

What Is Blindness?

Jim

I am a happy and well-grounded person. Incidentally, I am blind, without sight since birth. If I had been sighted and then some event caused vision loss, I might feel resentful and deprived, however, having always been blind, it is the only way of life I know. I am quite functional in the sighted world—I just function differently than most.

The five of us—my parents, two siblings, and I—got along well on our farm in the Midwest. Early on, I had it pretty good. People took care of me, until my family learned I needed to know how to do things for myself. I am glad! A social worker visited our home and explained there was a residential school facility in the state for visually impaired children. So away I went for sometimes up to three weeks at a time. It was quite a serious situation for this young person. I missed my family and home terribly when away, but was grateful because the schooling was excellent, teachers were inspirational, and I believe my strength of character was allowed to develop. My family also provided a sturdy foundation for me and played a tremendous role in helping me to become the person I am. Our parents are now deceased, but I will always be grateful to them for giving me sure footing. Fortunately, I continue to be close to my siblings, though we are scattered in different states. One sibling and I e-mail almost every day, and we are quite concerned about the other sibling, who has become less communicative. We do see each other as often as possible through the year, and getting together is enjoyable for all of us.

After graduating from high school, I attended college at Central College in Pella and went on to receive my master's degree at the University of Iowa in Iowa City. While attending graduate school, I worked an internship for the Department for the Blind. I also interned for a time at a nearby Independent Living Center (ILC). ILC agencies help people with disabilities remain living in the community rather than live in an institution.

It seems the internship at the Department for the Blind was extremely valuable, and I was quite pleased to be hired. I have maintained this position and enjoy my work very much.

I have the experience of living life as most people do. I ride a shuttle bus to work each day, about an hour each way. I have a hired driver at times, I walk many places, and when I am feeling particularly sociable and they are available, friends will offer to drive me. I have a reader who comes to my home during the week and tells me about bills I have received, newsletters, and other items that have come in the mail. I also take and type up meeting minutes and create newsletters for groups to which I belong.

There are numerous assistive devices available for me to use, many of which I utilize both at home and at work. I have screen reader software on my computer, which reads to me what is on the screen. I make use of other computer software, which functions as a Braille laptop with calculator and calendar. Another device I sometimes employ is a Brailler. It is similar to a typewriter, although the Brailler uses six keys and Braille paper to produce a document readable with touch. These and other items allow me to have normal and productive days. It is all about thinking differently and works out great for me.

I do find there are advantages to being blind. I consider myself extremely fortunate, because were I sighted, I might work in a different profession and enjoy myself less. Also, when speaking to others, I find that verbal information is often more understandable, because it is described to me more fully, more thoroughly. Now there is a benefit! There is little doubt that people can adapt to many different situations; blindness is just one of those situations.

One of my most memorable events took place in the summer of 1977. The baseball team from my hometown went to state. Being allowed to accompany them was tremendous. It was wonderful getting to know the players and their families. Winning a tournament game and playing two other closely contested games provided enough excitement to last a lifetime. Loving baseball as I do, I have traveled to attend professional baseball games in St. Louis, Missouri. I also happen to have a special softball so I can play. The ball emits beeps so it may be easily located. There are times I visit the park just to hit a few; it seems I cannot get enough of the game.

Another experience I have enjoyed is travel. I love traveling and have vacationed all over the world. I have been to places like Russia, New Zealand, Mexico, Costa Rica, and England. The experience of different cultures comes to me through smells, sounds, the weather, and the people, especially the people, of the particular location. My excursion to Costa Rica was a hiking trip. Learning of the plant life and animals in the area, added to the usual experiential methods, was great. It was quite fun and interesting.

Already I have mentioned how successfully I feel I can live and work within the sighted world. I use a cane to help me navigate when walking. Occasionally people forget I do sometimes need additional assistance, and this can create some awkward situations. At those times, what I try to do is to create a more comfortable environment. Recently, I encountered a person greeting customers when entering the restaurant I was visiting. I asked where I might get change and I was told, "Oh yes, right over there." Perhaps you will understand how those directions were less than helpful, so I said, "Could you guide me a bit?" The person graciously complied. When buying groceries, I have my cane with me, because I walk to the store. At times, the person at the checkout counter will ask if I need help out to my car. I often say, "Would *you* ride with me?" We enjoy a laugh, after which I am on my way—my cane, groceries, and I.

In the future, I look forward to meeting a compatible soul, living our lives together, and retiring in Florida, as warmth suits me more than cold. The lowest time in my life came when I heard some anecdotal information that only one woman in a million would marry a blind man. I took this to heart and felt a sense of worthlessness—that I had little to offer a woman. Over the years, I have come to understand that, just like much anecdotal information, this hurtful statement was completely false. I enjoy opportunities for dating; I just haven't met the right person as of this time.

I have worked for the same employer for sixteen years as a project manager. I have helped people with disabilities in many ways, once by creating more accessible voting sites for people with disabilities. I have been on the board of the state's Department for the Blind for three years. I did own a condominium and now own a house, which I believe is quite an accomplishment. Of this I am particularly proud. I excel at what I do, I have accomplished much, and I look forward with anticipation to what I will yet achieve.

Blindness

— Is/Cause

A) Kids Health informs us vision problems can develop before a child is born. Other causes might be accident, diabetes, or cataracts ~ http://kidshealth.org/kid/health_problems/sight/visual_impaired.html.

B) The World Health Organization says blindness due to uncontrolled diabetes is increasing worldwide, even as blindness due to infection is decreasing ~ http://www.who.int/topics/blindness/en/.

— Symptoms

A) The New York Times-Health Guide explains that partial blindness means very limited vision, complete blindness means there is no vision and light is not visible ~ New York Times-Health Guide, April 28, 2009 ~ http://health.nytimes.com/health/guides/symptoms/blindness/overview.html.

B) Medicinenet explains that when a person is blind from birth, or when it happens gradually, it is easier to accept than if it were to happen suddenly ~ http://www.medicinenet.com/blindness/page2.htm.

– *Tips*

A) Medicinenet tells us that in different countries, treatment depends on the cause of blindness and might be cured by changing nutrition, cataract surgery, or medication for infection ~ http://www.medicinenet.com/blindness/page3.htm

B) The Unite For Sight Organization states cataract surgery replaces the affected lens with an artificial one and has a high degree of success ~ http://www.uniteforsight.org/eye-health-course/module2.

Step 1. See "Blood, Diabetes," this book.

Step 2. Consult a professional.

WHAT IS GLAUCOMA?

Rose

Growing up in a rural area of the Midwest was an extremely pleasant experience. We were a close family: my parents, sibling, and I. The most striking memory I have of that time is a non-event, because when my parents argued, we did not know about it. If disagreements did occur, they were conducted out of children's hearing. What an effort that must have taken, but what wonderful results! We have carried on the tradition for our own progeny. My sibling is eight years younger than I, and I enjoyed being the protector as well as a "parent." As I aged, I grew emotionally and intellectually in many ways, but did not grow a great deal taller. That is okay, as there always has been a person handy who can reach what I cannot. My first spouse and two of my children were/are quite tall. I also realize now how resourceful I can be. My resourcefulness has especially come into play with vision. There will be more discussion about that later.

Dancing seems to be a theme in my life, as this is how I met both of my spouses (spouci?). I can hear you saying, "Both?" My first husband and I had three children, all the same gender. This fun-loving and wonderful person passed away with cancer when the children were young adults. They are now grown. One child is a high school science teacher who is great with students; even they say so. One child is self-employed and the other is general manager at a business. What terrific adults they have become! When marrying my second husband, I inherited three more children, about the same ages, two more the same gender, and one different. Boy, when we get together with children, grandchildren, and great-grandchildren, it is a p-a-r-t-y! I am incredibly proud of my whole family and tell them so often.

But I am straying from the topic. That can easily happen when speaking of loved ones! Dancing—it is extremely enjoyable. I need only minimal vision, it is less strenuous than other activities, and is a great way to socialize. I love all kinds of dancing: ballroom, square dancing, any kind of dancing. I guess I just have the rhythm in me. I also love to socialize, so it is a double plus. We have relatives who will drive many miles to dance to a particular band. We are less devoted fans and will enjoy whoever is playing the music. Dancing has remained a constant and a favorite pastime.

My vision trouble started about ten years ago. I had difficulty focusing on print while reading and seeing in the distance was an added issue. I could tell my eyesight had changed, so I went to the optometrist, thinking I needed new glasses. Imagine my surprise when I was told I had glaucoma and cataracts. I was also told that the glaucoma pressure had to be reduced before the cataracts could be removed. Wasn't I fortunate? I had been using compensatory measures, such as driving with a co-pilot, however, I thought things were at least okay. Anyway, off I went to see an ophthalmologist, who gave me eyedrops and said, "Even if you use these, you will be blind in two years." That shook me to the core! I realized then how very important the eyes are. Imagine if that happened, I would never again see the faces of the people I love or beautiful sunrises and sunsets. I would live in a world of darkness. Was that frightening? Oh yes!

What helped me get through this period was my faith that God would guide me and that He would help me cope with whatever happened. I prayed for some kind of miracle.

After faithfully using the drops for a time, I started to notice some loss of vision in one eye. It has been permanent, but one does adapt. Finally, I thought, *I am seeking another opinion.* Thank goodness I did, because the response from the second doctor was, "Sure, we can do laser surgery." It was the miracle for which I had prayed! I believe all things happen for a reason, and my experience has shown me how to appreciate the many wonderful things in life.

The surgery involved using the laser to pierce one eye in several spots to relieve pressure, waiting, and then the other eye was pierced to do the same. Next, more waiting was involved, using eyedrops before the cataracts could be removed. I am enormously thankful for the divine guidance to seek the second ophthalmologist, who was knowledgeable, positive, and helpful. With twice yearly checkups, I remain sighted. I am so blessed!

I take credit for being wise in some areas, because I have had several sad and some marvelous experiences. When one child was three years old, two doctors were consulted and a diagnosis of diabetes was made just in the nick of time; we were almost the parents of two instead of three. The illness and death of my first husband was a learning experience for me. We grew quite close during that time, and the grace and joy one person can display under dire circumstances made a lasting impression on me. Each night, though it may take some time, I focus on the day's positives. What a marvelous gift my former husband passed on to me. I am so fortunate. Having been married thirty-five years, my second husband and I have enjoyed many good times. We do things like Halloween costume parties at our home, couples' bridal showers, some fabulous vacations—like to Hawaii—and we go south every year for the winter. Yes, we are "snowbirds," and we enjoy it very much.

We spend our time wherever it is warm, waiting to leave the South until long after others have left and arriving early fall, before the Midwest weather cools. Whether we are in the southern regions or farther north, we are social butterflies. When we are at home, our days are packed full of going out to eat, out-of-town trips, visiting relatives and friends, family reunions, celebrations, fishing, ball games, any other excuse to have a get-together, and dances. When we are south, we go out to eat, swim, visit with neighbors and friends, take bike rides, fish, entertain visiting friends and relatives (northerners), travel to another country, bowl, find any other excuse to have a get-together, and go to dances. Do you see any similarities?

I am happy whether I am south or north. I enjoy people, and if relationships are any indication, people enjoy being with me. I fill my days with positives, having learned this from parents, now gone, my sibling, my children, and my marriages. These crucial interactions have helped me deal with a recent, additional, health issue that has surfaced. While I need some time to grieve for healthy days gone by, I am most grateful for having the ability to be a good wife, mother, grandmother, and great-grandmother. I do like to have a good time, and there is no better time than gathering with family. I am also grateful for sight, functionality, and, thank the Lord, for each healthy day that presents itself. As long as I am enjoying myself, I think I will just keep dancing!

Glaucoma

– Is/Cause

A) The Glaucoma Organization says it is a group of eye diseases that can damage the optic nerve and cause vision loss – http://www. glaucoma.org/glaucoma/.

B) The Mayo Clinic goes on to explain that increased fluid pressure inside the eye usually causes the damage – http://www.mayoclinic. com/health/glaucoma/DS00283.

– Symptoms

A) According to the Mayo Clinic, there are different types of glaucoma. Open angle has gradual peripheral vision loss and, when advanced, tunnel vision – http://www.mayoclinic.com.

B) Signs of acute angle-closure glaucoma could be severe eye pain, nausea and vomiting, and blurred vision - http://www.mayoclinic.com/health/glaucoma/DS00283/DSECTION=symptoms.

Author's Note—The open/closed angle glaucoma is confirmed by several other sources.

– Tips

A) The National Eye Institute states that glaucoma can be treated, and with early stage open-angle glaucoma, progression of the disease can be delayed. Medication, laser surgery, conventional surgery, and eye drops can be used for treatment - http://www.nei.nih.gov/health/glaucoma/glaucoma_facts.asp#4a.

B) National Glaucoma Research speaks of additional, potential treatments - http://www.ahaf.org/glaucoma/treatment/.

Step 1. Consult a professional.

WHAT IS MACULAR DEGENERATION (AMD)?

Marie

When I was a youngster, we were a family of eleven, living in a small Midwestern agricultural town. There were two parents and nine children. Within the family, we had enough players for a baseball team, so we took advantage of our numbers. As a matter of fact, it was through baseball that I met my future husband of sixty years. We had mutual friends at the games and we were attracted to each other. I digress. Before my siblings and I were vaccinated for respiratory diphtheria, I was fortunate (?) enough to come down with the infectious illness. One other sibling also contracted the disease. The family was quarantined for two weeks, and two family members stayed away from the home for that time. It is unknown whether diphtheria is related to some of my future health experiences. I have had difficulties regulating heart rhythm, which once required a stay in the hospital, and have recently discovered this could be related to having had diphtheria. Respiratory diphtheria can infect the muscles around the heart.

Sewing and knitting clothes for the family was almost an occupation from early on. I became proficient in my abilities and sent articles of clothing, during WWII, to those fighting the good fight. We all did our part. When the conflict had ended and my future spouse had returned home, we were in contact. We dated two years before marrying and clearly made a wise decision when we chose to wed.

Following our marriage, my spouse attended college. We moved from one Midwest state to another as he selected the medical field for a career. We were away from home four years while my husband learned a profession. It was during this time that I became ill, months before his graduation, and required bed rest and one surgery. Upon returning home, an excellent and wonderfully gentle practitioner was added to a very distinguished field. This kind and quietly intelligent person was loved by all. After a time, it seemed we were prepared to be parents. Because of my previous health difficulties, we adopted two children and now have a grandchild ready to enter the armed service. Both children live less than an hour away and both are in a service occupation. I am quite proud of this and their other superior qualities. We are a family that cares for others.

Before the diagnosis of macular degeneration, I noticed blurring of different objects and had trouble with night vision. Hmmm ... this could not be my glasses. I kept cleaning the lenses anyway. I quit driving at night altogether, because vision was difficult enough during the day. I have also used several items as aids to my vision. A lightbulb brighter than any regular bulb helps me when trying to focus on pictures or reading, a magnifying glass can also assist when reading, and a tint to my eyeglass lenses is helpful.

Eye examinations had been a yearly routine for me for some time. About ten years ago, my eye doctor noticed the beginning stages leading to macular degeneration. When I asked what the treatment for this illness would be, the doctor said, "Well, we pierce the eye with a needle to inject medication." My eye? A needle? This I had to think about for a while! After talking to others and some consideration, I thought, *If this is the treatment I will do it. After all, what else is there?* I could live with injections or let my eyes become worse. Injections turned out to be only a mild discomfort. I have had treatments in both eyes, one is better than the other. I am now grateful that progression of the disease seems to have halted.

I have always continued to sew, and take pride in my work. Perhaps this led to becoming a vendor at craft shows. Whenever I displayed the items I had created, it was a family affair. My spouse and one offspring would set up the tent and tables, while the other offspring and I would display my wares and collect the money. I thoroughly enjoyed these efforts, from family participation to making saleable items, to meeting prospective buyers of my product. When I started having trouble seeing well enough to sew frequently, I stopped attending craft shows. In the past, I have sewed gifts for others, making beautiful articles of clothing, if I may comment modestly. Now sewing is undertaken only for repair, if at all. My darkest days have come since I cannot sew. The needle of the sewing machine is too small for me to thread! The first time this happened, I was alarmed and thought, *What is this? Maybe it's my glasses.* Then I had to get someone else to help me with the threading. The interest to sew is gone, so now I focus on family.

Family is of supreme importance to me. Our immediate family and the family of one sibling in particular, spent a great deal of time together and we still have outings. When our two children would meet with the others' four children, it was quite a time. We were both quite social families, which is how we came to belong to the square dance camper's group. I can hear you saying, "The what?" As a family project we learned how to square dance. Because we camped with a trailer, it seemed natural to combine the two, so we did! We would leave home on Fridays, after my spouse was finished working, and meet the rest of the local group at a predetermined location. Many couples had children the same age as ours; their families had also learned to square dance, and we all camped. On Saturday night, we would all dress up in our square dance finery and dance. After the dance, we would have "finger food," which might have been prepared on-site. My husband, with my assistance, was the National Square Dance Camping Association president for eight years. It was an effort, as well as quite an honor!

One constant throughout the years has been our dedication to religion and our attendance at weekly services. The children attended religious schools, and I have volunteered for the church in many capacities. I have collected coupons, served thirteen years on the board of a fundraising group, and took advantage of other services offered by the church. My husband and I used the church hall to host our fiftieth anniversary, and we renewed our vows for that anniversary during a church service. My spouse, sadly, has passed away. An accomplishment of which I am most proud is being married sixty years and I miss my companion each day.

Now I try to look forward; I delight in the new puppy who has entered my life. Other things I look forward to are for others rather than myself. I look forward to the end of fighting, so men and women can come home to be with their families. I look forward to people being able to find jobs. I look forward to continued happiness for my children and grandchild. I am extraordinarily proud of them and their service to others. As you can tell, my rural upbringing leads me to focus on family, and I love them mightily. Additionally, I truly believe service to others is the highest calling one can achieve!

AMD

– *Definitions*

Macula—the central portion of the retina.

Retina—the light-sensitive tissue that lines the back of the eye.

– *Is/Cause*

A) According to AMD Awareness, AMD is a chronic disease causing central vision loss and affects mostly people sixty years or older – http://www.amdawareness.org/asrs/?cid=luc_we_F001053_P000517 &gclid=CKCNu83ygakCFcO8KgodnVnGVQ.

B) Medlineplus states AMD is a disease in which the sharp, central vision is destroyed. central vision allows seeing clearly and is needed for things like reading and driving ~ http://www.nlm.nih.gov/medlineplus/maculardegeneration.html.

− Symptoms

A) Lighthouse International states there are different symptoms for wet and dry AMD. Wet AMD symptoms might be wavy or distorted objects. Dry symptoms might be trouble with reading, driving, and watching television. It is important to get a complete eye exam regularly ~ http://www.lighthouse.org/about-low-vision-blindness/vision-disorders/age-related-macular-degeneration-amd/wet-amd-symptoms/.

B) Medlineplus explains the destruction of the macula can cause blurred, distorted, and dim vision ~ http://www.nlm.nih.gov/medlineplus/ency/article/001000.htm.

Author's Note—the author learned that wet AMD can be more severe and dry AMD can happen in stages.

− Tips

A) The American Foundation for the Blind has suggestions for living with AMD. Possibly learning to look out the right or left of side of the eye, or a goose-necked or press-on lamp might help where vision is needed ~ http://www.afb.org/Section.asp?SectionID=93&DocumentID=5217#tips.

B) Prevent Blindness also has tips to see better which involve light. Painting rooms light colors and buying sheer curtains to allow more light could help. There are also other suggestions ~ http://www.preventblindness.org/resources/factsheets/AMD_tips_MK15.PDF.

Author's Note—Low-vision aids, such as goggles by Opti Vision, are worn on the head and can magnify smaller items. Such goggles can possibly be found where craft items are available.

Step 1. Consult a professional.

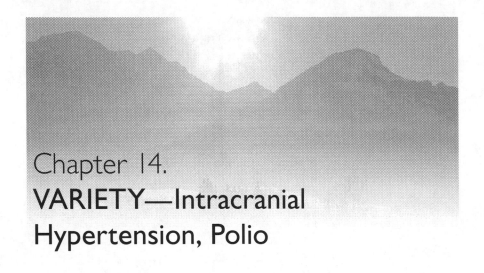

Chapter 14.
VARIETY—Intracranial Hypertension, Polio

WHAT IS INTRACRANIAL HYPERTENSION (IH)?

Felicia

People have often said I am a free spirit, and my friends have often called me "gypsy." Perhaps that is the reason I enjoy my current job so much. My husband travels with me, and our daily schedule is never the same. We visit different towns, different hotels, and see different people. This life suits me well.

About fifteen years ago, I was working as a waitress. Without a doubt, my dream job is very different, but at that time I was still searching. At least as a waitress I got to see different customers coming into the restaurant each day, and that was enjoyable. Then I started having horrible headaches! The first one went on for three days—and they kept happening! What was the reason for this much pain? The headaches were so bad they were interfering with my job and my life. Along with the pain, I would have dim vision and blurring. Sometimes there would be a sound in my ears, a whooshing with a rhythm which matched my blood pulsing. To make it even more awful, the pain would be in different areas of my head on different days. Was this a migraine? It seemed that the headaches were even worse than that!

It took only a few of these to send me to the doctor seeking help. That first visit, I was given heavy painkillers for migraine headache and sent on my way. I started taking the medicine, but it didn't touch the pain. I thought I would die when the headaches happened repeatedly, maybe death would have been a blessing. It seemed that I would have the pain forever, as if it hadn't been already! After months with no diagnosis, I had to wonder if I *was* going to die; actually, I wished for it. I couldn't live this way; I wasn't much good to myself or anyone else. I was living from blinding headache to blinding headache and it was impeding my life! I wondered what people would think if I committed suicide. Would they forgive me? Would God forgive me? How would my family survive without me? What would my children do?

It was my children who saved me. I realized that I couldn't leave them, because there were yet many things to tell them which only their mother could help them learn.

There were many trips to the doctor, seeing several doctors with many tests, and eight weeks later I was diagnosed with intracranial hypertension (IH). The doctors found I had a high level of cerebral spinal fluid (CSF), and only appropriate medications helped lessen the pain. The most common drug used is acetazolamide (Diamox), and, thankfully, it works for me. Also, I have learned that lowering the pressure in my skull relieves the headache, so lumbar punctures, or spinal taps, to remove the quickly regenerating CSF could ease an IH headache temporarily. Possibly a shunt would be a consideration to make the process easier.

Since the diagnosis, I am very frustrated that there is little awareness about IH. When I go to a new doctor, it seems that I know more than he/she does. The most frustrating of all is that people do not understand the pain I go through. When I talk about my headaches, someone always follows up with, "Oh yeah, I get migraines, too." Or they'll say, "Yeah, I know when I had my epidural before labor, it was awful." I promise you, it isn't the same thing. I have found that it's important to take medication records with me everywhere I go. When people with IH have an episode, we don't feel like giving a lesson about IH. Immediate relief is our goal!

I am inspired by the others who have IH and their efforts to promote awareness. Before my diagnosis, I was unaware of IH, as is often the case with such a problem. It's important to get the word out. My way of living life is to take things day by day, and I try to enjoy the days that are good. I'm living my most memorable times now, because I can work my own hours, we travel, and I spend most of my time working from hotel rooms. I can enjoy myself at work and in the off-hours. We do lots of sightseeing in this beautiful country of ours, and I can now enjoy it.

IH has made me a much stronger person. I am always learning—about people, my job, and about IH. Doctors are a necessary part of life and yet my viewpoint toward them is extremely cynical. Perhaps I've had my fill. Recently, I lost forty pounds, and I continue to keep my weight down so it is not an issue. I feel terrific, and it helps with the IH! I look forward to retirement, and I think life experiences make you who you are. It is my choice that those experiences are positive.

IH

— Is/Cause

A) The Intracranial Hypertension Research Foundation (IHRF) explains that three components, CSF, blood, and veins work together in a delicate balance. The skull is made of bone and cannot expand, so an increase in the volume of any one component is at the expense of the other two - http://www.ihrfoundation.org/intracranial/hypertension/info/C16.

B) The IHRF states that intracranial hypertension means the pressure of the cerebrospinal fluid (CSF) in the skull is too high - http://www.ihrfoundation.org/intracranial/hypertension/info/C16

— Symptoms

A) The IHRF says most people with chronic IH have three particular symptoms: severe headache, visual changes, and a whooshing sound in one or both ears correlating with the tempo of the pulse - http://www.ihrfoundation.org/intracranial/hypertension/info/C18.

B) Medlineplus states there can also be a buzzing sound, dizziness and nausea ~ http://www.nlm.nih.gov/medlineplus/ency/article/000351. htm.

– **Tips**

A) According to the IHRF, medication and surgery are often used to treat IH ~ http://www.ihrfoundation.org/intracranial/hypertension/ info/C31.

B) Suggestions by Emedicine Medscape tell us treatment concentrates on maintaining optic nerve function, while the increased IH pressure is managed. A further statement is that weight loss is a cornerstone to managing IH pain. They go on to explain

- It's been shown "as little as a 5-10% weight loss" can help.
- Consulting a dietician is important. ~ http://emedicine. medscape.com/article/1214410-treatment.

Step 1. Consult a professional.

What Is Polio?

Marco

Education of young people was my life for thirty years; teaching was truly my calling, as I loved every minute of it. My mother was a teacher, and it seemed to be a natural development for me to follow in her footsteps. I began my career instructing beginner students and then transferred to the middle grades of elementary school. There was an opportunity to move into administration, but I knew where my talents lay and chose to stay with what I loved. It was the most rewarding decision I ever made. Besides my mother and father, two sisters round out my family. There are several nieces and nephews, who have also provided joyful times over the years.

When I was a child, maybe five years old, my friends and I played in an irrigation ditch. There were about a dozen of us and most did not become ill. However, two of us did. I went inside and carried on as if nothing was wrong, but little did I know life-changing consequences were about to take place. My symptoms at first seemed like a cold, almost pneumonia. Then came the fever of 103 degrees, when I lost control of my limbs. A four-month-long coma followed, minus two days. What I remember then is waking up in an iron lung machine at the hospital. An iron lung is a machine used to breathe for a person when that person's muscle control is insufficient, like a ventilator. A plastic tent, providing oxygen, covered my chest. At five, what was I to think? I had been diagnosed with polio. Other people might know the disease only as an abstraction; well let me help them out. Polio viral infection is caused by direct, person-to-person contact, contact with mucus from an infected person, or contact with infected feces. I have the worst of three types: 2 percent or less of people contracting polio have paralytic polio. I was one of that category.

More than anything else, my right leg was affected; I used crutches when I left the hospital. Three adults, my mother, father, and grandmother worked my legs and massaged them to help my legs limber up and support me as I walked. We had to strengthen my back muscles as well. Without this assistance, I would have had much less function these many years. My family was great, I loved each of them, and I am indebted to them all. By walking with braces, I astounded the doctors.

As I got older, I wondered how I was going to make a living. I was afraid I'd never be able to be employed and amount to anything other than an invalid, which I had been called all the way through school. As a senior in high school, I began to wonder, "Where am I going after this year?" I was very limited in my physical abilities and had no job training to gain an income after this. I then buckled down and decided I had to go to college, but when I did, I thought I would never make it through! With encouragement from my parents, I did make it. The hand of God was in there, too. I worked to prove that just because I walked differently, it wasn't going to mean I couldn't make a good life for myself. I was a better college student than high school student. I was able to put myself in the classroom for thirty years and loved it.

My parents were industrious people, and following their example, I am industrious as well, though circumstances are limiting. I tried to make learning fun and colorful for my students, and I think I was successful in that effort. When I graduated from college and started working, I had summers off so I would help my dad. We did room renovations and painted inside or outside for people. We were moonlighting, you might say. We *were* pretty handy as a team. He had many word-of-mouth referrals, so people must have been pleased with the finished product.

Since retirement, I have been having post-polio symptoms for about the last ten years. This illness strikes about 25–50 percent of people who had polio as a young child. Post-polio is somewhat different from polio. Symptoms are muscle weakness, muscle pain, and fatigue. Yup, I am three for three. Also, my right leg is shorter now, so I am a little lopsided. My lung muscles are also weaker, so I breathe via supplemental oxygen. I get to pull my tank wherever I go. It tends to bother me to have people staring and wondering, *What is the reason for the tank?* I wish they would just come over and ask me instead of staring. Asking me if I object to questions could be a good conversation starter. My back muscles are also weak, so I tend to walk and stand bent over. It's hard to ask for help, but an assistant does stay with me at night. We are now quite comfortable with each other.

There are two things I would like to recommend to people. The first is to all mothers: have your child vaccinated! The second is to anyone who is healthy and thinks it's clever to park in a handicapped parking place. Yes, it's closer. Do you suppose there's a reason? Likely, there is someone who really needs the space.

I think polio has impacted me in a positive way. I have learned a great deal about myself and am understanding of others. I also understand my situation and have avoided bitterness; that would be useless, pointless, and hurt only me. I'm reminded of something I heard on television about bitterness being like taking poison and hoping the other person dies. It's unhealthy. Well, I am sixty-eight years old and have grown up with my limitations, so as far as I am concerned, it is the way it is. Fortunately, any pain is mostly alleviated with aspirin a few times a week.

I do wonder if I will ever move out of my current phase and when it will be. My body is going, and I wonder which part will be the next effected. Pain is a constant companion, and I can no longer work or travel for distraction and enjoyment. It's hard for me to continually worsen, and the doctors seem unaware of any possibilities to help. I keep going, as I want to prove that I can come out of polio's effects again. I have a lot of support from other people, which is great help. There are many people worse off than I, and I try to remind myself of this daily.

Staying as healthy as possible is crucial for most people, so I go to the gym each morning. I walk the treadmill, slowly, and ride the bicycle. We are a chummy group, the people who come to the health club in the morning. It is good to have friends. A man spoke to me the other day when I was doing my routine. He explained that he belongs to the club, is healthy, and has neglected coming for some time. He said I was an inspiration to him, so he will come more often. Well, that is exciting news for me, because I enjoy being around and talking to people. If what I do inspires others, it makes me feel better. Inspiration is important for everyone!

I feel good about being a productive contributor during my working years. I have bought and sold a couple of homes and live in my house alone now; independence is important to me. I will be going north shortly, to a cabin I own. A gentleman comes to the cabin once a week to check on me when I am there. I do enjoy my solitude. I also still get excited about helping others learn and I'm sure that will continue!

Polio

— Is/Cause

A) The Mayo Clinic explains polio is caused by the poliovirus and that the last naturally occurring U.S. case was diagnosed in 1979 ~ http://www.mayoclinic.com/health/polio/DS00572.

B) According to PubMed Health, there are three ways to spread the virus: direct person-to-person contact, by contact with infected mucus or phlegm from the nose or mouth, or by contact with infected feces ~ http://www.ncbi.nlm.nih.gov/pubmedhealth/PMH0002375/.

– Symptoms

A) Medicinet explains most people infected with the virus have non-paralytic polio. Those people might have flu-like symptoms such as fatigue, fever, headache, or sore throat – http://www.medicinenet.com/polio/page2.htm.

B) The Mayo Clinic says the very serious paralytic polio will show signs within a week of infection, such as loss of reflexes and muscle aches or spasms – http://www.mayoclinic.com/health/polio/DS00572/DSECTION=symptoms.

– Tips

A) The Immunization Action Coalition states there is no cure. Supportive therapy is what is needed along with fluids and bed rest – http://www.immunize.org/catg.d/p4215.pdf.

B) The Mayo Clinic says focus is on increasing comfort. It may involve antibiotics, moderate exercise, and a nutritious diet – http://www.mayoclinic.com/health/polio/DS00572/DSECTION=treatments-and-drugs.

Step 1. Consult a professional.

SECTION C:
RELATED ISSUE

There are two ways of spreading light—to be the candle, or the mirror that reflects it.

Edith Wharton

Caregivers are angels. They give their time and energy to make the lives of others more comfortable and bearable. Please know that your efforts are noticed and appreciated.

Chapter 15.
CAREGIVING

WHAT IS CAREGIVING?

Lisa

My first husband and I were born and raised in different western states, but our futures were cast in the stars. We met when I was in high school. He managed the ice cream shop where we worked, and he was my boss; we'll call him Greg. After serving ice cream for a while, it was clear to anyone looking that we had fallen for each other. Unfortunately, when we became engaged, we had to find different employment. Even so, it was mighty exciting, as a senior in high school, to be the only one in the class engaged to be married! As concerned parents, mine stipulated we wait one year before marrying. This was fine with us, and we actually waited thirteen months before the wedding. Greg and I were married twenty-eight eventful years.

Just starting out, we worked and saved our money. Then we purchased a restaurant in a different city, moved, and raised our family. It was well known that our restaurant had the tastiest seafood around! We also took many vacations around the United States with our sons. It was an idyllic life, doing what we loved with the people we loved.

Then we decided to sell our business, and Greg went on to work for a country club. It was while he was working there that my husband began having symptoms. Symptoms of what, you ask? Well, we were just as curious, but the country club decided to let Greg go anyway. Does that sound fair?

Greg was an area manager for a chain of restaurants when the symptoms really flared up. He was numb on all of his left side and had difficulty with balance and coordination. Greg stopped working then, but afterward, the owner of the restaurant chain really went to bat for us. He helped us modify our house to be accessible, and even delivered the eulogy at Greg's funeral. We still stay in contact. What a special person!

At the beginning, when Greg initially went to see his doctor, she didn't know of a diagnosis for his symptoms. Greg was told, "Go home and live with it." This was unbelievable to me and totally unsatisfactory. When I researched a bit more, I found a neurologist who diagnosed multiple sclerosis (MS). Well, we had an answer, but I was very angry. The thought of leaving Greg came and went; I loved my husband, and the kids were looking to me as a role model. I vowed we would do something about MS instead! The doctor prescribed steroids. The steroids helped Greg rally for a time, but eventually led to many IVs and cravings for frozen pot pies and milkshakes.

Instead of death in six months to a year, as this doctor thought might happen, Greg lived on. By golly, my kids were going to keep their dad a while! We were having none of the doctor's prediction, and thirteen months after diagnosis, Greg said, "I guess I showed her." He actually lived for fifteen more years. What a brave soul Greg was. He would throw a baseball with his sons, sometimes sitting while he did. We would camp out in the backyard. Greg might have to drag himself out of the tent and need help to stand, but sleeping outside was something he wanted to share with us. He did what he could for as long as he could.

It was eleven years following the diagnosis of MS that I became a caregiver for my husband. I had no idea where this role would take me, and it was helpful that I was unaware what the future held. It was hard, probably close to hell, but my children and I survived. Looking back, I wouldn't change a thing. Greg needed us there, to not abandon him, and we were a family united.

Every day I would think, *It will be okay if things just stay as they are.* However, things always changed and progressed, so I always had more with which to deal. Because my husband was unable to work, I worked two jobs in addition to my duties at home. With two boys to raise, I feel our family did incredibly well to come through the illness as positively as we did. My younger son was always aware of his dad's being sick, but my older son had to deal with much confusion. He had memories of baseball and numerous other activities with his dad, when Greg was mobile. Fortunately he handled it okay, because I had other issues that needed my attention. My days were filled with necessary things to do, such as getting the boys up for school, making sure Greg was fed breakfast, getting ready for work, and going to work. Then, after working the morning shift, I would come home for lunch, make sure my husband was fed, and go back to work. When that shift was over, I went home, made sure Greg was fed, and that he had all his meds. Around ten, I would make sure he was comfortable, so hopefully he had all he needed for the night. I would go to bed with a baby monitor from his room to mine. Eventually we built a handicapped room. I had little time to think except for what needed to be done. I kept it together by remembering the words of my mother like a mantra: "You never give up and never give in." It helped me through many days!

My mother's words were already a well-learned lesson when I was young. My parents divorced when I was four years old, and I was their only child. Though my father had custody, I lived with my aunt, because my father worked nights. My aunt was the most loving, giving, caring person I have known, and I miss her dearly. My mom would pick me up on weekends and eventually remarried. My stepfather is a great guy. Even though my sister and I have different fathers, she is absolutely awesome. She is as close to me as any sister could be. I feel the same about my brothers. My family was a tremendous support system throughout my trials. Often they would drop whatever was happening in their lives to drive to our house and assist us with ours. What angels they were! I lost my father to suicide when I was an adult, before my caregiving venture began. I miss him very much. It seems I was close to adversity from the beginning, so caregiving wasn't frightening for me. For this reason and others, it came naturally.

Fortunately, during the last two years my husband was at home, I was able to receive assistance from Medicare and Medicaid. Also, others were able to take some of the workload. That was a relief! We also had some lighter moments. My sons would be in their dad's room, would change the TV to a channel he hated, and then leave the room. Someone was always close by, so they could change the channel for Greg, and he would grin and say, "Those ornery kids!" During the last year of his life, Greg was in a nursing home. Neither of us liked it, but it was the most practical option at the time. Greg really understood.

Throughout years of caregiving, unquestionably, I had strong emotions to confront. The man I married no longer existed; I grieved for the loss. My children had to become caregivers because they needed to feed their dad. I worried how this was affecting them. I always had worries over money. I often felt anger, almost rage, but it wasn't directed at any person, and that darned MS seemed to always progress. Another issue that bothered me was the concern others had for my husband. I was always appreciative, though there was little understanding of my situation. At times, I was so weary and bone tired that I could barely function. Where does one go to find relief? I had to carefully avoid showing any of my feelings. Again, I would think of my mother and hear our mantra. My sons, as always, were also part of my comfort.

Would I do it again? Absolutely. Through the experience I learned countless lessons, such as the extent of Greg's strength, and mine. I know now I have the courage to take on tremendous challenges, more than I thought possible. Now I know I can manage! Life is tough and unfair, but we do what we must. To anyone reading, I recommend, "Appreciate all of your blessings, all of the time."

The moment of truth came in December of 2003, right before Christmas. My husband passed away peacefully upon his ninth trip to the hospital. It took some time to recover from Greg's death.

Five years following my family's loss, I decided it was time to begin life anew. My sons have seemed to take their experiences in stride and have also moved on. Match.com helped put me in touch with a second fabulous gentleman. I confess sheepishly, I did ask him if he had a chronic illness; he does not. He and I have been married one year, and we are totally devoted to each other. Fortunately, my husband is a very understanding person, who lets me cry, vent, or ponder as needed. It seems I have hit the jackpot twice. Am I am lucky or what?! Looking forward, I see lots of great things and enjoyment in our future!

Jane Rominne

Beginning in the fall of 2009, I worked for a year in a home to care for people who are developmentally disabled. We were located in an urban setting in France, and there were three of us to help seven people. People usually have developmental disability to varying degrees, as did the seven sharing this home. However, people should know that those with handicaps are more intelligent than is generally realized. I respect those people for their awareness.

For one month, I worked at training and learning to know the people living at the house. This time was valuable and helped all of us to become comfortable with each other. That way personal care was less shocking for the people who required help. I was anxious at the idea of giving showers, and at the same time, I was excited to learn. Another person already knew everyone well, and she helped me as I gave showers to three of the residents. She was able to show me the movements to be used and to what we must give attention. When there was time, we would talk to the individuals about their lives. We were privileged to hear the stories they shared.

Isabelle was forty-three years old, and lived with her parents until her mom died of a cardiac arrest in front of her eyes. After that, she was placed with a host family, because none of the four brothers and sisters could welcome her into their home. Isabelle goes to an occupational workshop during the day, where she does many activities, one of which is equine-assisted therapy. She dances, performs in plays, and does manual activities like playing cards and making necklaces. She paints, makes desserts, cooks meals, goes for walks, does group relaxation, and has beauty classes. It sounds like fun, doesn't it? At the workshop they try to help the residents maintain and increase their skills by providing diverse types of things to do.

Marie was seventy-four years old and has been at the Arc for thirty years. Before that, she had lived with parents, where she helped them with the bar by washing dishes. Roger was seventy-nine years old, and when he was younger he lived with his parents who moved to Venezuela for ten years. They then returned to France, where the parents passed away. After that, he lived with his sister until he had grown so much she needed others to take care of him. He then joined the Arc. Catherine was sixty-six years old, and began living at the care center in Compiege when she was eighteen. Her family left her there, because they felt it was necessary.

Jaques was sixty-one years old; coming to Arc from a host family. Harry was sixty years old, and lived with his parents until they could keep him no longer. Emile was twenty-three, and lived with his father until the father died as a young person.

Jaques, Harry, and Emile go to an ESAT, an establishment where people with disabilities can work. Jaques' forte is the small business sector, and he does ornamental ironwork and mosaics. He opened the ironworks and now teaches others to create, even as he continues to do. Jaques is quite a passionate artist, and the pieces he designs are extraordinarily beautiful. Harry works in the section that is half-time occupational workshop, and he gardens half time. He loves to work in the garden and see things grow. He and others produce and sell fruit and organic vegetables. Emile, the youngest, is in green space. That means he goes to different individuals or companies and maintains their lawn or green space. He does things like cut trees, mow lawns, and scarifies, which is scratching the surface to encourage growth. This is something that Emile really enjoys, and being close to nature is soothing for him.

The different ages represented were a good mixture, because the active youngest helps keep the older among them to stay motivated and in good shape. Marie, Roger, and Catherine stay at home. They need time to wake up and get ready for the day. We helped them wash up, comb their hair, dress, etc. It was important to finish helping Marie, Roger, and Catherine to get ready though, because we had the cooking, cleaning, and ironing still to complete. Those three use power wheelchairs, or are able to walk inside the house and are able to sit in an armchair. We would also spend some time with each of them to connect on a personal level. It is essential to make this connection, because very often tenderness is absent from the lives of people with disabilities.

If the capabilities of a person change, or even if they want to do something different because they think it might fit them better, they may change occupations. If the person likes their work but is unhappy, we speak about it with their socio-medical team to see how we can help them be more comfortable with their job. I attended several of these focus meetings, and we do have input, because we are close to the individuals so much of the time. Many times we can say what will or will not fit the person. We always want to provide benefits to the residents!

The French standards for the houses of people with health challenges are very strict, so the home these seven people shared was quite spacious. Add to that its warm and jovial atmosphere, and the residents are very comfortable. Each client has his/her own room, as does each caregiver. The individual is able to personalize the room to his/her taste and can spend time there, but must also participate in the life of the house. Each day, the caregivers were there to provide input to a group of professionals for the people in the house, and to help direct their activities.

On the weekend, all of the residents assisted with domestic jobs. They would help us cook, clean, and make the house presentable. In our spare time, we would go shopping, to the movies, and sometimes four-wheeling. On Sundays, we would meet others and would have an alcoholic beverage before a meal. We would share a moment of friendliness around a festive table and eat good food. Residents do tend to be a bit overzealous sometimes, and we had to be careful they stayed within their voucher allotment of funds. Getting together was crucial, because eating out helped us maintain our brotherly links.

When it was time for me to leave this admirable group, many tears flowed, but the people will live forever in my heart. The group sang a song to me. It represents what we mean to each other. I was in charge of teaching the song, and we sang to each other, saying how we felt. It said, "I will keep forever the pleasant memories of this past year with Isabelle, Marie, Roger, Catherine, Jaques, Harry, and Emile when there are bad moments. We'll remember the good fondly."

I was close to all of the residents, even if sometimes they were hard on me. I had been very reserved because I had a difficult childhood. With their help, I came to understand that I had to bounce back and to appreciate every moment of life. We were a little bit similar that way, so I was glad to help the residents however I could. Thus, I left with an immense sadness and undeniable joy for having gotten to know these wonderful people. We rejoiced in our time together; we had all benefitted!

Kathy

A day in March of 2008 was destined to be a turning point in our family's lives. There were many others who would also become instrumental in our future. On this particular day, my daughter Krystal, twenty-three, was in a horrible car accident. However, the events leading up to the accident were almost as remarkable.

Krystal had just graduated from high school and married her husband when she was eighteen. From a parent's point of view, the situation was less than ideal, but from an eighteen-year-old point of view, what do parents know? The marriage was happy until Krystal's husband started using drugs, and was unable and unwilling to change, so she left after only one-and-one-half years. A few months later, her husband went to court because of the drug situation. Then a few months after that, her father died suddenly. She had tremendous difficulty dealing with this loss. Then her husband went to jail. These would have been traumatic events in anyone's life. Krystal took one body blow after the other, but being the resilient person she is, she put her life back together and forged ahead.

Krystal had met a new boyfriend and kept on working, but she started having car trouble. Actually, she phoned me the night before the accident, and talked about getting her car fixed. It kept stalling, and always at the most inconvenient times. Piecing the circumstances together, we think we know what happened. It seems that Krystal knew someone with a place where they fixed cars, and had gone to see about hers. When she got there, the shop was closed. Upon leaving, she was exiting a small side road, intersecting a highway. The road was at the bottom of a hill, and just as Krystal pulled onto the highway, her car stalled. She had to be absolutely frenzied at the frightening situation! Additionally, a nightmare scenario developed when a Suburban came over the top of the hill, driving sixty or seventy miles an hour. Was there time for the driver to stop? Of course not! What stopped the forward motion of the Suburban was hitting the driver's side of Krystal's car.

Completely oblivious at home, what I knew was that Krystal was coming to my house to help her brother move in, and he was to meet her here. I was waiting patiently for them both when the phone rang. It was a woman, telling me that Krystal had been in a car accident, had been taken to the emergency room (ER), and I should get there. That was all the information she would give. I was panicked beyond belief! I wondered, *How bad was the accident, how badly was Krystal hurt, and was anyone else hurt?* but my overriding concern was Krystal. I waited, impatiently now, and when my son arrived, we tore away from the house in his car. We sped the whole way to the hospital. Unknowing, we tried to think through all the possible scenarios as we drove as fast as we dared. Just what had happened? Talk about being frenzied, now it was our turn!

Arriving at the ER, what I learned from the nurse was that Krystal was alive. Oh, what a relief! She had been wearing her seatbelt, which broke her pelvis and collarbone, but saved her life. She also had a collapsed lung and a brain injury, among other physical damage. The doctors worked many hours to try to mend Krystal's broken body. When we were allowed to see her, she was a mass of bruises and swollen body parts. We had been afraid for her life from the time of the phone call, and seeing her lying broken and in a coma added to this dreadful thought. I had faith, though I knew that if she were to recover, it would take time and effort to repair Krystal. Even so, I was sure we would get there. I knew my daughter!

At the beginning, Krystal couldn't do anything for herself; I had to help her with everything. After receiving physical, occupational, and speech therapy, in addition to psychological help for five months, Krystal learned to walk, dress, shower, and do most things for herself. It still took several months before I could leave her alone, because she would lose her balance and sometimes fall. I still have to fix Krystal's hair and help her put jewelry on. She limps and has lost the use of her left arm and hand. She is disappointed to be viewed by men as disabled, but I tell her she is beautiful inside, and a worthy person will see it. Even after extensive therapy, Krystal still cannot use her hand very much, only to carry things like a piece of clothing or something very light. She lost some memory; for example, she has forgotten how to do math. She has also forgotten what a lot of words mean. Krystal sometimes has trouble understanding conversations. She has lost the ability to cry, is very impatient, and is much less mature than before her injuries. My daughter does retain her independence, though, and wants to do things for herself, so she won't let anyone help her if she can do it. We have to monitor Krystal, because she is having trouble making wise choices. The decisions she does make are sometimes dangerous. There are downsides and upsides to her experience.

There are a couple of funny stories when Krystal was coming back to life, as I like to call it. At first she couldn't talk; she couldn't get the words out, but she would try. It sounded like jumbled-up words. Then, when she was transferred her from Spartanburg Regional Hospital to Roger C. Peace Rehabilitation Hospital, she thought she was being kidnapped. She thought the doctor was the ringleader, and the nurses and therapists were in on it. But they apparently had seen something like this before, and continued to be nice to her. When she first went to the rehab hospital, they had to put her in what they call a safe bed. It has a net over the bed that is then zipped up, so the person can't get out or fall out. Krystal could not walk or sit up by herself, but she didn't realize that, and these were two more reasons she thought she had been kidnapped. She also said that her brother gave her a pocketknife, and she tried to saw her way out of the net. Her brother explained to her that he never had a pocketknife, and even if he had, wouldn't have given it to her.

Krystal's oldest brother came to see her and asked her if she wanted to go outside. She said, "Yes." Krystal thought he was trying to rescue her from the kidnappers. He pushed her outside in the wheelchair and then, when he brought her back into the hospital, she was saying, "No! No! No!" The only thing is, she couldn't really communicate. She was just very agitated and yelling. Her brother and the nurses thought she just wanted to stay outside, but it was getting dark, so inside they remained. It was an eventful evening at the hospital; Krystal leaves her mark wherever she goes!

Then there was the time that the doctor was checking Krystal over and raised her bad arm. He asked her if she was hurting, and because Krystal was starting to talk, she said, "No." Then the doc raised her arm up higher and asked again if it hurt. Krystal said, "Well, I wasn't hurting, but I am now, bitch!" Krystal never, ever said things like that, but she still thought the doctor was the kidnapper! She was told by the doctor to write down the kidnap story when she recognized how things actually were, and send it to him. Apparently he was very interested.

Another time, Krystal's brother took her tubing on the local Green River, and as they were floating, he fell out of his tube. Krystal's tube, with her in it, got away from him, and she was floating down the river alone and enjoying the ride. He had to swim as fast as he could, churning the water like a paddleboat, to catch up with her. If she had fallen out of her tube, she wouldn't have been able to swim on her own! He was a nervous wreck, and she was laughing her head off!

Krystal's friends won't take her anywhere like that, because they think she can't do anything. She has only one friend that will take her to the lake or pool, and her brothers take her places like the movies, and out to eat. We are planning a trip to the beach in September. The Brain Injury Alliance is having a Summer Blast at Shaw Air Force Base for adults, and young adults with disabilities. They will have tubing, swimming, canoeing, kayaking, jet skiing, fishing, boating, and wheelchair sports. We will try to go to that. Something else she might be interested in is writing. Krystal used to write a little, and there are software devices that will write when she speaks. Whatever Krystal chooses to do, she will be confident enough to accomplish. I'm very proud of her for it!

Caregiving

— Definition

Caregiver—an unpaid person, usually a family member or friend, providing assistance with the daily needs of an elderly person or person with a disability.

— Tips

A) Vital Connections provides names of caregiver support organizations - http://www.vitalco.net.

B) The National Alliance for Caregiving has a newsletter that can be received, or where an e-connected caregiver might find help - http://www.caregiving.org.

SECTION D:
STORIES PLUS

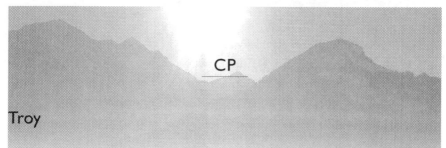

CP

Troy

Since birth, I have dealt with cerebral palsy (CP). CP doesn't define who I am, nor has it ever; it is just a part of my life. On a typical day, I get ready in the morning, and I can do it by myself. I do whatever I can and do it well. Working during the day mostly requires that I speak on the phone, and I can speak understandably. When it's needed, I can write, with effort. I drive my own chair just about anywhere I want to go. I can pull myself to my feet and need help only for watering the plants, fixing meals, feeding my cat, showering, and getting ready for the next day. I feel good about it. However, others have tried to define me as a "CP person." I learned early that this attitude could give me the push I needed to succeed.

My mother died in childbirth, so I already had a strike against me when I was born. My father remarried when I was young. This could have been a positive situation for me, except my stepmother was a "definer." To her I was a CP person, not a person with CP, and I was a burden. Strike two. My consolation was school, and I reveled in it. Each weekday, I'd go to a building housing twelve grades of only people with disabilities. The educators were caring, understanding, and I blossomed with their teaching. A hit!

In high school, one of the teachers had a saying by which I have lived my life: "Sometimes the tide comes in, and all is wonderful. Sometimes the tide goes out, and all is not so wonderful." This saying has sustained me through many unfortunate times, as well as through the good times.

Following graduation from high school, I worked as a telephone solicitor. When I had saved enough money, I moved from the East Coast to a place in the Midwest. I had heard that in the heartland there was a place for people with disabilities, they were welcomed there, and I have found it to be true. Contact between my father and me was non-existent for the three years following my move. Now it seems very unfortunate, because my father then passed away. I started working for a government agency after moving. I have been there ever since, find the work different every day, and it's extremely rewarding.

Before "the accident," I walked with crutches, so I was a bit slow but ambulatory. One fateful winter day I was going home after work. Living in an apartment in the winter means snow and ice removal from walkways is crucial for me. Trying to navigate with crutches *anytime* is a challenge. This is magnified tenfold when snow and ice removal is neglected. This day, the walks had not been completely cleared. As I was going up the apartment steps, one crutch landed squarely on a patch of ice, slipped out from under me, and I felt myself fall, tumbling down the steps. After catching my breath and taking stock of the situation, there I lay, helpless and forever changed. *Damn* it was cold, my leg was severely broken, and man-oh-man did it hurt! I was freezing *and* in pain, a world of misery. I had only arm movement, so I yelled myself hoarse before a neighbor came to help. Little did I know this was only the beginning.

After many weeks of recovery and rehabilitation, and lots of hard work, I needed to use a wheelchair full time. I have therapy yet today. I had much time to think during my rehabilitation and I decided to consult an attorney. The lawsuit I brought against the apartment building owners was successful, and I received a substantial settlement for my efforts. The compensation for my changed circumstances also changed my life in many ways. First thing, I had a choice to make; I could spend the money or I could invest it. I chose to partially invest in stock and partially invest in me. I attended college at the undergraduate level, a very worthwhile venture indeed. Because of these decisions, I am able to live, carefully, on the rewards of the choices I made.

I now live in an apartment close to work and businesses, so I can go to places I want with my electric wheelchair. It is wheelchair accessible. At home, I have help from students attending a nearby university, and a county van service takes me where I cannot travel by wheelchair. I do many extra-curricular speaking engagements. In my work, I have seen a huge change from mostly institutionalization to mostly independent living, with assistance, for people with disabilities.

It seems I live what we seek to promote at work. You see, those classes were worthwhile!

One day following the accident, a sunny, summer day, I went swimming. I was sitting on the edge of the pool, relaxing and enjoying the frolicking of other swimmers. Not thinking about much, I suddenly heard a dreadfully loud noise behind me. My fight-or-flight response took firm hold and flight was my answer. I didn't think, just reacted instantly, and jumped into the water! Oh boy, this was a fine kettle of fish, considering I had little leg movement. Fortunately, there were others close by, so I had only to keep my head above water for a few moments before being rescued.

Being insatiably curious, I have traveled to many other countries. Stops have been England, Wales, Australia, New Zealand and Africa, among others. The method of getting around is always the same and works well.

A personal assistant accompanies me, I use a manual wheelchair, and with his/her assistance, we enjoy. When I was in Africa, I had an opportunity to ride on an elephant, and other countries have provided similar unique opportunities. What memorable adventures!

At work, I help people with disabilities adjust to life as it is, help them to adjust to new surroundings, or help them arrange for and get used to independent living. I also speak at many forums at the university to students studying the disability area, and I conduct weekly television interviews of people with disabilities, or of those working in the field. My hope, and the reason I'm working where I do, is to see equality across the board for people with disabilities.

How do I feel about my life? I feel extremely fortunate to have had the advantages I have, whether hard times or easy. I experienced hard times a while back when I suffered heart failure. I spent five days in the hospital and will require medication for the rest of my life. I qualify as a senior now, which has its advantages, and I still feel great about the work I do helping others. I have generally good health, and after a time, I hope to travel again. I am currently in the middle of writing a book about my life with CP and the changes that have occurred in my lifetime. I am quite lucky really. Life is truly great!

MS

Suzy

Everything Can Be a Gift, Even Chronic Illness:
Aging Gracefully with Multiple Sclerosis,
Fibromyalgia, and Essential Tremor
Suzy

One of life's fascinating surprises is that situations which are challenging or even tragic can turn out to be blessings in disguise.

For example, while I would not have chosen to have multiple sclerosis (MS) for the past thirty-seven years, fibromyalgia diagnosed twenty-four years ago, or essential tremor diagnosed five years ago, what I have learned through dealing with these and other health challenges has been a precious gift.

The ongoing challenge is to live each day as fully and positively as possible within the frame of reference of chronic illness and pain, and to integrate these health challenges into a life of graceful aging, love, and service.

— *Symptoms I've Experienced*

From the age of five, I have had significant muscle and joint pain, as well as dizziness and fainting. This affected my ability to participate in many school activities, especially choral groups, which was sad because I loved singing, but often could not because I couldn't stand for long periods of time. Many times I would become dizzy or even pass out.

Throughout college and my first several years of teaching, I experienced increased difficulty talking, standing, or walking for more than a few minutes at a time. Two years after starting teaching, I began to experience something new: tingling sensations which felt like I had used a lawn mower then turned it off, but I could still feel the jiggling and tingling. I also had increasing bouts of double vision.

In my first year of teaching, 1968, my friends and fellow teachers encouraged me to seek medical attention for the symptoms that I was experiencing, and which they were observing. However, the first doctor

I consulted was very dismissive, saying, "You're so young; there can't be anything wrong with you. It's all in your head." Stunned after that negative experience, I just tried to "tough it out," avoiding medical care until it was absolutely necessary. I am grateful that medical science has come a long way since then, and caring and responsive doctors are becoming more prevalent.

— Physical challenge accommodation

By 1971, I was having so much difficulty staying strong enough to teach my classes that I finally decided that I would have to seek some other sort of employment where I could sit down to do my work, and where I didn't have to manage a large group. Although that broke my heart, because I loved my students and greatly enjoyed teaching and learning with them, I requested a transfer to teach in an alternative school within our school district which had fewer students and a more manageable schedule. That was a wonderful experience, working with students who blossomed due to the smaller class size, one-on-one tutorials, and I'd had the opportunity for a second chance.

Several years later, when even the alternative school situation became too physically challenging, I moved to a different state to participate in a clinical trial for MS, got stronger, and returned to education, eventually working in educational administration, which I greatly enjoyed. I learned that one can be student-centered and compassionate, and still be a good administrator.

However, the weakness and pain continued, and I had increasing difficulty with tremors and temporary loss of vision.

— Current employment situation

Four years ago, after nearly forty years in the workforce, minus the seven times I had to stop working for at least a few months due to MS flare-ups, I took early retirement due to disability and two months later was approved for Social Security disability benefits. Last year I became eligible for Medicare. I now live in an independent-living center for seniors and people with mobility impairment. While I have had to scale back on possessions, I have discovered that I really enjoy living simply. Although I had been an active community volunteer for much of my adult life, during the past two years I have been withdrawing from most community leadership activities because of physical and cognitive challenges. However, I still tutor non-native speakers of English, serve on our Resident Association council, and continue to be active in my church, when I am able.

— *Most helpful treatments*

I try to limit the number of medications I take. The medication I have found most helpful for the MS is Rebif®, or interferon beta-1a, which I inject three times a week or approximately every fifty-six hours. I take Primidone for the essential tremor and Cyclobenzaprine for the muscle and nerve pain associated with fibromyalgia.

However, the treatment modality that helps me the most is chiropractic. For nearly thirty years the same woman has been my chiropractor. She is a Bachelor of Science in Nursing and former public health nurse, who later went into chiropractic care, and now is a clinic supervisor and tenured professor at Palmer College of Chiropractic. She uses a combination of techniques, depending on how I feel at each appointment. She is warm, caring, highly skilled, and she stays current on research for possible techniques that might be helpful as she provides care.

— *Life these days*

Life is good . . . not easy or without pain and/or other challenges, but good! I live in a small, handicap-accessible apartment, in the downtown area of a city in Iowa, a few blocks from the Mississippi river. I enjoy living simply, and I keep scaling back on possessions. I have a lovely river view from my apartment, which is quite soothing, particularly on days when I am unable to move much, or at all. I read books, magazines, and the Internet voraciously, I listen to many different styles of music, and stay in touch with family and friends by phone, notes, and email. A part-time caregiver comes one or two mornings a week and helps me do the things that I am not able to do. She is warm, encouraging, and helpful.

Because I am having increasing challenges with balance and walking, I move as much as possible to try to alleviate muscle spasticity, and keep my muscles functioning. Fatigue is a huge challenge and I monitor my situation so that I do not get overtired. I try to keep my apartment cool, since heat exacerbates the MS, and my MS condition is becoming progressively more challenging. I'm also having increased bladder incontinence and difficulty with swallowing.

— *What I have learned from managing chronic health conditions*

I have learned so much:

- Everything is gift, even though we sometimes have difficulty discerning the gift when we are in pain or denial.
- While we cannot control some things that occur, such as illness or disability, we definitely can control our response so we can look for the gift, and life lessons to be learned.
- Faith is an incredible gift.
- Family support means so much.
- I have learned to slow down and be still. That is great for physical, emotional, and spiritual well-being.
- Words matter and help shape our reality, so I try to use words and phrases that express gratitude, hope, and a positive attitude. Attitude is ninety-nine percent of being whole and well, or as well as possible given our health challenges.
- I am grateful for everything, even the challenges, and I express gratitude to God daily for all gifts – family, vision, ability to move, etc.

All in all, I live a rich, full life, and I am grateful for the Social Security disability benefits and the fellowship and generosity of my family and friends. I enjoy moving and walking when I am able, as well as being still, having the freedom to rest when necessary, and watching and contemplating the ever-moving Mississippi River from my window outlook.

Nicole

We were a family of nine, two parents and seven children, when I was growing up in the Midwest. As you might expect, from my view it was organized chaos. We must have been a handful! Stories I have heard, tell of one sibling passing away from leukemia at seven, however, I was just three at the time and I was minimally affected. One parent was frequently absent from the home, focused on working in the community, so we were some of the original latchkey kids. We children were often cared for by local college students our parents affectionately called "big sisters" and as a result we had many parental-type influences. We all got along fine and having been diagnosed with MS as an adult, I continue to get along fine.

My life has been full of fascinating experiences and I have lived it as an honest and forthright woman. I attended a state university after high school, but after staying three years I found I preferred working to sitting in classroom…so I worked! Interactions with six brothers and sisters and challenging life events helped to nurture the qualities of independence and determination in me. Fortunately, those traits have aided me in living most of my life as a single mother of one. I have moved all over the country for my employment, working in numerous capacities over many years for a single employer. I have settled, for the last fifteen years, in the southwest and love it. The show "Friday Night Lights" is an accurate reflection of the feelings in our small community—football is king—and the weather is pleasant for much of the year. I stay in the air conditioning when it becomes too warm because heat can make me as limp as a cooked noodle. My child has graduated from a southern university and lives in the east working to gain experience in a political capacity. What more can a proud mother say? Believe me, you will hear more!

I fit into the timeframe when people are commonly diagnosed with MS, I was in my thirties. I have little knowledge how MS symptoms might be triggered, however it seems very close to the birth of my child, or shortly after, when I had my first major episode. One morning I went to reach for my offspring—to pick up the baby—and had no feeling on my right side. This was odd! As the day wore on and I was at work, I could function less and less because my right side became totally useless. I would think, "Move my hand" or "Move my foot," but it wouldn't happen and there would be no response. I thought I must have had a stroke. A substitute was called in to work for me and away I went to the hospital in an ambulance. There I remained for four days. I endured many neurological tests during that time and was undiagnosed upon leaving—it was disturbing and unhelpful for peace of mind. I was unable to work for a month afterward. Was I crazy? One thing is certain; I knew the symptoms were certainly real!

Four years following the first attack a different symptom popped up. Because of eye difficulty, I visited the optometrist and learned I had optic neuritis in both eyes. Waiting for just two weeks before I returned, the optometrist found my eyes were quite a bit worse! I was referred to a neuro-ophthalmologist. This kind and intelligent person, after many, many tests, was the one to diagnose MS. Upon discussing it with me, the one piece of advice counseled by the doctor was to avoid watching telethons as I would see only worst case scenarios. So I have. We grieved together, which helped me to cope and go on living my life. On an outpatient basis, steroids were prescribed and I was treated for only four days. I absolutely had to terminate treatment because I was climbing the walls and awake at all hours. With a baby this was less than ideal because allowing the baby to sleep was much more preferable. From the very beginning, my child and I have practiced mutual love and respect for each other. Since that first time, I have declined the use of any medication prescribed for multiple sclerosis.

After this trauma, it seemed to be a good idea to move to another state and be closer to parents. That way, when I had terrible difficulties with night blindness and short term memory loss, it was easier to bear. I stopped driving at night and I would compensate for dysfunctional memory by using measures to compensate, such as parking in the same spot each week when attending church. This way I could remember where I had parked the car. How proud I was to have a small victory!

Upon learning of the MS diagnosis, my child had fears about my illness being transmitted to him. To ease his fears, together we learned about MS by accessing the internet and other written material. I also promised to be able to walk at his high school graduation. Keeping promises is important to me and this one was exceptionally important to both of us! I am, again, quite proud of myself because I can say I followed through with my commitment.

Now that my child has graduated from university, given the commencement speech at his graduation, and spoken of his unnecessary MS concerns about us, I recall my promise to walk at my son's high school graduation. Acknowledgement of my continued determination was also recognized during his commencement address. I was surprised, extremely honored, and humbled by his mention of this attitude. My son is a marvelous success and saying I'm proud does not sufficiently describe my feelings. Bursting is much more descriptive! This amazing young man provides hope for me every day and in the future I look forward to being a fabulous grandparent.

As I think back, perhaps meeting my only spouse was an emotional reaction to the MS diagnosis; of this I am unsure. However, prior to our marriage my husband and I spoke only over the phone. We had a whirlwind, three month telephonic courtship and I chose to, again, move out of state. This may seem somewhat impetuous; however, we had made plans which probably fueled our conversations with excitement. With my previous managerial experience and my ex-husband's knowledge of business we pooled our talents, married, and started our own company. It seemed like a great fit to us.

For fifteen years our small business flourished, supported our family, and was economically successful. Unfortunately my ex-spouse and I are now divorced, I am unemployed, and unemployable in a full-time capacity. For good measure, I have also had two heart attacks. It's quite something and I'm determined to avoid doing that again! I watch my diet and have found that worry and stress can be extremely detrimental to one's health, so I choose to stay positive. I believe thinking positively has been enormously beneficial because a recent MRI demonstrated that the MS is currently inactive in me. Noticeable MS symptoms can be leg twitches and a slight limp on one side, which is barely discernable. Before, some days I would fall, while on other days I would feel I could run a marathon. Perhaps my situation will remain as it is now; the MRI suggests so! Through many challenges, my strength and sustenance comes from my son, my family, and just a few words, "I have MS, it does not have me." Positive, that's how I live my life. My son, my family, and my words are all the encouragement I need!

Tanya

Growing up in a Midwest suburban area was enjoyable. We were a happy family of five, consisting of: one parent to begin with, two older siblings, me, and one younger sibling. We were minus my dad until I was about six, when my parents reconciled. We lived across the street from a person my age, whose mother has a diagnosis of MS, just as I do. This will become significant.

I was diagnosed in high school with scoliosis. I have lived with this and have never had trouble, of which I am aware. After the diagnosis I went to cheerleading camp, as I was on the high school cheerleading squad. I started noticing how weak my legs were after a day's workout. Because this was so close to the scoliosis diagnosis, I thought scoliosis was the reason for my leg weakness. As I know now, this symptom, along with leg numbness in different areas and severe pain in my knees, were early MS indications. I remember also playing tennis with someone and hearing the comment, "If you don't move your feet, you can't get to the ball." What in the world was happening? Now I realize life is a learning process.

After graduation from high school (by the way at least four friends from school have since been diagnosed with MS) I went to a two-year school in the medical field. My future spouse attended a four-year college and entered the business arena. We wed three years after high school graduation and have been married thirty-four wonderfully close and loving years.

My spouse is a remarkable person. We have three fabulous children, who continually make us proud, and two grandchildren we adore. Two children have gone into business, while the third is in education. I worked full time until our children were born and then split between full and part time. My family has always been helpful to me.

MS symptoms tend to be erratic and multiple. One of mine has been a balance issue; my spouse says to keep my cell phone with me at all times when I am alone—very wise. Falling has plagued me, after which I have to get to a stable piece of furniture, use the leg on my strong side, and heave myself upright again; it takes quite an effort. I also experience horrendous burning in my feet and lower legs, which is unpleasant to say the least! Oh yes, just stepping out of the shower can be an issue because lifting my foot up over the lip to step out is almost impossible. Sometimes I am so weak I cannot lift my foot, so I have to wait until I cool off. Brrr. Add to these symptoms trouble swallowing, bladder difficulties, and issues resulting from taking medication; MS can be a maddening illness.

One of the most frustrating things in dealing with MS is its unpredictability. Some days would be better if I wore a rubber suit to protect against injury. One of those days I was at the top of the stairs, walking carefully as always, lowered my foot to descend, tripped, and fell to the bottom of the whole flight. Fortunately, after assessing my injuries there was pain, but I had avoided broken bones.

My husband had anticipated such an incident: the cell phone was with me! Some days, I feel strong and have no problems. It's great when those days happen. One symptom reared its ugly head recently; please know that I am somewhat sheepish in divulging this information. I was searching in the garage for something and had to use the toilet, immediately. This means I knew I could not reach accommodations soon enough. So, having limited control, the garage became the appropriate place to relieve myself. Yes, things like the stairs and the garage really happen, in a heartbeat, with no warning! It keeps life interesting.

What gives me hope? When I was first diagnosed, the neighbors of whom I spoke took me to an MS support group meeting. At that meeting, attendees were talking of a cure for MS in ten years. As a new person to this, or any MS group, a ten-year timeline truly was encouraging. However, it seems the prediction was a bit optimistic. Where could I turn? It was natural for me to wrap myself in family warmth, and I have been rewarded ten times over.

In coping with MS, family always comes into play. I am extremely thankful I was more functional when my children were young, and my spouse and I delight in their accomplishments. Children are our greatest success. The kids, having been aware of my MS for most or all of their lives, are quite willing to help and go out of their way to assist. I use a walker now, so my family, parents, siblings, husband, and children, are very concerned and caring. I rely upon them for much assistance. Family is quite vigilant, because fatigue can be an issue with MS. My husband shops for groceries and takes care of most household tasks. At this time I do laundry, dishes, and whatever else

I can do. No matter what the issue, we can work it out. MS is truly a family affair.

Reflecting on my life, I would rather live without MS, but at this point, what other options are there? Actually, I expect a scientific breakthrough soon, and it seems to come ever closer. I am so excited! Throughout my life I have been active in sports and other activities, so being slowed as I am is difficult to accept. My supportive husband says, "I wouldn't have it any other way," which is wonderful to hear, and then he cheerfully does the next helpful item on the list. Amazing! I look forward to being as mobile as I can be, for as long as I can. It's not really a surprise is it?

My family deals with things as they are and we adapt quickly. My granddaughter loves my walker, and when we visit their house, or they visit ours, she immediately claims the walker as her plaything. Sometimes when my husband and I go for a walk, I use the wheelchair, my spouse drives, and my granddaughter sits on my lap. We have a whee of a time! Simple joys.

Family is the core of my life and continues to provide support and sustenance. Echoing the words of my husband, "I wouldn't have it any other way."

Sonya

Growing up in a small urban area of the Midwest, with four siblings and my parents was terrific. My siblings are married and are now parents themselves. I am thankful for my many nieces and nephews. I have enjoyed watching them grow, interacting with them, and reveling in their achievements.

As we were growing up, my father worked in the auto industry, while my mother waited until the kids were older before working in auto-related manufacturing. It was ideal from the viewpoint of a child!

When it came time, I moved to another state and attended a university for my freshman year. I was a young person, ready to experience all that life had to offer, and I met someone. Moving farther away from home, I lived with him for several years. When the relationship ended, I moved to yet another state, which was actually closer to my roots.

After working a few years, I wisely decided to finish my degree in educational challenges and moved further away from home. While completing my degree, I discovered I was unsuited for this particular type of work. During that time, I also discovered I had multiple talents in the education area, so my career was revealed to me.

My eventual worksite and abode are, once again, located closer to the home of my youth. I have worked in my profession since my undergraduate years and am thrilled to be in an occupation that remains filled with variety, is rewarding, and is uniquely stimulating. It was during my first year of working in this occupation that I began to experience some symptoms. This was unfortunate, as my longtime employer required a contract to be signed prior to employment. It had a clause prohibiting long-term disability payments if symptoms appeared the first year of working. Disability benefits would resume if the person was able to work ten years. Of course, when signing the contract, I was asymptomatic and had no thoughts this could possibly apply to me. Little did I know! Since that time, two fortunate circumstances have occurred: the requirement no longer exists, and I have passed the ten-year timeline. I am still working and continue to enjoy going to work each day.

I imagine you are asking, "What were these symptoms?" and, "What did the symptoms mean?" I remember the first indication was numbness in my arm from shoulder to fingertips. It was like I had lain on my arm, it had gone to sleep, and had stayed asleep; there was no sensation. This seemed pretty freaky to me, and I was curious.

When I visited a neurologist, the doctor initially treated it as a pinched nerve. That was okay with me, though I had no idea how it could have happened. A month later, I developed a second symptom, optic neuritis. With it came searing pain and blindness in one eye. Absolutely, this was when I felt the worst about my illness. I had totally lost sight in one eye, and I was worried about vision loss in both eyes soon. What a distressingly frightening thought! It didn't happen, though. And fortunately, peripheral vision in the one eye has returned, for which I'm heartily thankful. I went back to the neurologist when I went dark on one side. I was informed that the two symptoms, optic neuritis and numbness combined, could indicate a diagnosis of MS. That suspicion led to an MRI and a confirmation. I never thought, *Oh woe is me, what will I do?* What I did do was continue to work and learn as much as I could about this thing called MS. Talking about it was another matter.

Shortly after the MS diagnosis, I was helping a friend move. I hadn't adjusted to the loss of depth perception yet; the absence of central vision in the one eye tended to throw me off. I was going out of my friend's house, down some steps, carrying a dresser drawer full of boys' clothing. I missed the last step and fell forward, directly on top of the drawer. It was smashed flat! Thankfully, the old drawer came apart easily at the corners, and the clothes softened my fall. I wasn't hurt. I hadn't told anyone yet about my health problems, so once everyone knew I wasn't hurt from the fall, it was so easy to laugh with them about MS and the results! I think this was right up there with the best of them—Laurel and Hardy, the Three Stooges, and Chevy Chase!

Still uncertain about the future, I talked to people, read literature, went to support groups, and talked to the neurologist. After that, I felt more comfortable knowing what was happening. It has been quite a while since then, and I am grateful, at least in my case, that progression has been extremely slow. No matter what my circumstances, I will remain cheerful and upbeat. I love talking to people. I am a people person and riding the bus, which I do frequently, is perfect for getting to know others.

Because of slow MS progression, I have been able to acclimate to the changes happening with the lessening of my abilities. When attending support group meetings, I heard from people who had symptoms which progressed very quickly and who viewed MS as an intruder. Now that I know what others' situations are, I am less angry at MS. Would anger help? Not me. I find anger to be unproductive.

I consider myself fortunate to have avoided hospital stays for MS. The one surgery I did have was unrelated and went well. However, immediately afterward I had a fright. I was just waking up from anesthesia, still half asleep and half awake, and for an instant I felt totally paralyzed! I could not move, and I wanted to scream, "Is this what my future will be?" Needless to say, it was more than a little bit alarming but lasted only momentarily. It certainly left an impression!

When I am at home, I use a walker to move from point to point. If I will be going distances, I use a scooter. I seldom drive, and when I do, it is usually to destinations in the community. On some occasions, I drive home to visit family. Most of the time, I will use local transportation to attend community events, go out to eat, sometimes see a show, go to movies, and enjoy life. Did I mention I am a people person? I like speaking to and meeting people; it is my joy in life, besides my other joys, of course.

I am happy to have a good life, family, friends, and acquaintances. I am also happy to be independent, able to work, and be on my own. I have accepted MS and have learned many things since my diagnosis. One of those lessons is to desire only what I have, while appreciating its existence. Also, I know better now what is important in life and how patient one can be. There was a time, when driving, I frequently used my horn and drove in the fast lane. I have learned to slow down and smell the roses.

My family is not overly concerned about me, while being completely supportive. My father used to be overprotective and tried to make decisions for me. It is likely you already have an inkling how acceptable that was! My family and I are an outgoing group, who delight in each other's company. Home has always been a sure foundation for me. I love my profession, my life, and having a happy family. A joy of mine is visiting with others and with the family I love.

STROKE

Dennis

Lots of sand, shrubbery, and sagebrush have been the landscape where I have lived my whole life. It is the most appealing vista to me! You see, trees, bushes, and flowers sort of clutter up that pristine view and block out the light. A clear view brings a kind of clarity.

Active is the way to describe my lifestyle until 2007. Frequently, I would make after-work plans with my buddies. We would rent ATVs and ride the desert, we would drive into Oklahoma, or we would visit establishments serving beverages because activities can work up a powerful thirst! On a weekend, we might even drive to Dallas or Ft. Worth. Things are different now. I am still a young man, twenty-nine, yet I live as if I am much older. Stroke and its effects sidelined me three years ago. How could this have happened, you ask?

In 2007, I lost consciousness at work and was rushed to the hospital. After a few quick tests, it was determined I had a brain tumor and surgery was necessary. By this time, I had regained consciousness, and even though I was informed of the surgery risks, I just wanted this growth out of my head! Into surgery I went, after which I knew nothing. Nothing, that is, until I woke up. Along with the terrible pain in my head, I had this weird feeling on my left side. Actually, it was an absence of feeling. Also, I was mostly blind in my left eye. Oh man, this was worse than I thought! So what did it all mean? I would soon find out. The first time I tried to take a sip of water, it dribbled out the left side of my mouth onto my chin. What the heck? When asking about many unusual circumstances, I was told by the doctor I had experienced a stroke during the operation and had almost died. Whoa! I guess things could have been worse.

My long recovery was about to begin. When I tried to move my left arm, it lay helplessly at my side. What an uneasy feeling! To think, I used to move this appendage whenever I wanted. Moving my left arm with my right hand would be a new adventure. It was unbelievable to me, and to have only one useful eye, what would my future be like? For now, I stayed focused on things I could control, like standing upright. After a few days, I began rehabilitation.

My legs were still very unresponsive, and I really wanted to walk again so I could have some bit of normalcy. For a few months I used a wheelchair, all the while practicing and building up the muscle mass and nerve connections that had gone from my legs. I am now able to walk, with an aid, when I'm out and about. I use an AFO on my left leg at home. AFO stands for ankle-foot orthotic. It is a device that is fitted to a person's leg and holds the foot up to keep it from dropping. Otherwise, I tend to trip when walking. This way I am able to stay on my feet.

About two years after my stroke, I finally understood that my physical condition would probably never change. I thought, *There's nothing modern science can do to fix me!* I would think, *I'm just in my twenties!* and, *I'd be better off if I killed myself.* What I have done instead of concentrating on the negatives, is to focus on the positive. It's all about coping with what I don't have and just being thankful for what I do have. I also keep a strong relationship with my Lord. He gives me the strength to keep going, so I must be here for a reason!

I have learned much from this experience. I know now there are many ways to compensate for one's limitations. Rehab was eye-opening. Compensation for limitations can be with expensive equipment, or there may be simpler ways to get things done, depending on what's needed. Sometimes, willpower alone works, and other times, I can readjust the way I do things. I have also learned that there are unexpected emotional feelings which may result from something like a stroke. I am working through depression and thoughts of suicide with a psychologist. I saw a psychiatrist and am now taking anti-depression medication. I thought my life was over, but have mostly gotten through those thoughts, and I am coping. The most important thing I've learned is that the strongest muscle in the human body is the heart.

My life has changed drastically and understanding why this happened to me has been a challenge. I need help to walk, I have less vision, and I cannot drive. That I am able to walk and see at all makes me glad and I can still think. However, there are times when despair washes over me. When that happens, I go to the computer and message with my many Facebook friends. Just talking those feelings out helps me enormously. I understand now that bad things happen to good people, and I am a good person; a chosen person. Yes, my physical changes have impacted me greatly, but I am more than a physical body. Will my capabilities always be the same? We'll see. What am I doing about it? I plan to live! New discoveries are being constantly made, and new medicines and technologies are being developed even as this is written. Faith in God is my inspiration, so I truly believe anything is possible.

EPILOGUE

People have willingly spoken about their lives and experiences. What courage it must have taken! I'm most grateful for the openness, candid remarks, and sharing of information. Contributors are to be commended! Those helping others in some way also deserve praise. Just by reading this book and understanding, *you* help. Together, all of us are an unbeatable group!